# FINDING YOURSELF IN PRINT

# FINDING YOURSELF IN PRINT

## A GUIDE TO WRITING PROFESSIONALLY

### BY RILEY HUGHES

NEW VIEWPOINTS/VISION BOOKS
*A Division of Franklin Watts/New York/London*

New Viewpoints/Vision Books
A Division of Franklin Watts
730 Fifth Avenue
New York, New York 10019

Selections from "The Crop" from *The Complete Stories* by Flannery O'Connor. Copyright © 1979 by the Estate of Mary Flannery O'Connor. Reprinted with the permission of Farrar, Straus, & Giroux, Inc.

Selections from *A New Age Begins* by Page Smith. Copyright © 1976 by Page Smith. Reprinted with the permission of McGraw-Hill Book Company.

Selections from *Vanishing Cornwall* by Daphne du Maurier. Photographs by Christian Browning. Copyright © 1967 by Daphne du Maurier and Christian Browning. Reprinted with the permission of Doubleday and Company, Inc.

Selections from *Store* by Nan Tillson. Copyright © 1978 by Nan Tillson Birmingham. Reprinted with the permission of G. P. Putnam's Sons.

Selections from *International Book Year 1972*: A Programme of Action by The United Nations Educational, Scientific, and Cultural Organization. Copyright © 1971 by UNESCO. Reprinted with the permission of UNESCO.

Selections from the *Pen Standards* compiled by the Standards Committee at Pen. Reprinted with the permission of Pen.

Shirley Graves Cochrane's "Middle Distance" is reprinted with the permission of *The Washington Review*.

"Princess In Thrall" first appeared in *Four Quarters* and is reprinted with permission.

Library of Congress Cataloging in Publication Data

Hughes, Riley.
    Finding yourself in print

    Bibliography: p.
    Includes index.
    1. Authorship.  I. Title.
PN147.H75        808'.025          79-18306
ISBN 0-531-06369-0
ISBN 0-531-06752-1 pbk.

Copyright © 1979 by Riley Hughes
All rights reserved
Printed in the United States of America
5  4  3  2  1

# CONTENTS

## Acknowledgments

To the staff and visiting speakers of the Georgetown University Writers Conference I owe too many indebtednesses for inspiration and information to be easily recalled or recounted. I owe thanks as well to the many editors who sent me their Guidelines for Writers and sample copies of their magazines, confirming the data they had given to *The Writer's Handbook* and *Writer's Market*, my original (along with current market notes in *The Writer* and *Writer's Digest*) and invaluable sources for this information. Both my undergraduate and Continuing Education students keep me constantly informed and inspired. Thanks go most of all to my wife, Josephine Nicholls Hughes, whose critical intelligence and unending patience have helped me immeasurably in finding myself, once again, in print.

*Riley Hughes*
*Georgetown University*
*Washington, D.C.*
*12 April, 1979*

*Again for my wife; also for my students who have found and are finding themselves in print.*

# FINDING YOURSELF IN PRINT

# PREFACE

It is the object of this book to guide the reader to a professional approach to writing. Clearly, if it is to be worth the effort, writing must satisfy certain objective standards and attain a level of skill that results in communication that is direct, forceful, and unique. This takes work. Constant application will almost inevitably produce a habit of writing, one that will remove initial difficulties and make the exercise of the newly acquired skill less arduous and at times even exciting. But to promise that writing of publishable quality can ever be made "easy" comes very close, it is equally clear, to being fraudulent. "Easy reading," someone has said, "is damned hard writing."

In the very presence of difficulty lies the acceptable challenge. Nobody can promise the writer, part-time or full-time, beginning or professional, a rose garden instead of a rockpile. Whether or not one is a "bleeder" (for whom words come one at a time, like drops of blood) or one for whom words seem to flow freely and copiously, there are objective requirements that measure achievement. These requirements derive from the nature of language, the canons of art, and the demands of the marketplace. Through continual practice one learns to use words logically and idiomatically, to master the basic techniques of, say, the forms of fiction, and, by the trial and error of submission, to requite the current longings of editors. This is writing made rewarding—writing made professional.

Anyone who engages in fitting words together into formal structures should consider doing so for compensation as well as for recognition. Without quite agreeing with Dr. Johnson that anybody who writes and does not do so for money is a blockhead, one may reasonably hold that getting into print is a sensible goal for those who spend the time and effort that writing requires. The only sure way of knowing whether or not one can write anything of publishable quality is to have it published. And to be published is, necessarily, to "go public." Private gratification with what one has written must always remain tentative and inconclusive if the test of publication is not ventured.

Ventured, not necessarily achieved. As with a sport or any other hobby, there is no point whatever in not knowing the rules of the game, nor, even worse, is there any merit in making up the rules as one goes along. Therefore even the dedicated amateur will be wise to refrain from adding an Alice in Wonderland quality to the writing game. He or she will write to the rules even though it is a performance without an audience. That such a silent performance can afford pleasure to the one performing cannot be denied. Although this book attempts to inculcate a professional approach and attitude toward writing, it will not withhold satisfaction from those whose purpose is to experiment with writing as an aid to self-knowledge or self-expression, or to learn, as Gertrude Stein would put it, how writing is written. These are respectable objectives.

The greatest fulfillment, however, in undertaking the difficulties of communication through an art form will come from seeing one's own work made public. It can be said with confidence that anyone who can compose a grammatical sentence, arrange sentences into paragraphs, and articulate those paragraphs into a coherent entity can, in a sense, "write."

And anybody who can, in these terms, write, can publish. Not anywhere, not everywhere, of course. Yet innumerable markets exist for those who are willing to start modestly. "Aim low and hit!" is not an unacceptable motto for a beginner. Upon hitting, one should not stop there, but attempt to hit again. One should also raise one's sights.

The beginner's suggested target, then, is publication. The paths to appearing in print are fortunately many and diverse, and it is one of the purposes of this book to examine the possibilities open to the new writer. Experimentation with one genre after another, with the forms of nonfiction as well as those of fiction, will serve to lend specific purpose and direction to the weeks and months of one's apprenticeship. Part of the process of the new writer's self-discovery will be to try out various professional approaches to expression. Curiosity is part of a writer's equipment, and the new writer will be unable to resist the challenge each untried approach poses. Hence these pages contain exercises and suggestions for experiment in both fiction and nonfiction, as well as lists of likely markets for finished work.

These markets are modest ones, within the range of the serious, hard-working beginner. It is insufferably elitist to suggest that everyone who can write at all can immediately join the ranks of highly paid magazine contributors or those of the authors of best sellers. For the published professional to intimate as much to the beginner is to perpetuate a cruel hoax. What the beginner needs is the quiet encouragement of understatement, not extravagant promises leading to frustration and unrealizable hopes. Therefore the beginning writer, often the nonprofessional of talent, the writer for whom this book is intended, is far, in the early stages, from requiring, or being able to secure, the services of an agent. Nor is self-publication a reasonable goal for the average beginner. The new writer should aim both low and accurately: at the freelancer's marketplace.

*Finding Yourself in Print* offers a challenge to new writers, whether they come to it individually or in the classroom or through writers' groups. This book has certainly been a challenge to its author, an invitation to sort out the lessons of varied experience in writing and in instruction. The result is an attempt to put down on paper what has been learned from teaching continuing education courses in writing as well as conventional literature courses to college undergraduates, from publication in all the forms treated in these pages, from magazine and book editing, and from the founding and directing of an annual writers conference.

Above all else, this book is based upon a passionate conviction of the importance of technique. It attempts to discover and explore the means, part method and part magic, of communicating information, emotion, and experience. Form comes first. Content without form is mere formlessness. For it is through technique and structure that one acquires the power to express, however falteringly and at whatever cost, the reality of the *I-thou* relationship. This will be found worth all the ardors of apprenticeship.

# CHAPTER 1
# LOOK AT YOU!

The reality to begin with is not pencils, books, or typewriters, but yourself. You—all you are, all you have been, and all you will become—are your own writing capital. From your experiences, from your observations of the life around you, and from, as Mark Van Doren puts it, "where your mind has been" will come all your emotions and ideas. You are your own "usable past." Even more than what you eat, you are what you think. Writing is thinking organized. To write is to place in order, to give form to those sometimes vagrant impulses of your consciousness through which you become articulate to yourself.

"How do I know what I think, until I see what I say?" writes W. H. Auden. All writing is the decoding and presentation of those arrangements the mind struggles for in coping with the self and the other, with the subjective and objective findings of the probing, registering intellect. That is to say, all writing is autobiographical. There can be one exception: autobiography. There you can be on your guard. You can leave yourself—parts of yourself—out. A striking example occurs in that American classic *The Education of Henry Adams*. The author's twenty-first chapter (out of thirty-five) is entitled "Twenty Years After." Through that evasive device Adams omits two decades of his long life, a period in which he married and his much loved wife committed suicide. Such concealment would be impossible to the novelist.

You are what you write—you write what you are. It is impossible to leave yourself out totally. Something of you will be discernible on the page, no matter how far your subject is from your emotional experience. But words cannot fail, at the very least, to reflect your intellectual biography. You are, let us say, the author of a high school mathematics book. I, the reader, can perhaps deduce from the problems you include ("If I have four apples...") some small inferences about your political leanings, or where you stand on economics. You wrote a text in college physics? If there are differing schools of thought in your field, your text will give the reader a clue to your position and commitment, (for example, do you accept or reject the big-bang theory?), however austere your treatment of the subject.

Admittedly, these are extreme examples, and the autobiographical information they contain is slight. They are given to point out that anyone who seeks complete anonymity, who has no wish to share himself or herself, cannot ever achieve the professional level in writing. Such a person cannot—and this is not being extreme—even achieve publication. Writing is sharing. At a minimum, it is sharing objective thought with oneself. That most intriguingly intimate and greatest of secret journals, the diary of Samuel Pepys, was written in a unique code, a fact which might argue that Pepys was attempting to conceal his real thoughts from others. But he took considerable care with style and other matters of technique—and he took care also to will his manuscript to Oxford.

The nineteenth century gave us two of the most influential and highly regarded poets of twentieth-century publication: Emily Dickinson and Gerard Manley Hopkins. Both published only a mere handful of poems during their lifetimes; the great bulk of their work came out posthumously and under conditions that have made them our contemporaries. Emily

Dickinson was a recluse, a "New England nun." Hopkins, a Jesuit, put himself under religious obedience and published only with the permission of his religious superiors. Both were extremely reticent persons, both painfully reserved, and yet they were true artists, genuine professionals. Because they were professionals, they longed to communicate with others, to "go public." "Are you too deeply occupied," Dickinson asked when she sent her poems to a literary critic, "to say if my verse is alive?"

This is the question most of us want answered. It is why we write, and why we publish when or where we can. We wish to know whether or not our work is alive. And, unlike Pepys, most are unwilling to leave the judgment to posterity. We will also do well not to make serious inquiry of family or friends about the merits of our writing. Partiality will prevent them from being objective; further, they are unlikely to be acquainted with technique or the requirements of the market. But, like all generalizations, this one is subject to exceptions. One thinks of Jane Austen reading her novels aloud to a large and appreciative family. For most of us, though, families are no longer large—or particularly willing to subject themselves to being first audience for what we write.

Whether or not our work is designed to attract private or public attention, there is no disguising the fact that to write is, in the words of François Mauriac, "to surrender." Not everybody is willing to sacrifice a lifetime as a Mauriac or a Henry James did. Nor is there anything dishonorable in the refusal of some published writers to engage in fiction, because fiction requires a greater degree of surrender. They are unwilling to accept that intimate giving over of self the act of writing fiction entails. In quality fiction, reality takes on an overpowering abundance. In fiction, because the subconscious as well as the conscious mind is involved, revelation of the most intense kind is inescapable.

The paradox at the heart of the matter is that to write is both, and simultaneously, to reveal and to conceal oneself.

There is the private I (who rises daily, and bangs out words slowly in longhand or on the typewriter,) and the public I (who assumes the role and mask of narrator in nonfiction or fiction). To test this, ask yourself whether you can (assuming there is no evidence in the text itself) determine if what you are reading was written on a Tuesday or a Thursday, or if the writer had a headache, was behind in payments on the car, or was planning a golfing weekend. No, you cannot. The author disappeared, so to speak, into the text and has no personal existence. In one sense, the author permeates the work; in another, the author is invisible and does not leave a trace.

Perhaps the most difficult problem the beginner—of whatever age—must recognize is this duality out of which the work arises. It is, indeed, one's first professional lesson. I must be myself, the writer must learn. I must use the words and phrases as well as the experiences that are *me*, and yet I have to assume at the same time an impersonal role. I must treat myself as the other. I cannot be the objective observer or spokesperson in nonfiction, or achieve universality of utterance in poetry, drama, or fiction unless I assume a mask, put on a persona. The beginning writer is all too likely to believe that everything he or she has thought about or that has happened to him or her is a news item the world is waiting for. Or (although this is rarer) the beginner is likely to be too diffident and to see his or her ideas for nonfiction as either hackneyed or trivial and to view ones' experiences as too limited in interest or applicability to be usable in fiction.

Anyone, then, who would write must learn, and quickly, to see oneself objectively at the same time that one calls upon the subjective self, one's inner resources. The writer of prose particularly must speedily discover where his or her natural bent lies. Is it an inclination in the direction of nonfiction or in the direction of fiction? Neither is superior to the other, neither is more "creative" than the other. But the two are different. (A writer friend infuriated by the claims of fiction to be the more creative refuses to employ the conventional terms for them but refers to the two as nonfiction and "nonfact.")

The bent that the natural, the "born," writer of nonfiction has may be likened to that of one who constantly hears an inner monologue. All questions have to this kind of writer one side, or better perhaps, one emphasis. There is one voice—the writer's own. This is not narrowness but strength. One voice steadily heard can result in writing that is calm, factual, logical, and persuasive. That voice does not beat down opposition but weighs it, probes it, subordinates it. It is the voice of clarity and wisdom, but it would not be successful in undertaking fiction. Inner monologue predetermines; it seeks out issues and it settles them. It leaves no room for the indeterminations of conflict, does not allow for cliff-hangers.

The writer with the innate knack for fiction is one who hears not one inner voice but many. This writer's mind is engaged in a continuing dialogue that is tentative and various. He or she listens with an attention that responds to continuing conflict, not to instantaneous conviction. The frame of mind of the fiction writer is a probing one also, but it probes for a different kind of discovery. It waits, without impatience, to be told. It is curious, many-sided, watchful for the tentative and mysterious in the human personality. T. S. Eliot made the point with his customary sardonic touch when describing that master of modern fiction Henry James: "He had a mind so fine that no idea could ever violate it."

You can tell which of the two inclinations is natural to you by asking yourself which engages your interest more often: the examination of ideas or the study of people. If you read for the facts, for the ideas in things, if you are constantly concerned about issues, perhaps with a strong urge to set things right, or at least to set out the fact of the matter, yours is a natural inclination toward nonfiction. When you learn of a new set of circumstances—or when you review an old one—your instinct is to classify, to arrange, to categorize. Make no mistake about it, if this description fits your cast of mind and your personality, you have a wonderful gift. The facts, the situations, and the issues your mind can feed on are without number; the market for the products of your discriminating mind is ample.

On the other hand, it may be a "human comedy" that most often engages your attention. You do not pursue ideas, because your interest is people. Jane Austen reports in a letter that when she went to a museum in London she could not keep her eye or mind on the exhibits; she was too busy watching the other people present. Hers was the classic reaction of those for whom fiction itself is an issue, a cause. As usual, Emily Dickinson had words, few and precise, for it:

*The show is not the show,*
*But they that go.*
*Menagerie to me*
*My neighbor be.*
*Fair play—*
*Both went to see.*

If you spend an exasperating half hour or so in a public bus and come away with your mind filled with sociological data and suggestions for transportation remedies, clearly you are a born writer of nonfiction. But if you leave the bus and the experience with a warm visual and aural memory of the others who were sardine-packed with you, then you have the makings of the fictionalizing mind. You gravitate not toward issues but people.

Now all this is a question of inclination and emphasis. There is nothing to prevent someone who has a latent talent for fiction from making a success of nonfiction, or vice versa. But for the beginning writer to go against the grain may result in some period, often extending to years, of disappointment. I have observed many participants at our annual writers conference at Georgetown University coming to us with the dogged ambition, say, to write fiction, and to publish it not after long apprenticeship but right now. They may know how to write, may have a knack and a professional attitude, but with one exception: their insistence on committing themselves to a literary form uncongenial to them. One of the reasons I have always maintained an "open" conference, and not one where the participant must sign up for one or two forms only and miss being exposed to all, is that among the beginning writer's first discoveries, after the discovery of himself or herself, should be that of a congenial form.

There are many reasons why those professional writers are rare who, after trying out forms experimentally in their formative years, excel at or even practice more than one genre. George Bernard Shaw wrote five novels, all of them failures, before finding himself and his proper medium. Playwright Tennessee Williams has written one novel only; F. Scott Fitzgerald, one of the most polished and successful writers of both short and long fiction, wrote one play—and it was a disaster. Our greatest novelist, Henry James, was literally hooted out of the theater. C. P. Snow notes that writing for the theater had an inordinate attraction for nineteenth-century novelists. James, for example, wrote a number of plays, all of them lacking the brilliance and conviction of his novels. Yet others have since turned his books into successful plays or screenplays. There seems to be something to Irwin Shaw's contention that the theater offers a "magnificent morass" to the novelist.

The pleasure of publication—as the beginner may not always be aware—can be postponed or deferred permanently if one chooses to bypass a modest success at the moment instead of reaching out for an achievement not yet possible. To have modest and attainable goals at the beginning seems more sensible than to aim too high. If publication is your tar-get—how do you truly know whether or not you can communicate unless you see your communication somewhere in print?—it makes sense to be moderate. Try a low-paying market first: attempt a feature article in a Sunday newspaper in your region or a magazine of small, if national, circulation. It will be in your interest to get into print in order to build up a few credits you can mention in a query letter. If this means putting off the Great American Novel for a while, so be it.

It should not be thought that because it is difficult to be successful with both fiction and nonfiction the two have no relation to one another, that they run on parallel, unmeeting lines. Although each is distinct, one borrows from the other. Of nonfiction this is especially true. This borrowing goes beyond the use of anecdotes in an article, the employment of the fictionalized example to make a point. It goes all the way, in fact, to the New Journalism. Here the author is, oddly enough, more present in the work than the fiction writer often is. Perhaps media news has had something to do with it; we all have noticed that the news comes to us via the tube stamped with the personality of the newscaster. Something similar happens in by-lined news items in the press as well. What Marjorie Holmes calls the "creative article" allows great scope to the personality (partly assumed, partly the mask, of course) of the author and permits the writer a wide range of inventiveness.

It would be worth it, I think, to consider generalizing first, then specializing. Try your hand—while you are still in the finger-exercise stage—at several forms, especially if you are uncertain. You "want to write"—but write what, write how? You had best shop around for a while, try your hand at various things. After appearing a few times in print, you will know more about yourself, learn the scope of your ambitions, become aware of strengths and limitations. Then it will be time to specialize. Also it will be time to be rebuffed by rejection slips again. Proficiency in one branch of writing does not automatically confer proficiency in another. Writing is a learned and constantly relearned accomplishment. Rightly regarded, that can be seen as part of its charm. There may be some consolation in knowing that the most experienced professional starts at the beginning, even as you and I, each time he or she begins a new work. His or her pages do not come pretyped any more than ours do. The habit of writing, it is true, will come to his or her aid, but it is a habit the beginner can acquire as well. Simply start.

I knew a writer who made an intriguing distinction in his employment of nonfiction and fiction. He was a self-supporting, full-time writer. He earned his living by his typewriter, and he had a high sense of himself as artist. He would not compromise his fiction by turning out, as F. Scott Fitzgerald did (bitterly aware that he was using up the same "nerve-ends") potboiler after potboiler. What this writer did was to use nonfiction as a means of earning his bread, letting fiction provide the jam. Nor would he slip into what James called "the second-rate trick" by using the slack stereotypes of popular fiction, out of fear that he would find himself automatically turning to them in his serious fiction. Instead, he turned out numerous articles and documentaries, nonfiction potboilers, including the "autobiography" of an operatic diva. Another writer, J. F. Powers, whose short stories of clerical life have become classics, says "I can always sell insurance" to avoid turning out potboilers.

Never deceive yourself about what you are doing. If, through inclination or necessity, you find yourself turning out potboilers, do not tell yourself that they are what they are not: art. Your integrity, and the integrity of your work, is deeply involved here. Again, what you are doing now should result from a total commitment—to the present. Never allow yourself to feel contempt for your work or scorn for where it is appearing. This is a dishonesty that corrodes talent. Never, even once, condescend. Whatever you are writing—whether it is a club meeting report for a newspaper or a sonnet—make it the best you can do. Believe in yourself, believe in what you are doing. Aim low at first, yes; but continually raise your sights.

Such ambition is wholesome and need not be concealed from yourself or even from your editors. The late A. S. Burack, who edited a magazine called *Plays* as well as *The Writer,* used to tell young writers who contributed to the former (a magazine that publishes plays for school reading and production) that he knew they would go on to other things, that they were just cutting their baby teeth in contributing to *Plays*. He said—and he meant it—that he was always happy to see one of his writers develop beyond the material he could use to something more demanding of their talents, to something more rewarding. He wisely knew that others would in their turn be coming along, that the flow of talent, like the need for communication, is endless.

You will make another essential discovery about yourself not long after getting down to the business of writing, of filling the forbidding blank pages before you. Ask yourself—you already know the answer—do I write with seeming effortlessness, fluently and copiously, or am I what is known in the trade as a "bleeder"? (Elizabeth Janeway once told me that she never heard the term, and apparently did not know the condition it is used to describe, but she may be one of the fortunate few.) A law of nature seems to be operating here. Some write effortlessly, often at top speed, and their only arduous chore is that of editing, pruning what they write. Others (I myself am one of these) compose with excruciating slowness—not one sentence at a time, but one phrase; not a phrase, but a word; not a word, but two or three syllables. It is hard to believe, or to convince others, that you are working when you proceed at such a snaillike pace. Yet it is impossible for you to write with speed; the words simply will not come. Hemingway was that kind of writer; so is Katherine Anne Porter.

Being a bleeder has its compensations. At least you are not wasting paper. At best, you are doing your editing, your cutting, as you go along. Your mind is directing your hand: pause, wait, now write. For some of us writing, unhappily, is a process of getting stuck, getting unstuck, and getting stuck all over again. Sometimes—you may have noticed this—the process of getting unstuck can be assisted by a change from longhand to the typewriter; other times the process is just the opposite. If you find you are a bleeder, learn to live with it. It can be grim. One remembers the Saroyan character who wrote a novel in one word: love. The bleeder wishes that were all there is to it—and thinks, guiltily, that even that would have taken a week. Make sure that you are not just being evasive, practicing some kind of avoidance, then face your problem honestly.

You may be able to increase your pace somewhat, but you are not likely to succeed in converting yourself from bleeder to gusher. With all the cutting down, throwing out, and revising to be done, the facile user of words comes out at the same place at about the same time. Hemingway spent the greater part of a day arriving at five hundred words. When he was stuck he would retype his last three or four pages in order to get unstuck and into his rhythm again. Katherine Anne Porter took twenty years to finish *Ship of Fools*. Writing became no easier for her. In a letter she acknowledges that she had great difficulty with one of her latest stories, "Holiday"—"the hardest story to write I ever did, not even excepting my first finished one."

One way to answer the question, How do I know I can write? is to ask yourself, Have I always been an avid reader? Compulsive and long-standing readership very often leads to the desire—one might almost say the instinct—to write. For one thing, as with any mode of communication the first stage of interest in an art form is that of being a receiver, not a maker. With some the urge to imitate, to create on our own, comes early. Playwright Eugene Ionesco wrote his first play when he was thirteen. He had been writing poems before that, and at eleven, he tells us, he tried to write his memoirs! Precocious as all that sounds, it was not originality: those forms already existed. We see the process clearly in the lives of painters: the stage of imitation and discipline in discipleship, followed by disavowal, ultimately resulting in the painter's own style.

The writer begins as an imitator, and the first imitating— the initiation—comes through reading. It is through reading that we first receive information in concentrated form. Through reading we first see story unfold before us. (If we are lucky, we have already been told stories in the family circle; less lucky but fortunate nonetheless if our first hearing was through television.) Through reading we first come under the power of words. Lord Bacon put the relationship between reading and thought pithily when he observed, "Reading maketh a full man; conference a ready man and writing an exact man." Omnivorous, compulsive reading in the future writer's earliest years used to be taken for granted, and most writers of an older generation are voracious readers as if by instinct. Anyone who has been an avid reader from early years has a distinct advantage. As if by a kind of osmosis, one has absorbed the rhythms of language; one's mind composes paragraphs; one thinks in idiom. The reader saturated with idiom becomes the "born" writer.

For the future writer of fiction there is no better preparation than acquaintance with the classics of English and American literature. In the novel, one should of course read Dickens, Jane Austen, Thackeray, Trollope, Hardy, and George Eliot. Some books not read early are perhaps best not read at all. They can come too late. If one has not encountered—on the printed page—Stevenson's *Treasure Island* when one is very young, it will be found too elementary, too unsophisticated. Let us hope you have read Conan Doyle early on, and perhaps *Robinson Crusoe* as well. *Jane Eyre* read at the right hour will be moving and powerful; come upon too late, it will seem an imitation of its thousands of imitators, for it is the great-great-grandmother of soap opera. The incomparable Jane Austen can be encountered with profit at almost any age. As for our own literature, it is best to start reading Mark Twain when you are young. Melville and Henry James can become acquired tastes later on; but Mark Twain, with his essentially juvenile mind and temperament of the prankster will seem as remote as Chaucer if put off too long. All these books can tell us where our language has been, can demonstrate that the forms we attempt today were born and practiced long ago.

Our imitation of such works should be general, not particular. One can imagine Dickens thriving today, in the era of book clubs and paperbacks, and yet even Dickens could not write now in the style he used in the mid-Victorian era. The rhythms of Dickens's sentences can suggest possibilities, yet slavishly followed would result in a curious, unusable pastiche. His sentimentality (based upon the hard facts of infant and child mortality in his time) would seem ludicrous to us today. Oscar Wilde thought that laughing over the death of Little Nell could be taken as a mark of tenderness. Yet the pulsing life Dickens gave his characters—and they still live on his pages—stands as a hallmark and a challenge to anyone attempting fiction today. To try to write fiction now without ever having read Dickens might, ironically enough, plunge one into repeating his worse excesses.

Should one read one's contemporaries? Of course. But as a second stage, not the first. For one thing, without some knowledge of the history and development of the form—I am thinking of poetry and fiction particularly, but not exclusively—one can have no appreciation of innovations. Unless one sees how today fits into tradition, today's denials, debts, and achievements cannot be seen or appreciated. There are practical limits, of course, upon the amount of time a writer, whether full-time or part-time, can devote to reading. It is best to have done the bulk of one's reading, particularly one's reading for literary background, not necessarily reading for information, in the formative years. As one begins to publish. more time should be devoted to writing, and it is not always wise to continue reading one's contemporaries. Why? There is the danger of unconscious, unintentional plagiarism, of picking up another writer's tricks of style. One critic sees, for example, imitations of Hemingway in some of the later stories

/

of F. Scott Fitzgerald. Saddest of all is the generally accepted impression that Hemingway ended his once brilliant career imitating Hemingway.

Unconscious plagiarism, the unwitting imitation of someone else's manner, is one thing. Intentional plagiarism is another. Nobody can own an idea or ideas. These are as impersonal as thought, as roving and random as the winds. You may not mark off, say, ecology as your subject and post a claim to it that forbids me or anyone else from writing articles, stories, or books that invade your territory. Topics are free and open to anyone. Plots, in the general sense at least (boy meets girl), are also free. The "eternal triangle" is well named indeed; it turns up, in one form or another, quite regularly. But the web of words you weave to present your views on ecology—that is yours. Your sentence rhythms, the way you place words one after another, their very ordering—that, not the topic, is what you obtain your copyright for. There your rights are proprietary.

For nearly all beginning writers a warning about plagiarism—a kind of literary shoplifting—is quite unnecessary. Nonetheless, every once in a while a deliberate act of plagiarism, committed perhaps out of a misplaced zeal, a good quality gone wrong, does occur. Two instances from my recent experience help make the point. In one, a young undergraduate, pressed for time and an end-of-semester deadline, abridged and modified a short story published in an annual volume of the O. Henry Awards series. The story sounded familiar; I checked and, as I had suspected, there was the original. The student had retained the story line, had given the characters new names, and had abridged the original. But word after word, with the exceptions noted, the story, which had first been published in a mass-circulation magazine unfolded before me. I returned the manuscript as unacceptable, first taking care to restore to the first two or three pages the words the original writer had used and the young plagiarist had edited out, perhaps as surplusage.

That was bad enough: the other instance was more serious. The plagiarist was a young man in his early thirties, the occasion a voluntary submission to a noncredit continuing-education course. Along with his short story he submitted a photocopy of stationery carrying the letterhead of one of America's most famous and prestigious magazines. The letter told him his story was being rejected with regret, and it went on to praise him, at some length, for many of the fine touches it contained. With the permission of the presumed author his story was read, anonymously, to the class. At the beginning of the next class session a man who had not previously spoken, angrily made a charge of plagiarism and asked to be permitted to submit proof. He did so. His proof was the photocopy of a newspaper column with a celebrated by-line, dated April 27. The rejection letter previously read to the class was dated July 17 of the same year.

Again there was no doubt. Some minor things had been changed; additions had been slight. Almost word for word, the words on the photocopied page were those of the short piece read aloud to the previous class. It was a shattering experience for us all. The person who had submitted the original non-original piece was present but remained silent throughout the discussion. One must be extremely circumspect on such occasions, yet the incident could not be passed over without comment. Leaving aside the legal consequences, about which only a lawyer could speak with certainty, I confined my comment to the harm such a practice could do to any writer as it was a direct assault on his judgment, on his very sense of himself and the integrity of his work. If ever the point that editing someone else's work is not writing needed making, this experience brought that point home. Imitation is a kind of remote flattery; plagiarism is utter dependence.

One might almost think that a proper reaction to incidents such as the above would be to read nothing at all. No, that is not the point. The beginning writer must refresh and inform himself or herself constantly with a knowledge of what is being done and how it is being done. And then one must go off and *in one's own words* try to do it oneself. The beginning writer must read. You cannot hope to write well and successfully what you are not willing to read. If you have contempt for poetry, if you avoid reading it whenever and wherever you can, it will be impossible for you to turn out an acceptable sonnet. Take, for example, *The New Yorker* magazine, that delight and despair of anyone who has attempted to write. If you read it with frequency, do you always skip over the fiction? And do you attempt to write fiction and send it out, to *The New Yorker* and elsewhere? Do you—an extreme but not an altogether unknown case—rather look down upon fiction yet attempt to write it and market it anyway? Obviously, something is wrong here. An editor will be the first one to detect your condescension, and will reward it appropriately—with a rejection slip.

Just as you cannot write with any degree of professional competence in a form that you look down upon, you cannot acquire professionalism, the touches that give a manuscript its professional air, its authoritative hum, by sheer accident. In one way or another, you have to slant. Some years ago I was a panel member at a discussion of creative writing for college students. Another panelist, an English professor and editor of a small-circulation magazine, declared that if a student of his turned in (and we all presumed there was no plagiarism here) a short story that might be worth sending to a mass-circulation magazine, he would not inform the student or assist the student in selling the story. The professor thought it would be bad for the student's morale and beneath his or her dignity to sell such work for a good price. I considered that the most arrant nonsense then, and I do so now. For one thing, any honest attempt to retrieve part of the cost of one's tuition is without question admirable and to a high degree character-forming. More seriously, it is impossible for someone to turn out a truly professional job without knowing one's craft. Writing may be an innate ability, everyone's birthright even—but not writing for publication in a major magazine. That's not nature, that's art.

A habit of reading is of inestimable value. Yet living totally in books, whether in the reading or the writing, is undoubtedly pedantic. There is here something of the chicken-and-the-egg dilemma for the writer; which comes first, life or the recording of life? Put another way, how can one prevent absorption and apprenticeship in writing from cutting one off from life, the very source of literature? One classic response to this dilemma—if one lives thoroughly and well, where will one find the time to write? if one writes, where will one find the time to live?—is the "cult of experience." The cult's two most famous American practitioners were Fitzgerald and Hemingway. Fitzgerald recorded in his fiction and his autobiographical *The Crack-Up* his hyperactive pursuit of literary material, at times taking him up and down the pleasure places of the French Riviera. The theory behind this frenzy was to live a social and emotional life so intensively that one's vibrant life would be the abundant source of one's material. With Hemingway the process was even more spectacular: flying planes, hunting water buffalo, breaking tradition and the rules as a war correspondent to fight in war—all "living-out," says Anthony Burgess, "strong-man fantasies in the literature he produced."

Others have found the Fitzgerald-Hemingway activist solution to be both excessive and unproductive. A writer who has based her work upon profound autobiographical soundings, upon what she calls her "remembering and transmuting mind," is firmly opposed to the experience cult. "If you want to write a novel about mountaineering," Katherine Anne Porter once told an audience at Georgetown University, "all you have to do is climb *one* mountain—part way." The implication is clear that there is a difference between fiction and reportage. Henry James put the position of those who deny the need for extensive experience when he said that a young woman could walk by a military barracks on a sunny day when all the windows were open and then go home and write a novel on regimental life. A middle ground between these two extremes of experience and inexperience recommends itself.

Sloan Wilson recommends that young writers would do well to live contented and interesting lives as the best preparation for writing novels. He seems to be calling for a new breed of writer. Most contemporary novelists, judging from what they have to say in their fiction, seem to have lived unhappy and frustrated early lives. However that may be, writers, young or old, stand in need of four personal characteristics if they are ever going to achieve print. They are the following: energy, method, persistence, and vanity (just a touch).

Energy is the first and perhaps the foremost. The physical strain resulting from prolonged application to writing (and very little can be accomplished through five minutes here and fifteen there) is considerable. Further, many people who aspire to write are engaged in occupations (such as teaching) that are energy-draining or, in one way or another, mind-depleting. Sling hash if you are serious about writing, Sinclair Lewis once advised, sling hash for a living and save your mind for your real work—writing. Clearly, writing is not for the languid, however sedentary an occupation it may appear to be.

Method, likewise, is not everything—but nearly everything. Admittedly, there can be madness in too much method; yet, as with any craft, a regular and orderly procedure and, if possible, a self-mandated time schedule are indispensable. Even seemingly trifling matters such as lining up sharpened pencils before beginning are not to be despised if they achieve results. What matters in method is what works for *you*. Remember Kipling's formula:

*There are nine and sixty ways of constructing tribal lays.*
*And—every—single—one—of—them—is—right!*

Circumstances will dictate your method. Circumstances and temperament. You decide whether or not, for example, you should rise early and put in an hour or two, or, as a night person, you should get down to it while the rest of the house is sleeping. Timing is part of method, so is place. One writer I know has a basement room, negatively equipped without telephone or windows, fixed up as his study. Upstairs, during his fixed business hours, his wife handles the mail and telephone messages. Flannery O'Connor wrote her great short stories with her back to the window, facing a blank white wall. Method involves sternness of will. Some things, of course, are not a matter of will alone. E. B. White observes that if being a major writer were a matter of will, there would be no minor writers. Nonetheless, being a writer at all is a matter of wishing to, willing to—and through method doing it.

Persistence, once the determination to write is made, is of equal if not greater importance. We all know, or have heard of, people who are gifted in all things but one: the gift of making the most of their gifts. Over the years I have observed that a truly gifted person, one perhaps too full of self-esteem, will be far less productive than the less gifted person (less a "natural" writer) who has a doggedness that will not be put down. Writers, someone has said, are people for whom writing is more difficult than it is for others. Often the very difficulty is the piece of grit in the oyster that produces the pearl.

Accompanying persistence must be an intelligent vanity, or rather a justified feeling of self-worth. One needs self-confidence, to the extent at least of thinking that one can write something that matters. If one's initial target is realistically moderate enough, everyone can do that. This means, of course, everyone who can think logically, write without cliché, and communicate grammatically. In grammatical terms, communication, the sentence itself, is a matter of predicating subjects. A subject given a predicate, another subject another predicate. Repeat this thousands upon thousands of times and you have a book. In order to be able to write with any degree of success, you need to possess that amount of assurance which enables you to master the means of saying and that you have something to say.

But if vanity should enter the writing process, it should not play any part in publication. In writing, your opinion of yourself matters a great deal. But in the acceptance of what you do, the opinion of others matters more. In fact, it is the only opinion worth having. It is something that can only be given freely; it cannot be bought. Publishing, whether in newspapers, magazines, or books, is the only remaining republic of merit. I am here and have created such and so. The editor is out there and will judge my work with relentless objectiviy. This is the professional way of things; this is the very integrity of letters.

What is chiefly wrong with vanity publishing (i.e., paying to appear in print) is that it means publication—of a sort—without benefit of objective judgment. You pay your money and you get—nothing. Vanity houses promise you a 40 percent royalty, as opposed to the usual 10 percent. But anyone can see the advantage of having 10 percent of someone else's money over 40 percent of your own. Vanity publications yield almost no royalties anyway, because they are—with rare exceptions—not bought. They are not bought because they are not reviewed. No reviewer in his or her right mind would request them, so the publishers send review copies out completely at random—right into oblivion. For around four thousand dollars, one of these slim, amateurishly dust-jacketed, badly bound volumes of butcher's paper can be yours—piled up in the darkness of your attic.

"Most people," Katherine Anne Porter once said from beneath the framework of a wide-brimmed hat, "don't want to write." She paused for the appropriate gasp. "They don't want to write; they want to *have written*." This reproach applies to us all, the published and the unpublished alike. An act of the will is involved, after all. And at times high purpose. At its most inspiring, and most exasperating, the task of placing words on paper offers challenges to which the response, however short of your ideal, will always be fulfilling.


## SUGGESTED FOLLOW-UP
## FOR THIS CHAPTER

### 1. *What to read*
Read biographies and autobiographies, of course. Dip into Boswell, and Walter Jackson Bate's almost equally plump biography of the great Dr. Johnson. If you can read only two autobiographies, make these *The Autobiography of Anthony Trollope* (a writer who tells all, his methods of writing and his earnings, in an engagingly straightforward style); and *The Education of Henry Adams* (mandarin in style at times but the greatest American autobiography to date, awesome in its prophetic scope). Somerset Maugham's *A Writer's Notebook* (first published 1947, reprint edition Arno Press 1971) and the journals of Arnold Bennett and Virginia Woolf are all noteworthy. The plight of the artist is the subject of several of Henry James's short stories. Read his story "The Lesson of the Master" for its exquisite portrayal of the demands of art and of life on the writer.

Make a habit of reading the obituary page in your daily paper. Here is biography of the anonymous in unending profusion. The astonishing variety of life stories you encounter on this page can be a fruitful source of ideas for both fiction and nonfiction. Most of all, it will plug you in to the life of your time.

### 2. *What to write*
For finger exercises only, try writing an autobiographical sketch. In the first person first. Then, treating yourself as a type—what categories do you fill?—in the third person. Start

keeping a journal. Record in it, among other things, snatches of conversation you overhear, to sharpen your ear for dialogue. On a bus recently I heard a woman say, "Laugh? I rolled around like a whipped dog." I am still trying to figure this out, but I like the imagery; it has an abrupt accuracy. Years ago I was walking on my beat as a reporter; a young woman and her child came toward me. As we met all three of us noticed a dead dog in the gutter. The mother reluctantly, after failing to distract the boy's attention entirely, acknowledged that the dog was dead. "Was he alive before?" the child asked. I have not been able to use that one yet, but the memory serves to remind me of the awesomely philosophical questions kids ask. Larry McMurtry says that he once overheard a conversation in a plane, some words that remained in his memory. It was ten years before he could use the remark in a novel. The point of the above is to illustrate the sort of things that can go into a journal, many of them impersonal and nonintrospective, yet in the true sense autobiographical.

### 3. *Where to send it*
Nowhere. The object of the above is to encourage the daily practice of putting your thoughts and experiences into words—into precise thinking, the kind of thought that can be communicated. Also, this can be a way of knowing yourself, perhaps even, as Bossuet put it, "to the pitch of being horrified." When you achieve that, it is time to, in Mauriac's sense, "surrender."

# CHAPTER 2
# LOOK AROUND YOU!

A young woman once inquired of Henry James what she should do in order to become a writer. "Be one of those," James replied, "upon whom nothing is lost." Then he added: "Observe. Always observe." In his *Notebooks* James is always reminding himself of his professional obligation to look around him. "I OBSERVE," he would write in capitals, and then add delightedly, "I VIBRATE!" Observation, with James, was not for idle reverie but for utility. To observe was ineluctably to see, and not with the photographing eye only, but with the probing eye of reason, the eye that told him what it truly was he saw. His response to the visible was to make it intelligible. He saw the ideas he was groping for as elusive fish and viewed himself as one whose business it was to grab them by the tail.

Learn to look around you, then. Much of your "looking" will be unconscious absorption, of course, as you go about intent on a number of concerns. It will be well, however, not to rely upon a casual imprint of the scene around you, but to be consciously alert. Keep your eyes and ears open, as the saying goes. Byron once sneered at Walter Scott for being so little the subconscious observer as to be required to dash outdoors with a notebook if he wished to describe a bird in his verses. Otherwise he could not have given us the color of the bird's tail feathers. It would be pleasant, like Lord Byron, to command such detail with the effortlessness of instinct, but if it takes rushing out, like Sir Walter, with a notebook, then by all means do so. Stephen Crane begins one of his greatest short stories, "The Open Boat," with this sentence: "None of them knew the color of the sky." The writer may not permit himself or herself to be like the men in Crane's boat. One must always know the color of the sky.

It will augur well for your success as a writer if you can train yourself to be a kind of radar screen, registering "blips" of all you encounter. To do this, you must move about, physically and mentally, on both the literal and figurative levels. On journeys to and from work, or for shopping or recreation, we all have hundreds, even thousands, of encounters with people and with things—with the dimensions of size and shape that appear, if only fleetingly, on our radar screens. Young Tarwater, the protagonist of Flannery O'Connor's *The Violent Bear It Away*, tells himself on his first visit to the city that thousands of people are seeing him there for the first time. Unless you are content to be a character in someone else's pages, reverse the process. Concentrate on seeing, rather than on being seen.

This can be done without staring. Keep your mind and eye in motion. What are the differing ways people carry umbrellas? Loosely, as items destined to be mislaid and forgotten, or tightly, as weapons? Notice the ways. How does a person break stride in order to look in a shop window? Does a man pause and linger one way, a woman another? Observe. What about crossing streets and the choosing of which side of the group to be part of in crossing with a traffic light? Something else you should take into account: Notice the way most people act when they place their arms and hands outside automobile windows, obtruding themselves on public notice. Do their dress and manners correspond? The appearance of people, the gestures and the sounds they make—take it all in. Objects, too, are constantly, insistently impinging themselves upon our vision.

Here you certainly can be aggressive and stare. Visit your neighborhood trees, notice the pitch of the roofs of houses, the way a fence stands, the frequency and contours of potholes. You are storing away in your memory landscapes for future use.

Utility is the key. You may become a more complex person, and perhaps a more entertaining conversationalist, if the product of your observation is reserved for your own enjoyment and not for other use, but it will not, under those circumstances, make you a writer. The writer always exploits—in the nonpejorative sense of the term—experience, and he or she is constantly looking for experience to exploit. A writer friend of mine tells the story of an unexpected experience he once had that formed the basis of a magazine article. (Perhaps implicit in what we have been saying so far has been the assumption that the gathering of images and impressions was for the sake of writing poetry or fiction only. Let us be explicit on this point then. Nonfiction as well derives from sources of direct observation as well as from books and libraries.) My writer friend found himself, one day, more than a half hour early for an appointment in a downtown office building. What to do? Half a corridor away from where he was going he happened to notice a glazed door with the words Artificial Eyes emblazoned within the outline of a human eye. More than curious, he scented copy. For him, a professional writer, this was invitation enough.

He knocked on the door and went in. A cherubic man, right out of Dickens, sat importantly at a desk. Behind him stood row upon row of cases containing unblinking artificial eyes. My friend quickly explained that he was not in the market for an eye but was only (only!) a free-lance writer. The other man beamed. He had a touch of the Ancient Mariner in him, it appears, and he welcomed an inquisitive visitor. Without any need for prodding, he revealed the whole glorious story of the artificial eye business. When he made or supplied an artificial eye, for example, he always kept an identical spare—

for immediate replacement. My friend felt a moment's uneasiness at the thought that somewhere out there an eye was being worn as mate to each displayed before him. The eye-maker took down one eye after another, as lovingly and carefully as though they were fragile eggs. "Now here's a special one," the zealot said. "The mate belongs to a very good customer of mine. Take it. Feel it. Do you notice anything unusual?" The writer held in his hand an artificial eye usual in every respect but one—in the iris was a tiny American flag.

"My customer is something of a prankster, I'm afraid," the eye-maker chuckled. "You see, when he is drinking at a bar, he will get to talking with the person standing next to him. At an appropriate moment he will make a switch, and then propose: 'Let's drink to the flag!'" His gesture as he replaced the eye in its container amounted to a salute. The writer had more than an article; he had his lead. This story even carries a moral. Another writer paid my friend the ultimate tribute from one professional to another—the tribute of envy. "For years," he exclaimed with exasperation, "I have been passing by that door on the way to my dentist, and I never once had the simple common sense to follow it up. Besides that, you sold your article to one of *my* editors—that's the final blow!"

The beginning writer is on the way to success the moment he or she becomes alert to the copy that experience yields. Everywhere the writer goes, material to write about is present, waiting practically in ambush. Recognizing subject matter in the constant bombardment of information that comes from the people, objects, and ideas that present themselves to us is a matter of attentiveness. What is needed is an alert and open mind. Marjorie Holmes tells of a young Englishwoman she met once, whose husband's career in service abroad had exposed her to a dozen cultures and had made the rearing and education of her young family difficult and exacting. "What can I write about?" she wondered aloud. "Why, about this—this too—and that," Marjorie replied as one humorous incident or vivid tale of woe followed another.

Sometimes all it takes is standing back for a detached look at ourselves. What do we prefer, what moves us, what do we think, perhaps most important of all, what do we remember? Memory tends to be selective, the result of un- conscious shaping of past events. What I remember about my childhood and about my growing up is highly selective (if you have any siblings, you can test this), an editing of what I was in terms of what I am now. This is how these events are *perceived*, not necessarily how they were. Nonetheless, they form the given, my capital as a writer. So does what I remember about the lives of others around me, and what I remember from books or formal training. By an examination of what I remember about history, for example, I can find a clue to what interests me outside myself. I have begun to block out a field for myself in nonfiction.

The main thing is to have a bump of curiosity, and to keep it working overtime. G. K. Chesterton once said that there are no uninteresting subjects, only uninterested people. For the writer, interest is perhaps even more important than original- ity. If our reaction to things we hear, see, smell, and experience is conventional—if we react the way anyone else would—what then? Simply put, it can mean that if we articulate what we think and feel, we speak for thousands. Our curiosity, on the other hand, may take a more probing, more complex, more individual turn. Ours may be the gift for expressing the minority voice, the tread of the out-of-step marcher who sees things differently, with a point of view that deserves respect—and articulation.

Conventionality of view, then, is no excuse for remaining mute. Nor is the conviction that one marches to a different drummer. Conformist or nonconformist, yea-sayer or nay- sayer, what is important is to be alive to possibilities. Observe and vibrate—in the manner of Henry James, and not in the scattered, impulsive way of the amateur. Alertness is all— alertness for use. We who would write must continually be in a state of receptivity; we should be willing, with King Lear to

> *hear poor rogues*
> *Talk of court news; and we'll talk with them too,*
> *Who loses, and who wins; who's in, who's out;*
> *And take upon's the mystery of things,*
> *As if we were God's spies.*

In the infinite mystery of things we can discover, in all but infinite ways, our own reflection and subjects.

The recognition of subjects is merely the necessary first step. That is all it is—a beginning. Awareness occurs when we wed subject to form. This is an idea! There is copy in that! Here is a "germ" for a story! To recognize these things is to be at the primary state of awareness. The true shock of recognition comes when the idea and its formal identity are simultaneous. Then ideas come clothed. This is a suggestion—this feeling, this image—for a poem. Here I have an idea for a documented article or a "think piece." With Henry James, I find a character instantly present to me, a character and his "story" coming "in a bound!"

You are most likely to see and grasp your subject in terms of the literary form you enjoy the most to read and write. If you tend to read fact most, it will occur to you to write articles; if you are a constant reader of fiction, stories. The rhythms and sentence patterns, the stanzas or paragraphs, the sizes and shapes of larger wholes—all these are urgent and palpable because they have, after long contemplation and usage, become the form of your thought. Patterns of prose or verse should constantly be in mastery of your mind. Your subject will not come to you already fashioned, a matter of "found art," encountered formed and complete on a beach or in a junkyard. It will be rather the stuff of scrimshaw, the sea-molded ivory ripe for the transmutations wrought by handicraft. Many times an idea that occurs to you will be susceptible to molding into only one or at most two literary forms. It might be a theory or a process that can be made articulate only in nonfiction prose—of article or book length.

Or the idea that occurs to you may be so tentative and fragile that it would support only the lyric moment of a short poem. It could, of course, come to you in the form of a few words, and yet be capable of ramifying into a novel of a thousand pages.

Arnold Bennett, in his preface to *The Old Wives' Tale*, tells how the idea for his lengthy novel came to him. As he was sitting in a café in Paris he noticed an old woman nearby, staring down at the glass of absinthe placed before her. The woman's drooping shoulders and her general air of desolation moved him to think, "She was young once, and loved." From his one glance, one thought, one swift perception came the elaborately detailed, many-peopled novel which is his master-piece. Liberated from the burden of additional knowledge about the woman—he gave her no second glance—he was able to move from the actuality of the café to the far more real world of his imagination. He was able to confer a sister upon the woman, now young, now beginning, and to weave a web of intricate relationships for her. He set his heroine and her sister down, for a time, in Paris, the Paris not of the actual world of the old woman but of the past, of the time of the Commune, following the fall of Napoleon III. His plot, his theme, and his characters all evolved from a seemingly casual encounter. If Bennett is not deceiving us (and himself) his is an account of a magic moment when what he saw before him and his skills from the long practice of his art instantly converged.

It should prove instructive to apply Bennett's idea, his "germ," to other forms. Obviously, if the encounter could yield a novel it could also provide the basis for a short story. One could take the same encounter and the thought it engendered for Arnold Bennett but decide the scene would be the café, the time the present, and provide just one other major character. Who might that be? A son perhaps. Make him the waiter. Bring him out so we can see him. Get them into a casual conversation and see what happens. Consider, for example, creating a brief altercation over the payment. The waiter pays for the drink, and leaves a tip for the woman. A bemused American tourist looks on in bewilderment. Or she is present to pick up a packet of a drug. A minor character comes in, an agent of L'Office Générale de la Répression du Trafic Illicite de Stupéfiants, to make an arrest. He sees the woman and is moved to pity. On second thought, the first idea is better. The second is too facile, too capable of decline into melodrama.

Try a poem. We have an idea here with enough body in it for a sonnet, indeed for a sequence of sonnets. What Bennett perceived when he saw the old woman he immediately intellectualized with the most useful of literary devices, the device of contrast—old woman, young woman; beauty, ugliness; then, now. Any one pair of these disparates will yield a lyric. Such a twoness of people, things, time is behind many of Shakespeare's sonnets. A perusal of sonnets 2 ("When forty winters shall besiege thy brow / And dig deep trenches in thy beauty's field."), 6 ("Then let not winter's ragged hand deface / In thee thy summer ere thou be distilled"), and 65 ("Since brass, nor stone, nor earth, nor boundless sea / But sad mortality o'ersways their power"), for example, will prove my point. Your poem need not have the formal structure of a sonnet, although working within the fourteen-line restriction affords practice and discipline. Free verse will do equally well. The point is to capture your impression, your emotion, your fleeting perception in a net of words.

Is Bennett's original idea capable of expression in nonfiction? Of course it is. Had Bennett been another type of person, a journalist, say, instead of a novelist, a light essay might have resulted. Try the idea, invoking the Impressionist painters. Place a Toulouse-Lautrec poster behind the woman's head, the poster face and body of a younger woman. The lettering announces a fancy ball. But that, you might argue, is to be one step away from—or toward—fiction. Very well, then, let us see whether or not our subject, Bennett's germ idea, is capable of reportorial treatment. For an investigative reporter the subject might prove no less attractive than for others. The old woman drinking her absinthe raises all sorts of statistical and sociological questions. Is she a representative figure? Does her society tolerate her, and on what terms? Can she be found, in greater numbers or at all, in Amsterdam, in London, in Madrid? A social historian with unlimited curiosity, and an ample expense account, could make much of Bennett's old woman.

"It is no use being a writer," Arnold Toynbee tells us, "if one is not *en rapport* with the world in which one is living." Toynbee's "world," of course, is a structure of thought and action as well as one of direct impressions and sensations. The writer of fiction as well as the writer of nonfiction will do well to inhabit this world. One owes it to oneself and to the integrity of one's work to be one's own contemporary, and this can best be done by being *en rapport* with the full range of communications of the electronic age. Newspapers, magazines, radio, film, and television—as well as books—keep one sensitive and responsive to the pulse of one's time. Retreat to some kind of academic ivory tower is unconscionable as well as being almost impossible. Information on what is going on now is obviously indispensable to the article writer; it is of equal value to the writer of fiction and the poet. Without it none of them can hope to remain relevant or even plausible.

For the beginning writer the public library and its librarian should be primary sources for keeping in touch with the outside world. They should be viewed as the writer's first line of communications with his potential readers. A good library affords the most convenient way for the writer to discover and explore new issues of magazines, the familiar and those offering new markets because of changing editorial policies. Check out such changes. Here one may study back issues of magazines to "slant" for and can check the Books Newly Received shelf to learn what topics are current. The librarian can be called upon for information on what types of books are in demand, and what subjects are most inquired about. For the writer of juveniles the children's librarian is more than helpful; she or he is likely to be indispensable.

For most purposes, the nearby branch of the public library will be more useful to the journalistic writer than a college or university library which may be accessible. The average public library is much more likely to house the "slicks," the mass-circulation magazines, and the trade journals. On the other hand, the college library is almost certain to have a much wider selection of quality magazines, of the quarterlies, and especially of little magazines of limited circulation. The last group is of special interest to poets and writers of short fiction. It is not too much to say that without them poetry and the short story would be nearly defunct. Whichever library is available to you and you feel at home in, visit it frequently and regularly. Never leave the periodical room without going through the latest issue of *Publishers Weekly*. Edit your own digest magazine, so to speak, by spending a few hours each month going from magazine to magazine, sampling the contents, taking notes. Read at least one magazine covering a subject you are familiar with but which does not interest you.

An effective sampling will include more than noting the contents, important as that is. After you have examined the contents of a typical issue (it will take the perusal of at least a half dozen recent issues to determine what is typical), noting the types of material used (any poetry? any fiction? how many stories in each issue?), you will have appraised the general tone of the magazine, taking into account level of language and the literary or political assumptions the contributors and the editors seem to share with their readers. Make particular note of paragraph length. The larger the magazine's circulation, the shorter the paragraphs in the articles are likely to be.

Examine the advertising contents with equal care. What is advertised in, say, *The New Yorker* and *Popular Mechanics* will tell you much about the expectations of the editor. The reading interests and the purchasing power of the subscribers to both magazines are being reflected in the copy and the advertising. Editors are particularly conscious of this relationship, and the free-lance writer should be too. The attitude

toward the people he or she is publishing for marks the difference between the magazine publisher and the book
publisher. The magazine publisher knows, or is persuaded that
he or she knows, the people out there who are regular readers.
Surveys draw all sorts of elaborate profiles of the readers; they
can be polled.

The book publisher, on the other hand, lives in almost
total ignorance, beyond a general educated guess, of who is
buying, and especially who is reading a particular work. The
reader does not bring the same identification to a book as to a
magazine. Someone might say, in irritation or disgust, "I'm
never going to read *The Atlantic Monthly* again!" or "That
does it! I'm canceling my subscription to *Newsweek*!" (One
remembers President Kennedy, in a misguided moment of
pique, stopping the White House subscription to the
*Herald-Tribune*. He quickly regretted it, and resubscribed.)
But no one would say, "This is trash. I'll never read another
Doubleday book!" Or "That's Harper and Row. No thanks. I
won't start it. I didn't like the last one." Book publishers have
almost no way of knowing who their readers are; readers, in
turn, are almost never aware of the imprint of the book they are
reading. This lack of product identification in the book world
carries far-reaching consequences for the writer.

The most important of these is that the book writer enjoys
freedoms from editorial restraint that the magazine writer,
especially of nonfiction, does not know. Book publishing has
room for variety in styles and approaches because in the public
mind very few publishers enjoy a definite profile or image. The
book editor knows a freedom of maneuver that the magazine
editor, more image-ridden, may well envy. A magazine is,
according to its nature and identity, required to appear at
regular intervals and with the same number of pages when it
does appear. The writer's contribution to an issue of a
magazine is a single item: an article, a story, or a poem. The
implication is plain that all the contributors conform in one
degree or another to a controlling editorial policy; they become

part of the corporate entity. They conform to the greatest tyrant of them all, the rigid limitations of space. Stephen Spender once commiserated with the American writer of short fiction for being condemned to appear in fragmented pieces framed by display advertising.

The book world presents no such limitations on utterance. If he or she has something to say, the book writer, in fiction or nonfiction, may be copious, even prolix. Even with heavy editing, he or she is likely to be asked to conform to his or her best self rather than to a pattern established and upheld by others. The great Maxwell Perkins intervened mightily, one has read, with Scott Fitzgerald and Thomas Wolfe, in both instances solely to free them to be more fully themselves, not to make them conform to a Scribner's house image. According to what Fletcher Knebel said once to a group of writers-conference participants, no book has a single author: every book is a collaboration between author and editor. At that time Knebel was smarting under the implications, as he saw them, of being only half a writer because his best-selling *Seven Days in May* was the result of a collaboration. (He has since gone on to write several excellent books all on his own, none of them best-sellers of the magnitude of *Seven Days in May*.) Certainly there are instances where an editor has taken a strong hand with a book manuscript, probably in all of them to urge the transformation of something inchoate into viable form.

Authors are not always the best judges of their own potential. Sometimes, like unsuccessful politicians, they lack a firm grasp of the art of the possible. An editor told me once about a published author who was on his way to becoming an unpublished one, at least as far as one particular book was concerned, because he was insisting upon the inclusion of two dozen plates in full color. He should have known, the editor complained to me, that he was pricing the book right out of the competitive market. There was no way anyone could publish this particular manuscript with these illustrations and not price the book out of sight. The beginning writer, of course, never would get to the point where his or her demands for color illustrations would even be momentarily considered. And that is the point: part of the craft of writing involves learning as much as you can about the mechanics and economics of publication. A poet is no less sensitive for being aware that one magazine will recompense him or her with a check for a poem whereas another will pay with only complimentary copies of the issue the poem appears in.

Learn as much as you can about the printing trade, about type sizes and styles, about graphics. Your public library may get *Printer's Ink*. Ask to see the librarian's desk copy of *LMP* (*Literary Market Place*, an annual publication) for information on names and addresses of book publishers, dates of writers conferences, literary agents, periodicals that publish book reviews, the addresses of syndicates handling literary material, and much more. As a free-lance writer, if you achieve any modicum of success, your work will be handled by people in a number of trades. The more you know about them, the more professional your attitudes and your work will become.

Even though it may be obvious that many matters peripheral to the art of writing can be learned, or learned about, a major question remains. Can writing itself be learned, or, to put it another way, can writing be taught? The question always draws a number of seemingly contradictory responses. Absolutists of the affirmative and absolutists of the negative are equally vehement in their answers. Here, as elsewhere, it is useful to make distinctions. Always distinguish, as the Aristotelians say. In the nineteenth centry young people were always asking the famous, "Have I a genius?" The implication was that talent was something innate; it might be discovered within, but it could not be put there. Clearly, nobody can be taught to become a major writer—a Ph.D. in English literature or even in comparative literature will not do it. Our schools and universities cannot produce artists or creative people with the facility with which they turn out physicians and lawyers, and no reasonable person would expect them to. But they can discover and cultivate talent already there. "Nobody can make a writer of someone whom God neglected to," Bernard De Voto once wrote. "But the right teaching can shorten the apprenticeship of an inexperienced writer, and it can sometimes do a lot for writers who regard themselves as finished products."

Writers and teachers are in agreement that certain shortcuts and matters of technique can be transmitted from teacher to beginner. Seán O'Faoláin, the Irish master of the short story, considers writing courses valid in their ability to convey technique and also for the stimulating effect they can have when a small group of enthusiasts get together under direction to discuss "the lonely, patient devisings of the craftsman artist." A course that requires a student to write—rather than merely talk about writing—has obvious value. It has the virtue of demanding work and of presenting deadlines. No one is ever going to write without having a method for producing work—and producing it on schedule. Ray Bradbury has taken on a few students over the years, setting "harsh" but "tonic" regimens for them. "I told them," he wrote for a symposium conducted by the editors of *Four Quarters*, "they must write one story, or its equivalent, a week, for fifty-two weeks a year, for five or ten years, in order to have the luxury of burning millions of words, in order to wind up with some good ones." He goes on to say, "I have yet to see great quantity that did not wind up one day as eventual quality."

Perhaps most of us are, for a multitude of reasons, either unwilling or unable to pursue the path to quality through overwhelmingly quantitative means. Nontheless, Bradbury points the way, the optimum way, let us concede, to fulfillment as an artist. For the worker in a craft (the cabinetmaker not the sculptor, so to speak) the way may be no less arduous—with one difference: One may practice the trade while still serving an apprenticeship. One may be appearing in print on less well paying levels while learning how to analyze and meet the requirements of much more demanding markets. As long as one writes, one is learning. Experience teaches indirectly; reading, daily sessions at the typewriter, membership in a club or group, or study under an individual teacher, offer direct instruction in the use of words, the writer's lifelong concern.

For those who wish to serve an apprenticeship in writing through formal instruction, the climate has never been more favorable. Degree-granting institutions throughout the country offer humanities programs that include a variety of noncredit continuing-education courses in writing. One reason for attending is to become exposed to the ideas and ambitions of others. The student body taking such courses, especially on an urban campus, can offer the beginning writer the shock of recognition that comes from association with others of similar purpose and goals. Such a shock may stimulate the spur of emulation (I can do it, too). Excuses for not writing frequently fade away when you discover the obstacles others face— particularly obstacles posed by other demands on the writer's time and energy.

As you look around you, you will discover others whose very presence in the same classroom is of considerable help to you. Perhaps they are more at ease when it comes to plying the instructor with questions, or they may have problems you recognize as similar to your own. It may turn out that you can look upon your own publishing credits with more satisfaction when you discover someone with comparable ones, or fewer, confidently setting out with a plan for publication. These are people who, at whatever stage of their lives, have found something to say and are determined to be heard. From my own recent continuing-education classes I can recall vividly several such cases. Among them: a young man who came with the completed manuscript of a first novel (since published and succeeded by two books of nonfiction); a woman who was an active and competent huntswoman and who made her new target magazine articles after having published Sunday features in newspapers; a woman who held a secretarial position yet found time to write a weekly column she placed, through her own unaided efforts, in nine newspapers. And then there was the successful non-success story of the retired Army colonel whose response to the rejection of his first novel by a half dozen publishers was to plunge with undiminished enthusiasm into his second.

Such contacts can stimulate envy—good, so long as it is emulative envy—in the beginning writer. If she can do it—can find time for writing as well as being a housewife and mother of small children—so can I. More important perhaps than the inspiration offered by fellow students is the help which a competent instructor can provide. Someone capable of professional response can be an objective touchstone for your work. Ideally, this instructor will have had practical as well as academic experience. It is very well to hear how Jane Austen may have handled a problem of characterization or how Mark Twain or Walt Whitman or Thomas Wolfe named, catalogued, and vitalized the places of the American scene. Historic precedents are helpful, and the craft, whether fiction or nonfiction, contains elements that are unchanging. But you need to know what is happening now, what editors are likely to be looking for, what newspapers or magazines are plausible targets for you here and now. If your instructor is personally battle-scarred from having received a full quota of rejection slips, along with some significant credits, enkindling sparks should fly from such a relationship.

Many colleges and universities offer credit courses and degree programs in writing. They normally make sense mostly for those of undergraduate or graduate school age. The M.A. program in writing at the University of Pittsburgh arranges its schedules "so that the degree is attainable by employed persons attending evening classes." The objectives of these degree programs are instructive; they show what in the view of many institutions can be taught. The University of Washington hopes to "fuse the vigor of the creative impulse with the discrimination of criticism." The University of Alaska has the goal of producing "good writers who will write with a sound knowledge of their own literary and cultural backgrounds and traditions." The University of South Dakota looks for "writers as interpreters of their region." Stanford University has as its aim the providing of a "critical and supportive climate." For Antioch University, the recipient of the Master of Arts is "a professional, dedicated artist, a real live word hero." Syracuse University looks beyond the individual student to "furthering imaginative writing in America." (For further information on the degree-granting programs, undergraduate and graduate, in American colleges and universities, write: Associated Writing Programs, c/o Department of English, Old Dominion University, Norfolk, Virginia 23508.)

Joining, or even establishing, a group for like-minded people interested in writing, a writers club, is a possibility the beginning writer might wish to consider. There is something to be said for the mutual support such membership could give. One often feels the need of a sympathetic ear. Yet if it is a group of the unpublished, one can see little advantage beyond temporary consolation in it. A group of published writers coming together in friendship and for mutual support could be quite another thing. Yet here is where the difficulties in such an association really begin. Even among newly published writers there tends to be inequality. Success of one member places that member in an awkward position in relation to the others. Success isolates; and it will be discovered, sometimes painfully, that the problems of those who publish regularly and of those whose work appears only now and then are by no means the same.

Then we have that unique and characteristic American institution, the writers conference. The first conference, the Bread Loaf Conference, was established in 1926 at Middlebury College, Vermont, under the inspiration of Robert Frost, who called for "a place where writers meet to see what they can get out of each other." For over half a century, every summer writers and editors and students have been congregating in college classrooms or lounges, or under giant oak trees, with ivy-covered buildings, lakes, or mountains for backdrop, to see what they can get from one another. Since most conferences last only a week or two, there are limitations to what they can give. A conference alone cannot "create" or even "develop" a writer, but it can have a precise role in that creation, that development.

There is a time in every writer's life, whether he or she be chronologically young or merely young in spirit, when it is right for that person and a conference to come together. It is helpful, for one thing, to learn early on that writing is a lonely enterprise that is nonetheless related to a whole community. A conference can give the untried writer an objective self-view. A conference can be an up-to-date source of market information, and it will help the untried writer to know where to aim with a hope of hitting. A conference can give the unpublished and the slightly published writer a focus through which to view the complex worlds of book and magazine publishing. A conference can give the amateur a promise and a glimpse and taste of the world of professional competence and performance. Perhaps this will be one's first opportunity to see and meet and talk with living authors, to realize they are people not pages.

A writers conference should inform. It can serve as the intermediary between the writer and the editor. It can prepare the fledgling writer for encounter with the latter—sometimes in person—at the conference itself. It can supply fresh market information; it can account for trends in publishing, or at least show that trends exist. It can define basic terms and qualify all sorts of confused concepts of the role of the editor or the agent; it can give information (available in books, but scattered) about contracts and other facts of the writing life. Most importantly, it can provide the immediacy and variety of the current literary scene.

A writers conference can and should instruct. There are two chief ways a conference instructs (aside from presenting speakers and panelists): through workshops and through manuscript consultation. Workshops are condensed courses in a literary form: verse writing, article writing, the short story. Some conferences limit the participant in the number of workshops that can be taken, often by running them concurrently. Others are completely open, allowing the indefatigable participant to sit in on them all. There is a distinct advantage to be gained from a conference that permits open scheduling. The beginning writer may not know what form he or she can be good at; he or she may have a romantic attachment to, say, the novel and be far away from success with it. He or she may have scorned the idea of fiction, on the other hand, and through the fiction workshop feel a hitherto unacknowledged interest. Manuscript consultation with a workshop director who has published in the form is a distinct advantage to the new writer. It is having an editor you can talk to, even if that editor must, to be honest, play the role of animated rejection slip.

Above all, a writers conference should inspire. A conference should not be conceived of as a one- or two-week sublimation for rejection slips, or as a surefire method for curing the same, but as a living example of what professional objectivity means. It is a genuine inspiration to come in contact with writers and editors and to see that writers, editors, and publishers all have a stake in occupying the same country. For there is no officers' country separate from enlisted men's country: they are one. The words of Mark Twain to a young correspondent ring true today. "As soon as his writings are worth money," Twain wrote in a Buffalo newspaper, "plenty of people will hasten to offer it. I wish to urge upon him once more the truth that acceptable writers for the press are so scarce that book and periodical publishers are seeking them constantly and with a vigilance that never grows heedless for a moment."

To the extent that it really and permanently succeeds, the writers conference has its effect not when the participant is still on campus, but later and long afterward. Sinclair Lewis is reported to have addressed the participants of a conference with impatience. "You're writers, are you?" he asked. "Then why aren't you home writing?" He has a point, of course. Yet many, perhaps most of the people he was talking to would not have been writing at all without the information, instruction, and inspiration they obtained from the conference. What is received depends, of course, upon the receiver. There is the impatient, ungrateful genius. Genius is young, talented, and fiercely self-protective. He or she will probably arrive and depart sneering. A conference that had too many young geniuses at one time would quickly be dismembered. A conference that never had any young writers of talent would not be worth conducting. They will stir others (some to disbelief or irritation), for they will circulate the idea of quality, of the worthwhileness of it all. The young genius will have an enlightening effect on others. So will the old retread, the participant who has published but for one reason or another needs to be reinspired, revitalized, rechanneled into another literary form. A conference can, as a recent Georgetown participant put it, "bridge a gap for a writer whose work has been interrupted for a few years." Another participant whose very presence is helpful to others is the writer by association— the teacher who comes to a conference out of interest in cultural richness and interplay—and whose students back home will profit from a week whose reverberations they know only by hearsay.

Let us suppose that you, the beginning writer, have attended a conference, combining activity and relaxation in an unprecedented way, full of impressions and memories, with notebooks bursting—and are now home again. If the conference has been worthwhile for you, the urge to be at the business of writing has become contagious; you picked it out of the conference air, from the program itself, from the celebrated guest speaker, from a sympathetic reading of your manuscript, or from the comments of a fellow participant. You have memories, let us say, of contrary points of view about agents or of a visiting writer who out of generosity of spirit made it seem all too easy, or the one whose spiky attitude said I made it, but can you?

You have had a week or so to listen, to talk, and to dream—nobody ever gets any writing done at writers conferences—and now the time has come to file away your notes and get down to the lonely, one-on-one—one person, one paper—business that writing unavoidably, inevitably is. If you have carried away anything valuable from the conference you attended, it is likely to be, from one speaker after another, from each of the workshops, that method and schedule are absolute necessities. It may have been possible, as the saying has it, for the British to obtain their empire in moments of absentmindedness, but that is no way to go about acquiring a book. Or even a newspaper article. Or possibly, if it has any length at all, a poem.

Regular hours, writer after writer will tell you—and doubtless have told you at the conference—rank high among priorities. For most of us, this means adding regular hours to those we already put in—at the office, at the plant, in the classroom, over a hot stove. So we steel ourselves to getting up early, when all the house is quiet, or staying up until the same condition of silence obtains, and staring at the enemy—the threateningly blank piece of paper. These solitary sessions should be frequent as well as regular. Ideally, they should be daily. It is not always possible to adhere unfailingly to such a schedule, but the daily practice (with no time off for holidays) should be one's goal. In his prime, Hemingway adhered to a daily schedule—and to a production of five hundred words—that allowed for an occasional day off fishing. To make up for that he wrung out seven hundred and fifty words a day, two hundred and fifty for each day away from the typewriter.

The time set aside daily should be at least an hour, a clock hour not an academic hour. It is further discipline not to shift around the clock with the writing hour, early one day and late the next unless circumstances make regularity impossible. Some writers are indifferent to the place they write in; others find it impossible to write anywhere other than at a certain desk (or in bed, as Mark Twain and G. K. Chesterton did) in a certain room. Some writers require familiar objects around them, with everything in place. Booth Tarkington had to have everything arranged on his desk exactly where it had always been, and he required a number of freshly sharpened pencils. Anatole France was the most finicky of all: he did his reading in a separate library building on his Loire valley estate; he wrote, robed and skullcapped a la Balzac, at a beautiful antique desk in his drawing room.

Time and place, however, are the mere disposing elements. They are important only as they dispose to action. If you have to be inside a trash can like a Beckett character, and nothing else will get you started, then there is the place to be. For the fortunate few this preparation may mean only a few minutes of concentration, of going over one's notes—and then they are off and running. The less fortunate, the bleeders, may require more. If Hemingway had trouble getting going on something he was already into—and this happened frequently—he would retype the last three or four pages of what he had previously written. Then he would be off on the new page before he really knew it. Write something. Even a letter to yourself complaining about the problem you have writing. Or make a fresh journal entry. Graham Greene used a journal as a way "to talk aloud to myself" and wrote about dialogue for novels he was gathering notes and impressions for, inventing incidents. Some of the random dialogue and disparate incidents he found useful and usable, others he did not.

One of the most remarkable results of a seemingly desultory beginning is recorded in Flannery O'Connor's remarkable collection of speeches and essays entitled *Mystery and Manners*. She sat down one morning, she tells us, with the intention to write firmly in mind, but with little else besides.

She started off by describing the women of her acquaintance, and the first thing she knew, as she dryly recounts, she equipped one of the women with a daughter who had a wooden leg. Then a Bible salesman walked into the story....

Most writing comes to be realized in a similarly spontaneous way—but only after one's powers of concentration, however artificially, have been bolstered, coaxed, and cossetted, by trivia even.

To paraphrase Sinclair Lewis: You are at your desk, aren't you? You have pencil in hand or typewriter at the ready?

Why aren't you writing?

## SUGGESTED FOLLOW-UP
## FOR THIS CHAPTER

### 1. *What to read*
Above all, and every month, read the two leading magazines for writers: *The Writer* and *Writer's Digest*. Both provide the latest in market news—new markets for the free-lancer, markets that have folded, new prizes and contests—the kind of target finding the beginning writer needs to know. The publishers of each magazine come out with an annual (or in the case of *The Writer*, a nearly annual) market guide. *The Writer* brings out at frequent intervals *The Writer's Handbook*, which contains how-to and why-to articles as well as categorized where-to listings. *Writer's Digest* brings out the annual *Writer's Market*, with a small amount of comment but an extraordinarily ample categorized guide to the markets. For the British market there is the fascinating and splendidly informative annual *Writers' and Artists' Yearbook* (London: Adam & Charles Black).

### 2. *What to write*
An opening suggestion—it may take up your time, but it will save you money—is to get off the telephone. Instead write to

people, whether in your code area or long distance, with whom you regularly have long telephone conversations. Don't broadcast the same form letter, as some people do with year-end greetings. Make each letter individual, shaped to the personality of the recipient as well as to your own. Pour out as much as you like, put as much of yourself into it as your correspondent can take without embarrassment or offense. You are getting *you* on paper, that's the point. Keep carbons or exact copies, of course. Remember the content of the letter belongs to the writer, not to the recipient. Your rights are protected under common law.

Another suggestion—is to clip and write fillers. This may seem like really beginning at rock bottom, but, again, that's the point. *The New Yorker* is the top market for these. An examination of *The Writer's Handbook* and *Writer's Market* will yield a list of magazines paying for fillers. They pay more of course if you are able to write a caption they can use. What are you doing when you are writing fillers? You are training your eye to watch for items you come across in newspapers— items that mirror the ironic, the pretentious, or the absurd in daily life—and you are practicing the art of writing the appropriate and pithy sentence. You are, therefore, on your way to becoming a writer.

### 3. *Where to send it*
Study the filler market, as suggested above, and then clip, comment, and enclose your S.A.S.E. (self-addressed stamped envelope) and take it off to the nearest mailbox.

# CHAPTER 3
# FIND THE
# RIGHT WORD

It is time to turn away from consideration of the self as subject. It is time now to examine our bedrock source for communicating the I-thou relationship: the resources of language. Everything begins with the word, the wellspring of what we think and say. Words are our tools as writers, our implements and our raw materials. From among these symbols of our daily meetings and traffic, from the very banalities of ordinary existence, we must pluck the precise instrument of our art, the right word—*le mot juste*—and place it in a context of other words, cogent and well chosen. The result, objectively, is style; the result, subjectively, is ourselves. Setting down proper words in proper places, as that canny manipulator of language Jonathan Swift put it, is the whole of the art of writing.

Whatever our ethnic background, whether English is native to us or—as in the instance of one of our greatest writers, Joseph Conrad—acquired, we have fallen heir to one of the world's great languages. Ours is a communications system abundant in vocabulary, extraordinarily rich in its literature, and each day more and more the language of international exchange in trade, in diplomacy, and in contemporary science and technology. A world linguistic map will show the vast areas of the globe where, for historic reasons of settlement and consequent cultural penetration, English is the first language.

Elsewhere, as in Scandinavia, it is taught in school as a second language, making that extremely literate part of the world an instantaneous market for the ideas of those who write in English. Our tongue has gone a long way, like it or not, toward displacing French in diplomacy and German in science. This geographic extension is of no little importance to the American free-lancer. "No foreign language," Stephen Crane once wrote, "will ever be my friend." And, writers like Conrad and Nabokov aside, the writer whose goal it is to communicate in English will subordinate other living languages to a thorough idiomatic saturation in the tongue of Chaucer, Shakespeare, Jane Austen, Hawthorne, Mark Twain, and Hemingway.

Our linguistic inheritance is enormous. An unabridged English dictionary contains the most extensive vocabulary available in any modern language. Because we have had no official monitor over what is acceptable or assimilable, no equivalent of the French academy to declare which words may gain respectability and which may not, ours is an unequaled word depository. Over the centuries, following the trade routes of commerce, exploration, or conquest, our language has picked up and absorbed the words of many countries and cultures. The result has been a literature of great flexibility and power. Yet the very copiousness of our word bank provides handicaps as well as opportunity. Because of the inheritance of a word bank limited and controlled by a literature of classic eloquence, the mayor of a small village in France can call upon the language of Racine and, on the meanest or most routine of occasions, achieve clarity and distinction. His American counterpart, faced with resources more ample but less disciplined, can only bumble in cliché and platitude. It is impossible to count the ways to be grammatically correct in English and yet stylistically deadly.

How did this come about? As suggested above, through the very abundance at our disposal, but also because of the history of English. The language of a small island has held a curious dominion over a nation continent-wide and with a vastly greater population. In terms of our language, our history will always have been English first. Old English, for example, comes into our language inheritance by reason of the fact that Germanic tribes, the Angles and the Saxons, came to conquer and displace earlier inhabitants of Celtic origin, who still earlier had been subdued and held in check by the Romans. At base, then, our language is a highly inflected one, as replete with case endings as Latin itself. Then the Danes came, the "hethene men" of the Anglo-Saxon chronicles; they came annually to plunder, to make coastal raids which carried off women and cattle. At last the Danes, reacting to pressures at home by even more savage tribes to the east, came to Europe's offshore island to stay. The linguistic consequences were considerable; they removed the inflections of Anglo-Saxon, giving us a language wherein word order rather than case endings controlled the sentence.

Even before the Danes, of course, the language of the English was enriched by the island's conversion to Christianity. Ecclesiastical Latin and the complex language of theology, of Greek as well as Latin origin, was grafted on to that of native stock. Then in 1066, a year known to every English schoolboy but perhaps negligible in the consciousness of Americans, there occurred another conquest, another occupation, again with lasting linguistic consequences. This was the Norman Conquest. A sophisticated feudal order, with an extensive new vocabulary, was imposed. The new language was French, or more properly Norman French, a language whose genius was in many subtle ways different from the genius of the Anglo-Saxon.

The Norman Conquest gave us—gave us as Americans!—doublets; words of Norman origin that are exact equivalents of words already in the language. (At that moment doublespeak was born.) Compare the Anglo-Saxon *begin* with the

Norman-French *commence*, which are no different in meaning. Or Anglo-Saxon *end* and Norman French *terminate*. Again the meaning is the same. Yet only the careless would write a sentence like "The day began with sunlight and light breezes and terminated in blustery winds and rain." Here is a stylistic error that is easy to commit, yet almost equally easy to eliminate. All one has to do is to check the word origin, in a good dictionary, Webster's unabridged if possible. As a rule of thumb, a good, effective (A.S. *god*, F. *effectif*) style will not be overly French, will have an Anglo-Saxon base. Communication so "pure" that all one's words would have Anglo-Saxon roots is neither possible nor desirable. It would be so pure as to be primitive. It would leave thought where it was centuries ago, would rule out the possibility of communication about the technological world we see all about us. On the other hand, sentences composed almost entirely (A.S. *throughout*) of words of Latin origin will, unless they are on scientific or technical subjects, sound pretentious, even bombastic.

The free-lance contributor to general magazines will take special care with the words to be formed into sentences. In general, the concrete words in our language are Anglo-Saxon in origin, the abstract ones of Latin or French origin. Latinate words tend to be polysyllabic, to express abstractions; in tone they tend to be hortatory, to "editorialize." Unless the subject is one that will not admit any humanizing whatever—and no subject is made up solely of technical terms and concepts— your first reader, the magazine editor, will stiffen at the sight of them. The editor will do all the editorializing there is to be done in the magazine and will not look to the free lance for assistance.

Just as words have their history—and time spent in dictionary-browsing, especially with *OED (The Oxford English Dictionary),* will be well spent—so do words in their context of sentences and paragraphs, words formed into style. On the whole, the stylistic journey has been from ornateness to simplicity. This is the route the elements of art have taken in the work of the greatest writers, of the painters, and of other artists as well. This progression holds true for architecture, for technology, and for invention. The computer industry alone presents living examples of growing complexity clothed in outward forms of increasing simplicity. In our literature the supreme example, as he is with so many things, is Shakespeare. His stylistic journey takes us from the punning and persiflage of the early comedies to the austerity of *King Lear* and the serene, uncluttered statement of *The Tempest*.

The following may serve to illustrate the changes, from elaboration to clarity, in form and rhythm of the English sentence in the past four centuries:

> *Among a number of ladies he fixed his eyes upon one, whose countenance seemed to promise mercy, and threaten mischief, intermeddling a desire of liking, with a disdain of love: showing herself in courtesy to be familiar with all, and with a certain comely pride to accept none, whose wit would commonly taunt without despite, but not without disport, as one that seemed to abhor love worse than lust, and lust worse than murder, of greater beauty than birth, and yet of less beauty than honesty, which got her more honour by virtue than nature could by art, or fortune might by promotion.*

This passage is a single sentence from John Lyly's *Euphues*, first published in 1580. From the title we derive our word *euphuism*. Before Lyly's century was out, Francis Bacon had achieved a firm yet flexible way of employing prose. In his essay "Of Truth" he writes:

> *Truth may perhaps come to the price of a pearl, that sheweth best by day; but it will not rise to the price of a diamond or carbuncle, that sheweth best in varied lights. A mixture of a lie doth ever add pleasure. Doth any man*

*doubt, that if there were taken out of men's minds vain opinions, flattering hopes, false valuations, imaginations as one would, and the like, but it would leave the minds of a number of men poor shrunken things, full of melancholy and indisposition, and unpleasing to themselves?*

Bacon is more direct than Lyly, yet in addition to forms like "doth" and "sheweth" one senses a remoteness and formality which imprison his thought in the past. His *Essays* (completed 1625) are nonetheless a classic of our literature, the first in modern prose. Ironically, Bacon was so unsure of the lasting powers of English that he wrote them originally in Latin.

In the prose of the eighteenth century we can detect method and movement that resemble our own. The contemporary magazine article can, with profit, employ the conciseness and the antithesis Dr. Johnson made his signature. The following passage, a model of Johnsonian style, is from the preface to his *English Dictionary* (1755):

*It is the fate of those who toil at the lower employments of life, to be rather driven by the fear of evil, than attracted by the prospect of good; to be exposed to censure, without hope of praise; to be disgraced by miscarriage, or punished for neglect, where success would have been without applause, and diligence without reward.*

*Among these unhappy mortals is the writer of dictionaries; whom mankind have considered, not as the pupil, but the slave of science, the pioneer of literature, doomed only to remove rubbish and clear obstructions from the paths through which Learning and Genius press forward to conquest and glory, without bestowing a smile on the humble drudge that facilitates their progress. Every other author may aspire to praise; the lexicographer can only hope to escape reproach, and even this negative recompense has been yet granted to very few.*

It is impossible, as one reads these words, to escape the vigor of a positive mind or to avoid the feeling that Johnson is somehow one's contemporary.

Eighteenth-century prose was not always formal and classic in proportion. It could be relaxed and easy, as in the following from Jonathan Swift's *A Tale of a Tub:*

> *The most accomplished way of using books at present, is twofold: Either first, to serve them as some men do lords, learn their titles exactly, and then brag of their acquaintance. Or secondly, which is indeed the choicer, the profounder, and politer method, to get a thorough insight into the index, by which the whole book is governed and turned, like fishes by the tail. For, to enter the palace of learning at the great gate, requires an expense of time and forms; therefore men of much haste and little ceremony, are content to get in by the back door.*

Except for the punctuation, the passage looks and feels modern. The eye and ear catch in Swift's sentences a use of words that is vivid and exact. The proper words in themselves and as they fit into their proper places make both the author's sense and sound instantly available to us.

If we would use our language to make the tenor of our thought available to others, we must choose words with care. Presumably we wish to use language to reveal, to expose what we are thinking, or feeling, what we have come to know. To reveal, and not, through accident or ineptness, to conceal. It is the task of the writer to subtract from, and not to add to, the body of sludge, the verbal pollution, forced upon us by those with bureaucratic minds and purposes. Hamlet is the great user of language to reveal, to call ugly acts by their correct names; it is the role of the usurping Claudius, Hamlet's murderous uncle, to employ words to bury deeds. Shakespeare shows the new king's true character by embedding a grotesque image in his greeting to Hamlet, when he describes himself

*. . . as 'twere with a defeated joy,*
*With an auspicious and a dropping eye.*

Try that sometime, crying with one eye and smiling with the other. Yet that is the kind of distortion that the deliberately devious or the thoughtlessly slipshod use of language inevitably involves. Whether the ambition of the free-lancer is to be a competent craftsperson or to claim to be an artist, language that conceals defeats both purposes. One avoids the deliberate misuse of language through integrity to oneself, and avoids the careless use of language through integrity toward one's materials.

Integrity of materials means the employment of words in their true definitions, not in qualified or debased ones. This is to write standard English. Standard English is not puffed-up words, the longest and most unusual possible. Most of the words in standard English are of reasonable length and the familiar designations of familiar things. (The word *house*, when properly applied, is always to be preferred over *edifice*, and *walk* always over *perambulate*.) A word is standard when it is defined in a good dictionary without a qualification. The chief qualifications are *slang, colloquial, dialect, poetic, archaic, obsolete*. A word without such a qualifier and in the part of speech you intend is standard. The stipulation about part of speech is important; some words are standard English in one part of speech and slang in another. Colloquialisms, the words proper to spoken rather than written language, may occasionally be admitted, but slang never.

Slang is attractive, of course, and the temptation to indulge in it is strong. Slang that is new to us seems to have a recommending freshness. Naturally so, for slang is a kind of wild poetry; its fault lies specifically in the fact that it is figurative and not literal. "You've got to hand it to her." Hand what? "This sends me." How? Where to? Clearly, the use of slang defeats communication. One man's slang is another man's poison. Even when the message can be conveyed through slang—by use of the phrases that are momentarily in the nation's consciousness—it is likely to become obsolete quickly, to become opaque instead of clear. Although it is true that some words might climb from slang to standard—the word *mob*, which Swift inveighed against, is an example—other slang words and expressions have remained unusable. Bacon used the phrase "cuts no ice" (does not impress or convince) in his essays. The expression has remained slang for centuries.

A manuscript containing slang identifies the author as an amateur. Slang phrases the writer is aware of and carefully contains within quotation marks are more objectionable still. They mark the writer as aware that he or she is using substandard language and also as unwilling or unable to do anything about it. Under two circumstances, however, slang is acceptable, even welcome. Use it in nonfiction for purposes of authentication of a certain period, for example, the slang of the sixties, or to indicate the thoughts and conversation of people who habitually and characteristically use slang. The same rule holds for fiction; it would be a serious violation of realism to convey the impression that a typical high school student or a garage mechanic employs the thought processes and speech of a clergyman or a college professor. Your characters, then, whether you are writing fiction or nonfiction, may, when it is natural for them to do so, use slang freely, but not to the point of caricature. You, the writer, when not contributing dialogue or reflecting the thought rhythms of others, may not indulge in slang. When you are describing a process, presenting an argument, reacting aesthetically to an object—or whatever—you must use standard English.

In addition to doing without slang entirely, consistency requires that you also avoid colloquialisms. Colloquialisms are grammatically correct, but they are proper to speaking and, when it comes to writing, to personal correspondence. For most periodicals, you must add the strictures of formal prose to those of standard English. These are easy enough to observe. Avoid contractions (*don't* for *do not*, *shouldn't* for *should not*) and the excessive use of abbreviations and numerical figures. Not all publications require formal prose; part of your study of a newspaper or magazine you aspire to contribute to should be a careful examination of the degree of formality of its content.

Slang is to be forsworn because it prevents communication with your reader; the cliché, or trite and threadbare expression, usually a word group, is to be shunned because it prevents the writer from communicating with herself or himself. The hackneyed phrase is stale, prepackaged, embarrassingly, boringly familiar. It prevents thoughts by choking them off. If I use the worn phrase "Little remains to be said" (one of the most bewhiskered), I have effectively precluded my saying very much; and a great deal may remain to be said. Wide reading will have acquainted most people with the cliché, but to young writers who have presumably read less, this form of verbal evasion may be difficult to identify. A good test when you are in doubt is to ask yourself whether the word group came to you word by word or all at once. "Last but not least" is a venerable cliché. Another is "May the best man win." The most shattering one of all is "Needless to say." All an editor can do is reach for the S.A.S.E. upon encountering such rehashed, shopworn phrases. Their presence indicates one thing: the absence of originality and thought.

The origin of most clichés is murky; like swamp gases, which have no certain beginning, clichés usually appear without parentage. A notable exception which allows us to mark the birth of what was to become a famous and much utilized cliché occurred when Winston Churchill, a master of language, coined the term "iron curtain" in 1946 in a speech at Westminster College in Fulton, Missouri. He spoke of an "iron curtain" descending upon Europe. It is instructive to note what followed. The wire services carried the phrase throughout the world before the day was over. Within two days it had found its way onto the editorial pages of the country's newspapers. Not long after that, it turned up in magazines, and within the year in books. For much of that time the phrase carried the freshness of cogency and of vivid imagery. Soon—and the point is linguistic and not intended to be political—the words "iron curtain" were clearly on their way to becoming hackneyed. What at first contributed to insight, or at least to a concise point of view, had become blunted by time and overusage—the words were common, on everyone's breath and Churchillian no longer. Variations began to appear, among them "bamboo curtain." Thus what began as freshness and novelty had declined to decadence. No writer can use the term today without risking being misunderstood, without his intent being taken for humor or parody. As Dr. Johnson sternly admonished, "Clear your mind of cant."

Slightly less damaging to intelligent discourse perhaps and yet to be held in abhorrence all the same is the use of jargon, the language of the in-group (itself a jargon word). Jargon, sometimes called gobbledygook, is the language George Orwell advised us against in his classic novel *1984*. He issued his warning in 1948, to, as the cliché expert would put it, "little or no avail." Jargon, like slang sometimes, has this excuse: it fills a need—it defines something that is discovered for which there is no word. But far too often slang and jargon intrude when they are not needed, when they are new words (admittedly sometimes colorful or pithy ones) for things that have already been observed to exist, things that have already been named. Jargon is more elusive than outright slang and thus more likely to escape the editorial eye. Often it bears institutional sanction, in the corporate world, in government circles, and, less forgivably, in adademic language.

Jargon offers easy thinking to the writer and reader alike. Unfortunately, it is "buzz word" thinking. This is nothing less than a form of snobbery—look what I know, and you do not know. Yet some words have become generally accepted.

Among jargon words or phrases that now seem to be firmly entrenched we may include *life-style, establishment, interface, low profile, meaningful, identity crisis.* Less certain of survival are such words associated with Watergate (itself a jargon word) as *stonewall, point in time, stroking,* and *deep six.* When we use such words in speaking or in writing (and we all do both), we simply are avoiding thought. In reaction to fellow academics using jargon, Professor John McCall of the University of Cincinnati suggested recently that his colleagues be fined twenty-five cents for each indulgence. His dean immediately sent in a dollar as conscience money.

The lingo of jargon may have its source in the academic fields of knowledge, but it is likely to be first seen and perpetrated in the columns of our newspapers. The daily newspaper is, after all, the most available, most repetitive source of the published word. Here is the word as everyone most often sees it; hence the importance of the impression the newspaper headline and news story make on us. Even in the age of television, the newspaper first fixes and holds the word for us. Hence the style and quality of the newspapers we read are of overwhelming importance. Newspapers are our most frequent source of information in print; hence certain visual images of usage come to us through this source. But the newspaper is not the customary market for the beginning free-lancer. The magazine is. And as magazines come out less frequently than newspapers do, they have the time to take more care with style and usage.

There is one new area that the editors of both newspapers and magazines find particularly sensitive: the language of sexism. As the *New York Times Manual of Style and Usage* observes, writers who think nothing of referring to Golda Meir as a grandmother would never designate Charles de Gaulle as a grandfather. Male writers, not aware they are offending, blithely use sexist terms. Even more so, they may operate, through innocence—or ignorance, as it must increasingly be seen—from assumptions that are sexist.

Editors are becoming more aware that the language contributors use may denote discrimination based on gender. The free-lancer who does not take this possibility into consideration and take steps to avoid *sexism* (a term analogous to *racism*) will not be welcomed in editorial offices. In the summer of 1974 the McGraw-Hill Book Company, publishers of a number of trade publications as well as books, issued a set of Guidelines "intended primarily for use in teaching materials, reference works, and nonfiction works in general." A staff team of experts worked out a set of attitudes and postures to overcome the effect of stereotypes in both male and female roles, "to show the role language has played in reinforcing inequality; and to indicate positive approaches toward providing fair, accurate, and balanced treatment of both sexes" in all magazines, anthologies, and textbooks McGraw-Hill publishes. The basic premise of the McGraw-Hill stipulations was that men and women are people and should be treated as such.

From such a seemingly simple and obvious premise several consequences, all of considerable moment to the free-lance writer, inevitably follow: Emphasis must not rest on people seen primarily as members of opposite sexes. Shared humanity is to be emphasized; hence neither men nor women are to be portrayed in sex-stereotyped roles. Women, therefore, should not be typecast in traditional roles. Nor should men be typecast after the assumptions of the "masculine mystique." Jobs or professions should not be sex-typed. Nor should roles in home maintenance. As the McGraw-Hill Guidelines put it, "Sometimes the man should be shown preparing the meals, doing the laundry, or diapering the baby, while the woman builds bookcases or takes out the trash."

The Guidelines, in general, seek to see to it that women and men are treated with equal respect, dignity, and seriousness. Women, in particular, need to be presented as part of the rule, not as the exception. The trivializing of either sex, or the stereotyping of either, should be avoided, both in text and illustrations. An important consideration for the free-lance writer is, oddly enough, to see to it that men are not treated with contempt either. One good rule here would be for the writer to refrain from doing what the advertisements on television fall into doing. In these advertisements the man is portrayed, when it comes to inhabiting the home, as either a bull in a china shop or a simpering idiot. TV advertisements patronize him unbearably; in equal swipes of unfairness they patronize the woman around the house as well. The McGraw-Hill Guidelines indicate that, "Men should not be character-ized as dependent on women for meals, or clumsy in household maintenance, or as foolish in self-care." Nor should women be described—by pen or camera—by physical attributes while men are being described by mental attributes or professional position.

Since customary usages and assumptions die hard, it is particularly important that those who write for children—and those who edit what is written for children—commit themselves to nonsexist attitudes and treatment. The Guide-lines call upon both to "show married women who work outside the house" and "treat them favorably." The assump-tion must not be made or the implication left that most women "are wives who are also full-time mothers"; the point must be made that "women have choices about their marital status, just as men do." Instructional materials "should never imply that all women have a 'mother instinct' or that the emotional life of a family suffers because a woman works." Publications, the McGraw-Hill statement points out, ought to reflect the reality of Labor Department statistics showing that an increasing percentage—it was over 42 percent in 1972—of all mothers with children under eighteen work outside the home.

The McGraw-Hill Guidelines statement recognizes that principles need the support of sane and balanced application, that excessive emphases can lead to inept wording and other awkwardnesses; in such instances principles need not be abandoned but only sensibly and practically applied. The following is a good example of the tact and common sense recommended:

> *When as a practical matter it is known that a book will be used primarily by women for the life of the edition (say, the next five years), it is pointless to pretend that the readership is divided equally between males and females. In such cases it may be more beneficial to address the book fully to women and exploit every opportunity (1) to point out to them a broader set of options than they might otherwise have considered, and (2) to encourage them to aspire to a more active, assertive, and policy-making role than they might otherwise have thought of.*

The free-lance writer, perhaps particularly the male writer, must see to it that his work avoids a patronizing or girl-watching tone.

Among the specific positives and negatives proposed for the writer by the McGraw-Hill Guidelines are the following:

| NO                                                         | YES                                                                                              |
|------------------------------------------------------------|--------------------------------------------------------------------------------------------------|
| **single words—**                                          |                                                                                                  |
| *the girls* or *the ladies* (when adult females are meant) | *women*                                                                                          |
| *girl* (as in I'll have my *girl* check that)              | I'll have my *secretary* (or my *assistant*) check that (or use the person's name)               |
| *lady* used as a modifier, as in *lady* lawyer            | When you *must* modify, use *woman* or *female*, as in a course on *women* writers, or the airline's first *female* pilot |

co-ed (as a noun)

*student* (Logically, a *co-ed* should refer to any student at a co-educational college or university. Since it does not, it is a sexist term.)

*housewife*

*homemaker* for a person who works in the home, or rephrase with a more precise or more inclusive term

*customer, consumer, shopper* (in purchasing contexts)

*career girl* or *career woman*

name the woman's profession: *attorney* Ellen Smith; Marie Sanchez, a *journalist* or *editor* or *business executive* or *doctor* or *lawyer* or *agent*

*mankind*

*humanity, human beings, human race, people*

*chairman*

*the person presiding at* (or *chairing*) a meeting; *the presiding officer; the chair; head; leader; coordinator; moderator*

| **NO** | **YES** |
| --- | --- |
| **word groups—** | |
| Pioneers moved West, taking their wives and children with them | Pioneer families moved West. |

*Pioneer men and women (pioneer couples) moved West taking their children with them. (The principle involved: Women should be spoken of as participants in the action, not as possessions of the men.)*

man's achievements

human achievements

Henry Harris is a shrewd lawyer and his wife Ann is a striking brunette.

The Harrises are an attractive couple. Henry is a handsome blond and Ann is a striking brunette.

The Harrises are highly respected in their fields. Ann is an accomplished musician and Henry is a shrewd lawyer.

The Harrises are an interesting couple. Henry is a shrewd lawyer and Ann is very active in community (*or* church *or* civic) affairs.

The sound of drilling disturbed the housewives in the neighborhood.

The sound of drilling disturbed everyone within earshot (*or* everyone in the neighborhood).

the best man for the job

the best person (or candidate) for the job

grow to manhood

grow to adulthood; grow to manhood or womanhood

The Guidelines suggest solving the pronoun problem by using the generic *he* freely in books when the statement is sufficiently given that masculine pronouns are being used for succinctness and are intended to refer to both females and males, and by rewording to eliminate unnecessary gender problems. Use *he or she* sparingly to avoid clumsy prose. Again, examples of nos and yeses:

| NO | YES |
|---|---|
| The average American drinks his coffee black. | The average American drinks black coffee. |
| | Most Americans drink their coffee black. |
| When you shave in the morning | when you brush your teeth (or wash up) in the morning |
| the consumer or shopper ... she | consumers or shoppers ... they |
| the secretary ... she | secretaries ... they |
| the breadwinner ... his earnings | the breadwinner ... his or her earnings |
| | the breadwinners...their earnings |

(The principle involved for the three examples directly above: Different pronouns should not be linked with certain work or occupations on the assumption that the worker is always, or usually, female or male. Instead either pluralize or use *he or she*, and *she or he*.)

A final thought from the Guidelines on the subject: Males should not always be first in order of mention. Instead, alternate the order, sometimes using *women and men, gentlemen and ladies, she or he, her or his.*

"Use the right word," Mark Twain advised, "not its second cousin." The right word for the writer comes from one of her or his three vocabularies: a reading vocabulary, a speaking vocabulary, a writing vocabulary. Each fortifies and enriches the other. Each, within reason, should be formal enough so that the transition from either of the first two to the third will be instantaneous and effortless. The writer, again within reason, will do well to think like a book, as it were, and speak like a book in order to be able to write one. She or he will do well, of course, to consider the interests and capacities of those who might, because of age or verbal sophistication, read what one has written. There are many ways and devices for maintaining awareness of the ease or difficulty in verbal level; one of the most immediate and attractive is to employ the Fog Count. By means of the Fog Count one can be alerted to a tendency to use difficult and abstract words, "Norman" words.

To apply the Fog Count to what one has written, simply award a value of 3 to polysyllabic words, all words of three syllables or more; allowing a value of 1 for all other words. A familiar word group which can be read at single clip; for example, "Chief Justice of the United States," would be awarded a value of 1 when appearing before the personal name. The theory is that a polysyllable stands for a "hard idea," one that takes a certain time and concentration before the average reader is prepared to move on. Place names as well as familiar personal titles would receive the count of 1 (for example, a total of 2 for the following: Providence, Rhode Island). A similar treatment obtains for names of months and days (Saturday, 30 March, 1985, would be given a total of 4). Even an amount of more than a million would, given in figures, rate a Fog Count of only 1.

The point of the exercise of assigning the values of 1 to 3 is to determine the transparency or the opaqueness of your sentences, their sound and meaning density. To determine the grade level of a piece you have written, first calculate the average Fog Count for it. To do this select a number of sentences—remembering that a compound sentence can count as two or three, depending upon the number of semicolons separating clauses—at random throughout your manuscript. Compute the Fog Count for each of the sentences you have selected, then divide the total by the number of sentences you have chosen. If the average Fog Count is 24, your reading level is that of the twelfth grade. You simply divide by two. If the average is 20, subtract 2 and divide by 2. Thus an average Fog Count of 18 indicates a ninth grade reading level. Clearly, the Fog Count, while not infallible, enables an educated guess as to whether you are writing above or below the comprehension of your readers. It can be especially valuable in indicating whether or not the vocabulary you are relying upon is too "Norman."

The following passage from Macaulay's *Literary Essays* will show both a moderate amount of "Norman" words and the difficulty of avoiding them entirely. Words of Latinate, non-Saxon origin are set in bold type.

> *Poetry holds the outer world in **common** with the other arts. The heart of man is the **province** of **poetry**, and of poetry alone. The **painter**, the **sculptor**, and the **actor** can **exhibit** no more of **human passion** and **character** than that small **portion** which overflows into the **gesture** and the face, always an **imperfect**, often a **deceitful sign** of that which is within. The deeper and more **complex parts** of **human nature** can be **exhibited** by **means** of words alone.*

Of the eighty-one words in the above passage twenty (eliminating repetitions) are "Norman." According to Fog Count standards, five of these (again not counting repetitions) are "hard" words. Not one word in the above of Anglo-Saxon origin is a "hard" word. The Anglo-Saxon proportion of the above can be strengthened (and the Fog Count slightly lessened) by the substitution of *land* for *province, show* for *exhibit*, and *share* for *portion*.

By now, if you have been counting and evaluating the density of the sentences you have been writing, you are only too painfully aware that what you have been doing is—again and again—predicating subjects. A subject plus a predicate equals a sentence. Sentence after sentence, paragraph after paragraph a subject is presented and then an action or state of being is attributed to that subject. Thus all writing involves grammar (and inefficient grammar is bound to strike the editor unfavorably and, in most instances, inspire rejection slips) and punctuation. Again, editors do not expect perfection in punctuation, but they do not invite chaos. And this language that is such a glory and a burden to work with provides special obstacles when it comes to punctuation.

Punctuation is a special problem in English because English is a language of position. Blame the Danes for this, if you care to, but in an uninflected language meaning needs the clarification of pairing and separation that internal punctuation provides. With a highly inflected language like Latin, for example, the position of any given word in a sentence is a matter of indifference, so far as meaning is concerned. Note the six ways of saying the same thing: Paul sees Peter.

Paulus videt Petrum.
Petrum videt Paulus.
Paulus Petrum videt.
Petrum Paulus videt.
Videt Petrum Paulus.
Videt Paulus Petrum.

Paul sees Peter cannot be switched around to Peter sees Paul and mean the same thing. Therefore word position and the signals that keep that position unambiguous are important in English. Punctuation provides the eye signals that identify and mark off thought units. What they do for the reader, and for the writer as well, is obvious enough.

The organizing of one's words in sentences is the final step in the selection of the words that will make our sentences live. For the writing of prose these words can be found in the fountainhead of language, poetry. "It is always a mistake not to be a poet," Lytton Strachey writes, and the successful writer of prose will almost inevitably be one who goes to poetry to stay in touch with language. Good prose has been called the proper words in the proper places. Those words are "proper" which have fresh relevance to observed actions and objects. The sonnet form demonstrates with deft economy words freshly, effectively at work. Fourteen lines and not a word wasted; it is a form that reflects the discipline of word-for-word choice.

It is by no means a mistake for the writer of prose to engage in the writing of verse, if only for insights into language and into the tactics of sentence formation. A verse form to start with is the *haiku*, a Japanese form capable of great delicacy and subtlety, of sharp imagery, and of mordant wit. A *haiku* is a poem composed of exactly seventeen syllables—five in the first line, seven in the second, and five in the third and final line. It may rhyme or be rhymeless. *Haiku* serve admirably for accomplishing two things: painting swift, vivid pictures; and making wry comment.

The three *haiku* that follow may serve to illustrate the fun you can have with this simplest of literary forms.

### Health Food Restaurant

*Natural, with this*
*Artificial additive:*
*Smiling waitresses.*

The first version (even *haiku* do not usually come to mind in final form but, like everything else, must be tinkered with) was written on a paper napkin. The device of contrast, the contrast between the natural and the artificial (a thought inescapable in the surroundings) controlled the content of this one.

### Plot

*A late blooming rose—*
*God's desperate strategy*
*To capture sunlight.*

Here the first line came to mind in the beginning, then the third line. The problem was how to connect the two—in seven syllables. (This is writing at a fundamental level; it involves knowing the rules and by remaining within them actually creating something where nothing existed before.) The initial form of the third line was "capturing sunlight." The word "late" suggested a kind of latent intent; "desperate" suggests a kind of dramatic necessity for the coming of the rose. The rationalizing and the line seemed to occur together.

### Playmates

*Ribbon and cat's paw*
*Agreeably disagree,*
*Dancing together.*

For "Playmates" there was difficulty with the middle line; the final line resisted but finally yielded to amendment. The middle line first read "In mounting disagreement." This was too abstract, too stuffy. Poor kitty, she was being made to be a philosopher. The substitute "Engaging in argument" was no improvement; still abstract, still "Norman." The final line did have the advantage of image but it was lacking in precision. "Spiral together" seemed inadequate when one considered that not all the action of the ribbon would actually be a spiraling motion. "Dancing" seemed more accurate; it also is far more playful; the contrast and contradiction of the middle line fit into the spirit of banter.

What went on with these three *haiku* was what goes on, constantly, when one writes: the discovery of language. The habit of art is here in miniature; the habit of choosing, sifting, revising, working image and idea one against the other. Success in even the slightest and simplest of forms provides the mirror from which the writer's own image emerges. What is reflected in that mirror is the elusive prize, the fish's tail Henry James grasped for: personal style. Train yourself, then, beginning with the word.

## SUGGESTED FOLLOW-UP FOR THIS CHAPTER

### 1. *What to read*
You should have several good dictionaries, first, in several sizes (one size for desk, another for pocket). *Webster's International* (1963), now in its third edition, is the one used in courtrooms. It is also the most complete; its relaxed standards on what words are slang have been bitterly controverted. *The Oxford English Dictionary* gives the historic origin of words, that is, their first appearance in manuscript or print. H. L. Mencken's *The American Language* (reissued by Knopf in 1977) is copious and valuable on the subject of word origins. *The Harper Dictionary of Contemporary Usage* (1975), edited by William and Mary Morris, includes the embattled results of the editors' polling of writers and editors on the subject of insidious new words and phrases. H. W. Fowler's *A Dictionary of Modern English Usage* (Clarendon, 1965) is a classic if crotchety guide to its subject, and J. A. Cuddon's *A Dictionary of Literary Terms* (Doubleday, 1977), ranges from *abecedarius* to *zeugma*. For luxurious browsing, a great grabbag of a book on words and those who work with them is Israel Shenker's *Words and Their Masters* (Doubleday, 1974), an ideal deskside or bedside companion. Sprightly, elegant, and enlightening are Edwin Newman's *Strictly Speaking: Will America Be the Death of English?* (Bobbs-Merrill, 1974), and *A Civil Tongue* (Bobbs-Merrill, 1975).

The standard reference on matters of word choice, spelling, punctuation, and type sizes is the University of Chicago's *Manual of Style* (1969), now in its twelfth edition. The U.S. Government Printing Office issues at intervals its *Style Manual* (1967), indispensable for forms of governmental report writing; it contains a guide to the typography of foreign languages, including Greek, Hebrew, Hungarian, and Norwegian. Two newspaper stylebooks are current and extremely useful in preparing copy for the free-lancer submitting feature copy: *The New York Times Manual of Style and Usage* (Quadrangle/Times Book Co., 1976), edited by Lewis Jordan, and *The Washington Post Deskbook on Style* (McGraw-Hill, 1978), edited by Robert A. Webb.

Two widely used books on style have come to be regarded as contemporary classics for their fresh approaches to the subject. They are *The Elements of Style*, (Macmillan Co.) by William Strunk, Jr., and E. B. White, and *The Reader Over Your Shoulder: A Handbook for Writers of English Prose* (Macmillan Co., 1944), by Robert Graves and Alan Hudge. *The Elements of Style*, originally published in 1959, has enjoyed immense popularity. The book had gone into its twenty-fourth printing by 1966; by 1979 it was in its third edition. *The Reader Over Your Shoulder*, the work of two English writers, was brought out in a revised and abridged paperback edition in 1979. Both are indispensable deskbooks.

As valuable as the above is *Fifty Contemporary Poets: The Creative Process*, (Longman, 1977), edited by Alberta T. Turner; the editor asked the contributors, living poets, most of them young, each to contribute his or her best poem and an account of the poem's evolution along with a statement on the poet's sources of inspiration and writing methods; if you own only one book on the poetic process, it should be this one. Available currently in paperback is Harold E. Henderson's authoritative and stimulating *The Bamboo Broom: An Introduction to Japanese Haiku* (Houghton Mifflin, 1934), which contains copious examples of classic Japanese poems in the form.

    Finally, there are a number of college handbooks. If you feel the need for a refresher on the basics of grammar, punctuation, and kindred matters and you happen to live near a college campus, visit the bookstore and see what the freshmen are using. An excellent example of the type, streamlined and practical, is *Bell and Cohn's Handbook of Grammar, Style, and Usage*, (Glencoe Press, 1976) by James K. Bell and Adrian A. Cohn. If no bookstore, campus or otherwise, is conveniently near, this book can be ordered directly from the publisher at 17337 Ventura Boulevard, Encino, California 91316.

### 2. *What to write*

Do mostly warming-up finger exercises. With emphasis on word choice, and checking word origins, concentrate on rewriting your own material, particularly if you have unpublished, rejected material. Try rewriting random paragraphs —with the same emphasis—from newspaper feature articles or magazine articles you encounter. Everyone is the recipient of gobbledygook in second-class matter received from government or private sources. Edify and calm your mind by recasting objectionable sentences and passages into more direct, supple, and vivid discourse.

### 3. *Where to send it*

Again, the finger exercises are for home consumption only. Be patient; you were merely marking time, not wasting it.

    Writing *haiku* can be another matter. There are nearly fifty American magazines specifically in the market for *haiku*. The largest group of magazines publishing *haiku* are those which publish poetry only, or the little magazines, which emphasize fiction and poetry. Among these markets the following may be noted: *In a Nutshell* (buys sixty to eighty poems, all kinds, a year; limit submissions to batches of four to six); *Lake Superior Review; Natchez Trace Literary Review; Pierian Spring* (90 percent written by free-lancers; "founded to provide another outlet for the beginning writer"); *Potpourri— An Anthology* ("100 percent free-lance; bimonthly); *Sequoia; Seven Stars Poetry; Western Humanities Review.* Specialty magazines are hospitable to *haiku.* Among them are: *Alaska Woman Magazine; American Dane Magazine; Big Bike; The Carolina Sportsman* ("would like to see poetry related to outdoors"); *Chesapeake Bay Magazine; Coffee Break* ("to brighten coffee breaks, lunch hours, commuting time, and other hum-drum lulls"; biannual; 80 percent free-lance); *Connecticut Fireside and Book Review; Ebony, Jr.; Educational Studies; The Horn Book Magazine* (everything related to children's books); *Mountain Review* (poetry "should relate, however metaphorically, to mountains"); *New Earth Review;* and *Skate World News.*

Look up the addresses—address to poetry editor's name when given—in *The Writer's Handbook* or *Writer's Market.* Remember to enclose S.A.S.E. (self-addressed stamped envelope). Most of the magazines mentioned above take a long time (six weeks seems to be the average) to reply, and they generally pay nothing or pay in complimentary copies. Yet acceptance means that you have found yourself in print.

# CHAPTER 4
# TIME TO
# BE CRITICAL

"A book review would be the best way to start," the editors of *Midstream* reply to a query about how to break into print with them. "Send us a sample review or a clip, let us know your area of interest, suggest books you would like to review." For one who has not yet seen her or his words in print, this is a beguiling invitation. It is one to be seriously considered by anyone who has not yet appeared in print and is eager to do so. It should be said at once that *Midstream*'s invitation is sincere. It is also—if the writer is willing to take pains and devote some hard thought and hard work to it—eminently practical. Book reviewing is indeed a very good, perhaps the very best, place to start.

The form itself is attractive. The review is a short essay; to anyone who can put sentences together and arrive at paragraphs, writing one seems a manageable challenge. One has the feeling that one has done this sort of thing already; some beginners have published reviews in the private print of a school or college newspaper. Most obliging of all, the review is a form of writing that provides the subject to write about: the book under consideration. Most beginners are stopped before they start when they ask themselves (and find no ready answer), What shall I write? The book review tells you.

Reviewing is perhaps the most widely opened door— admittedly a rear door—that will admit the beginning writer. It is the only form by means of which, on the basis of as little as a typed page or two, the unpublished and unknown can find themselves with an invitation to publish. This possibility is what the editors of *Midstream* suggest by the term "sample review." If you have a clipping or two of published work so much the better, but that is not beginning at the very beginning. The invitation this and other magazines and newspapers are issuing is more than holding out the possibility of appearing in print. It is an opening to a profession. Enter, it is saying, the harrowing and yet exciting world of deadline responsibility, of writing to order. Discipline is what is being offered, as well as opportunity.

Hilaire Belloc had the disciplinary benefits of book reviewing in mind when he observed of the form that "it vies with cricket in forming the character of an Englishman." And there is definite character formation in disciplining oneself to write by the clock or the calendar. The old romantic idea that one writes when the spirit moves is banished forever, as it should be, upon the undertaking of the basic professional challenge in all writing: the deadline. Someone else has set it, and not arbitrarily. After you submit your copy to the editor, a chain of events is set into motion involving a complex interrelationship of trade, business, and industry. By the very act of meeting a deadline you have become a professional.

To become a reviewer is to take part in a cultural event at the heart of modern communications. As it relates to that movement, a book review is news. In this country over forty thousand books are published every year—each in itself a news event. A book's publication merits news coverage in the newspaper and, by extension, in magazines. The book reviewer is primarily a reporter—and books are this reporter's beat. Actually—and this is one of the built-in problems of the book industry—because of the limitations of space only a small proportion of the books published each year—some two thousand out of the forty—can come to the attention of a leading newspaper in any one year. This situation means that even if the newspaper or magazine in which the review appears is a small and relatively unimportant one, the reviewer may well come to the attention of those who shape the book world.

Books are news, and the issuance of books is a planned news event. (An unplanned news event is, or should be, something like a four-alarm fire, a plane crash, a visiting tornado.) Like a baseball game, a concert, or the opening of a new play, the book appears at a predetermined and specified time: publication day. Publication day is a red-letter day on the calendars of authors, agents, and publicity directors; it tends to pass unnoticed by everyone else. Of course that is where, and why, the book reviewer comes in. The reviewer records the event, serves notice that it is happening now. Without the reviewer, the event, unlike a ball game or a play or a concert, would pass completely unnoticed, silent and invisible.

The publication date of a book is an artificial thing, not like a baseball game or a play, which actually takes place the very day and hour of the scheduled event. Pub date is always set for a month or more after the book is actually ready—printed, bound, dust-jacketed, just as you would find it in a bookstore. That is the reason, of course, for the artificiality of the event. A month is needed to get the books into the bookstores—and in the hands of the reviewers. Hence the deadline that the literary editor sets for the reviewer is not the editor's choice alone but one synchronized with the publisher's program of advertising and publicity. In other words, the reviewer's work is locked into the time schedule and other demands of a complex industry.

Publishers send out review copies of new books to newspaper and magazine editors and directly to reviewers who write regular columns, as well as to opinion leaders in various fields. The expectation is that the reportage that comes from these sources will be synchronized with the date set for publication. The sad fact is that the selling of books to the American public resembles the sale of fresh vegetables. Both must be on display when they are at their peak of accessibility, because even fresher ones ready to replace them are already on their way. A prematurely published review, even an overwhelmingly favorable one, can kill a book's sales. Most book buyers are impulse buyers; they want a copy of the book when they first hear about it, now, not tomorrow, not in two weeks. In two weeks it will be quite another review and quite another book that will be attracting their attention.

Books come to editors and individual reviewers directly from the publicity departments of the publishers. This is an important point for the beginning reviewer to note and consider. The knowledge should relieve him or her of any misguided sense of obligation to the publisher. The review copy should be considered a convenience, with no special responsibility attached. The review copy enables the work to be done, just as receiving tickets to the ball game or to the theater is a convenience for other types of reporters. One usually may keep the book after the review is accepted. It is the ticket stub, so to speak.

The review copy, then, comes from the publisher's publicity department, with no strings attached. It is important to note that the book is not sent by the publisher's advertising department. If that were so, then strings would be attached. The expectation would be that the reviewer would play a role in the advertising of the book; all reviews, under those circumstances, would be like the label on a can of beans—or the copy on the dust jacket flaps—fulsome in their praises. Few books would escape being called masterpieces. Although it would be gratifying to authors, perhaps, the situation would become all too benign. The relationship between author and reviewer should not become an adversary one, but a quizzical alertness on the latter's part is vital if the public is to be served.

The review copy looks the way the book does when encountered in the bookstore. (Still, there is nothing quite like the smell and touch of a mint-fresh copy of a book straight from its jiffy bag. For some reviewers the anticipatory excitement of being on hand at the creation of a new book offers a sensation that never becomes stale.) The reviewer's copy looks the same as any other, but it carries with it additional material spun in the brains of the publisher's publicity people. This material may take the form of background material on the author, generous amounts of favorable comments on her or his previous books, or a rapturous forecast of the success of the present book, sometimes accompanied by a schedule of the dates and places of the author's promotional tours.

Although the beginning reviewer will do well to be wary of the tone and purposes of the news release placed inside the copy, as some read suspiciously like reviews already written for the indolent, such releases often call helpful attention to the book's newsworthiness. A Times Book Company release on a book by Peer De Silva entitled *Sub Rosa* (1978) is intriguingly headed "Why We Need Spies." The release opens with a statement about the "media attention," none of it favorable, the CIA has attracted in recent years and then goes on to point out that *Sub Rosa* "presents quite a different point of view." In its two pages the release clearly sets forth the book's claim to the editor's and the reviewer's attention, all with a minimum of puffery. The Putnam release on Richard Lane's *Images From the Floating World* (1978) presents the subject of the book, the Japanese woodblock print, in terms that, without being extravagant, pique immediate interest.

Employed judiciously, the releases can be of service to reviewer and reader. They may be the source of biographical information about the author, for example, that might be difficult to come by otherwise. They can often alert the reviewer to useful data, facts about the subject intended to place the book in relation to other books on its subject. There is little judicious use, however, the reviewer can make of the most conspicuous vehicle of information the publisher provides: the flap copy on the dust jacket. While the factual information on the jacket blurb may be true and the evaluation of the book valid, the latter represents the publisher's stand, not the reviewer's. That is to be gained only through reading the book itself.

The reviewer will glance at the dust jacket only to ascertain the list price of the book, not to have the approach of the review suggested or its judgment anticipated. For the same reasons the reviewer will be content with only a cursory glance at any packets of information, however engaging the folders they come in. Ordinarily, the decision whether or not to reproduce a photograph of the author or of some other illustration from the book will not be the reviewer's to make. But there is one item that comes with the advance copy, tucked inside it, not to be ignored. This is the information slip giving the book's price, publication date, and the restrictions placed upon quotation without written permission. These slips request that you observe the publication date and provide two clippings of your review. One of the clippings will be filed for possible use in the publisher's advertising. The other will be sent—some publishers, mercifully, wait for six months—to the author.

Publishers vary in the demands they make of reviewers. Viking phrases its request for the reviewer's cooperation in these words: "Kindly send us two clippings or notification of broadcast of your review of this book." The Harper & Row slip stipulates that direct quotation in reviews be "limited to 500 words unless special permission is given." Doubleday makes the identical stipulation about the number of words that may be quoted, and adds: "No dramatization in lectures, television, or radio is allowed." The reviewer's slip from Coward, McCann & Geoghegan specifies the publisher's conditions thus: "This copy carries with it permission to quote in a periodical or radio review up to 750 words, provided full credit is given to title, author, and publisher. All other permissions to quote from this book for any purpose whatsoever must be requested and secured in writing from the publisher." Obviously, whatever stipulation the publisher makes on the slip enclosed with the reviewer's copy is to be heeded.

The reviewer's problem—and challenge—is to communicate meaning within a form severely restrictive in its length. The review cannot merely deviate into sense but has to meet it—and meet it head on. There is something fundamentally arrogant, perhaps, in the belief that you can convey in two or three hundred words what it took the original writer two or three hundred pages to convey. Yet what the reviewer performs is not the miniaturizing of larger originals. Ideally, the review is a work of art in and of itself. A sonnet, after all, is not a miniature epic. Thus the beginning reviewer is a professional, attempting an art form. It soon becomes clear to the tyro that the book review offers no shelter for incompetence. Quite the contrary. In the very act of offering to comment on the work of others you expose your own: it will not do to criticize another's prose in words that do not measure up to the style of the book under review.

As a reviewer you have the right to see your opinions in print—as you wrote them. The editor may not call "stupid" or "bumbling" a book you have characterized as brilliant. No negative adverb of the editor's may intrude. As a reviewer, whether of books, performances, or events, you have a right to your own language. That right protects you from all changes of your copy save one: abridgment to fit available space. Your editor may cut superfluous wording in your sentences and perhaps straighten out a word or phrase here and there (and the reviewer can profit from the indirect instruction). Permissible editing ends here. The editor's decision to cut, not tamper, must be allowed. The reviewer can avoid having the copy cut by writing to the space originally allotted.

Tight writing is not the entire secret of professional reviewing. Early on, the reviewer will have discovered that the form of the book review is like any other in requiring an absolute integrity. The reviewer must make a commitment that requires fairness, evenness of judgment, and integrity to the form and the occasion. The reviewer's sense of integrity toward the subject will preclude judgments that are too lenient or too harsh. Critics and reviewers have, ever since the emergence of a popular press and general reading public, been accused of either malice or favoritism. Edgar Allan Poe, book reviewer as well as poet and short story writer, considered editors and their reviewers too subservient and flattering, although he admitted there were a few editors, "very few," who accepted books with the understanding "that an unbiased critique would be given."

From the point of view of the authors of books, the other extreme—not flattery but ferocity—is equally to be feared. Certain authors seem to be favored targets, usually the authors of best sellers. Whether the unfavorable notices they receive derive from envy or from zeal for literature is difficult to conclude. Certainly a jealous regard for standards is a proper one for reviewers. Lord Byron put it best when in his preface to his satiric poem "English Bards and Scotch Reviewers" he wrote, "My object is not to prove that I can write well, but, if possible, to make others write better." So long as the reviewer avoids self and concentrates on the subject, solicitude for standards would seem becoming. Not every writer of books would agree. Many are sensitive to criticism; some show their resentment publicly. Frances Parkinson Keyes, whose novels were best sellers in the fifties and sixties, was stung by the "respected opinions" in the criticism she received. She was offended by what she considered inaccuracies—as when reviewers implied that she wrote hastily or (it seems to have pained her equally) that she used a typewriter.

Mrs. Keyes often wrote lengthy "notes" about the sources and the extensive research she engaged in when writing her novels. These she defiantly placed under the heading "For readers only, Reviewers please skip." Her overreaction to criticism had its point nonetheless. Reviews should be focused on books, not on their authors. The short review—any length up to five hundred words—should inform the reader on the book under review, and that alone. A longer critical article is another matter. Reviewers who observed Mrs. Keyes's stern injunctions would have deprived themselves of background material useful, perhaps at times essential, to forming their judgments on her book. If correct in her conviction that reviewers had already made up their minds before opening her books, she truly had a grievance.

Even the dullest books deserve more than abrupt and peremptory dismissal. The Victorian poet and critic Matthew Arnold was wont to greet a new book by comparing it with Homer and complaining, "This will never do." His contemporary Thomas Babington Macaulay tended to overwhelm the books he reviewed, replacing the hapless author and book alike in a long review which supplanted both through a learned discourse of his own. In reviewing a biography of Warren Hastings, Macaulay wrote (with an assurance no reviewer should ever emulate), "We are inclined to think that we shall best meet the wishes of our readers, if, instead of dwelling on the faults of this book, we attempt to give, in a way necessarily hasty and imperfect, our own view of the life and character of Mr. Hastings." And so on, for dozens of pages.

In an outburst at the end of chapter 5 of *Northanger Abbey,* Jane Austen vigorously deplores the then prevailing custom of novelists to deprecate their own craft by causing their heroines to declare "I am no novel reader," or "I seldom look into novels." Jane Austen will have none of this. "Let us leave it to the Reviewers," she writes, "to abuse such effusions of fancy at their leisure, and over every new novel to talk in threadbare strains of the trash with which the press now groans." The novel, particularly the first novel, needs all the friends it can muster, and the thrust of Jane Austen's defense of fiction has pertinence still. Happily, the reviewing of fiction provides a reasonably available field for the beginning reviewer. In the strict sense, there can be no "specialists" for a first novel. It is a new, unexplored territory to which the beginning reviewer is usually as eligible for passport as anyone.

A book review, then, should be neither an implicit bid for indulgence and sympathy for the book's author in deference to the struggles (self-assumed, after all) endured, nor again a reviewer's self-indulgence in pique or display of learning; a review shall be an honest appraisal of the book being reviewed. The reader should come away from the review enlightened by a number of related facts and by the reviewer's considered judgment on the book's success or failure. Certainly to be derived from the review is a firm and accurate notion of the type or category the book falls into. Nothing is more irritating than to finish reading a review without being told that the book is a novel, a selection of short stories, a biography, a fictionalized autobiography—or whatever. Precise information on this point (and fairly early in the review, not in the final sentence) would seem to be a minimal service for a review to perform.

Equally a service, but more difficult for the reviewer to convey, is an accurate and ample recounting of the book's contents. This should be done without resort to mere synopsis or flat summary. Enough of the content of the book should be indicated by the review to enable the reader to go from the review to the book itself with a sense of familiarity. The review should inform the reader about the book's setting in time, place, and action—in the intellectual action of nonfiction as well as the main plot lines of fiction. It would seem obvious—yet even veteran reviewers sometimes ignore the obvious—that in a novel of mystery or adventure the ending should not be given away, or even strongly hinted at. It should be the reader's pleasure to discover that the butler did it. Nonetheless, the information that a novel contains a murder that is solved at the end, that it occurs in nineteenth-century Rhode Island, and that political figures, some of them derived from real people thinly disguised—presuming these to be matters important to an understanding of the story—are all part of the rapport that should exist between reader and reviewer.

A report to the reader on an author's style is no less valuable than one on the book's substance. Indeed, it is part of substance: the *how* of the *what*. Style is more difficult to report upon than substance, of course, yet it should not be neglected in the reviewer's evaluation. Direct quotation from the text, if well and fairly chosen, can give the reader of the review a direct experience of the book—a sample of its content and a whiff at least of the author's style. Knowledge of an author's style is of equal importance to the reader of nonfiction as it is to the reader of fiction. Style is of the very substance of a book; it is not to be considered a garnish or topping—the sizzle separate from the steak. The prospective reader of a book of nonfiction, to put it another way, has the right to know how uphill the climb will be; to the assurance, if it can be given, that one is going to meet a mind, a personality, and not a mere heap of important but nonetheless inert matter.

Style may be thought of as the doing well of what needs doing, and the question of the need for a particular book is not always an easy one to answer. What use, Ben Franklin once enigmatically asked, is a newborn baby? The specialist will, naturally enough, be on more solid ground here than the generalist. Yet it does not take a specialist to detect an essentially silly book put together with the aid of scissors and paste, an extravagant bit of nonsense, or an exploitative, puffed-up quickie trading on public knowledge of some incident notable only for its scandal or horror. For this last a single magazine article would suffice. But this is the inflated era of book journalism, a time when political hangers-on rush to tell all, providing the reviewer with both occupation and occupational hazard.

Whatever the book, the reviewer will find that the task being assumed will require two things: (1) setting out the contents of the book; and (2) evaluating the book's quality. If the reviewer does the first alone, the result is not, properly speaking, a book review at all. It is a "notice," a report without even the implication of opinion one way or the other—a mere listing. Notices have their value; they are indispensable to the librarian. But their very neutrality means that they do not foster the critical spirit. Someone has described reading as the soul's adventures among masterpieces; less grandly put, the review is the mind's, and the spirit's, experience with new work. Masterpiece or not, a new book deserves to live in at least one reader, the reviewer, before passing into silence, or being placed in the deep freeze of a library shelf.

As a beginner, the reviewer may wish to separate the two: to explicate first and evaluate second. The reviewer thus will set forth for the reader something of the immediacy of impact the book may have on any reader who is interested in its subject. The author's major views and conclusions, the book's perspective—these are some of the matters which, in a review of nonfiction, the reviewer may wish to touch on first. Then comes the evaluation: a discussion, perhaps, of the book's originality, its relevance today, and its possible long-lasting contributions to its field. When these matters are handled with cogency, the reader comes into possession of the essential *what* and *how*. It is perhaps more evenhanded to offer the explication first. Then the reader possesses some insight into what is being evaluated; the reviewer's standards for evaluation can be immediately perceived.

The book under review is the primary, often the sole and sufficient, basis of information on its contents and value. The reviewer determines the appropriate approach to take toward the book and the tactics to be used in presenting that approach. A quotation from the book, if it is sufficiently arresting, can make an effective opening statement, as in the following:

> *"Picture me with my ground teeth stalking joy." This is one of the hundreds of striking images and phrases that light up the almost six hundred pages of* Flannery O'Connor: The Habit of Being, *edited by Sally Fitzgerald. These pages contain the hundreds of letters the late Flannery O'Connor, short story writer and novelist, wrote from 1948 to her death, at age 39, in 1964. The letters, like her fiction, are the product of a thoroughly original mind, a totally engaged personality.*

*Flannery O'Connor can be tentative and modest when she touches upon abstract matters, deferring to others; but she is serenely confident when discussing her art ("I'm good at it") and her Catholic faith, which was awesomely whole and vibrant.*

In the above, explication and evaluation are mixed, with the former predominating. The reader is given precise information on the length and category (nonfiction: letters) of the book, the dates of the life of the subject, and a glimpse of her personality. In the evaluation the tactic used is contrast: between "tentative and modest" and "serenely confident."

The following first paragraph of a review begins and ends with quotation. The second quotation has as its purpose the revealing of the style and point of view of the book's author.

*"If one considers the impersonality of the modern bureaucratic state," Louis Simpson writes in* A Revolution in Taste, *"it is likely that, more and more, poetry will be written to express the life of the individual." Simpson, a Pulitzer Prize winning poet, examines the lives and work of four contemporary poets—Dylan Thomas, Allen Ginsberg, Sylvia Plath, and Robert Lowell—for intimations of individual utterance he can understand and find himself comfortable with. "The poetry I like," he writes, "has a connection with the world we perceive through our senses. It is always calling us back to the heat and drama of human contact."*

The two-paragraph review from which the above is taken quotes a few short phrases in the second paragraph and ends with a quotation: "Critics love intricate poems like those of Plath and Lowell, Simpson observes, 'for it gives them something to look up.'" Once again, the reviewer attempts to give the reader an example of the author's informal, nonacademic approach to his subject. It is obvious, too, that the reviewer is exercising benevolent bias in trying to make reading about poetry attractive.

At times, beginning a book review with a summarizing statement proves a satisfying way of placing the subject of a book within its frame of time and place, as in the following:

> *The senior Oliver Wendell Holmes, friend as well as contemporary of Longfellow, Lowell, and Emerson, was Boston's Renaissance man. He rose to eminence as a physician, an experimental scientist, as dean of the Harvard Medical School, and as a poet, a novelist, and, most memorably, an essayist. Yet he was always something of an outsider, distrusted because so many-talented, as Edwin P. Hoyt shows in his biography* The Improper Bostonian.

The author's analysis of Holmes's position as an "outsider" in Boston and of his struggles to overcome the disadvantage of being a genius constitutes the major theme of the book—and thus of the review. The review ends with a final item of information useful to the reader: "Hoyt recalls it all with zest, and he includes the poems that made Holmes famous."

A summarizing beginning can be helpful in introducing a reader and a novel to one another. The following comprises the first half of the review's opening paragraph:

> Paloverde *by Jacqueline Briskin is a lengthy novel concerned with several generations of California pioneers. They all have a deep love for the soil and forests and waters of their state. Yet they are the first to begin its spoliation, in their search for oil, laying waste to vast areas.*

The above is all exposition. In this particular review evaluation is deferred—because of the desirability of first giving attention to the main contours of a complicated plot—to the end. The review concludes with this evaluative comment: "All the family's heartaches and the melodramatic events that touch the Van Vliets may not be convincing. Yet one must admit they are compatible with one's concept of the large-scale, violent truths of California's flamboyant history." The first of these two sentences alerts the reader who may prefer realism to melodrama to the possibility she or he may find the story unconvincing. The suggestion is put tentatively because another type of reader may well find melodrama appealing. The final sentence of the review may say as much about the reviewer as it does about the book.

Finally, here is a complete short review, one wherein evaluation is implied rather than stated.

> *The daily lives of four generations of American women are captured in the unposed photographs, accompanied by text and captions, in Annette K. Baxter's* To Be a Woman in America 1850–1930. *"Perhaps it is the knowledge that their labors are unending," the author writes, "that has given women a sense of being victims of time rather than the masters of it, seldom able to create works that are universal and timeless." The author's perspective is one of reaction to the stereotypes of "self-sacrifice, not creativity" in woman's traditional role.*

> *The archives of state historical societies are the principal sources of these moments of arrest by camera shutter of "women in the act of doing something." We see women at a sewing party; croquet in hand on a 1905 lawn; ice skating with protective males nearby; bending over a washboard or ironing on a board supported by chairs; garbed in a duster ready to go motoring; in World War I factory assembly lines; and even as tightrope walkers over Niagara Falls.*

The first and only indispensable rule for reviewing a book is one that cannot be overemphasized: read the entire book. The argument that you need not eat an entire apple to know that it is bad is sophistry here. Avoid reviewing the book at all if you cannot bear to read it all. A review based upon the partial evidence of a partly read book is certain to misfire. You say the character of the person next door is underdeveloped? The development of this character occurred within the chapters you skipped over. Nibbling here and there at a mystery story is obviously unpardonable, but leaving out whole gobs of a gothic is equally unfair. So, pencil nearby, along with the reviewer's slip to mark where you left off and to jot down notes, get on with it.

Reading fiction for review can be a pleasant enterprise, and nothing should be done to lessen that pleasure for the reviewer. Some reviewers, it is true, may feel that they have read the book twice—some recommend this—once to obtain the general idea, and the second time to check impressions, to take notes, and to marshal opinions. Ideally, if your book for review is not a first novel, you should read, for valid purposes of comparison, the author's first novel and other publications. As a reviewer of fiction you are like an astronaut walking on a new, uncharted planet. Nobody has been here before; the reviewer enjoys the excitement of fresh discovery. There is always the chance, and the hope of being the first to discover a book that will last.

Nonfiction contains more handles for the reviewer than fiction does. With nonfiction there is no excuse for the reviewer's failure to ascertain and convey the author's intention. The nonfiction book often includes an apparatus: preface, introduction, charts, maps, line drawings, photographic illustrations, and index. These supplement the text and are an integral part of the book's scope. The reviewer should give these items the same scrupulous attention given the text, to the last picture caption, the last footnote. The author devoted just as much care to them as to the text itself, and so should the reviewer.

The author's introduction is usually the most reliable guide to the book's intention. Unless it is absurd or illogical, or pretentious, the introduction should serve as guideline for the reviewer's evaluation. The author should not be criticized for not carrying out the intention of the reviewer. Never review a book not written, but the one before you. If the author announces in the introduction that the coverage of the subject ends with the year 1850, and gives excellent reasons for so doing, it would be ungracious and absurd in your review to express the wish that the book had extended the subject to the year 1900. You might consider, if feasible, rounding out your review with a sentence that, in a complimentary way, calls for a sequel to move the story forward.

In the limited space allotted to reviewing, critical remarks that could be supported in a longer essay are usually out of place. Unless misprints reflect a general carelessness, seemingly shared by the author and the publisher's editor, forbear from commenting on them. Unless a book lacking an index is intended to be authoritative or scholarly, do not occupy space with comment on the omission. In general, keep complaints like this in proportion. A critical attitude that seems to indicate a feud between the reviewer and the author is unseemly. The rule is to maintain civility while being exact and fair in judgment. Credibility is at stake here—that of the reviewer as well as that of the author of the book under review.

Book reviewing can of course be thought of, like the *haiku*, as a getting-ready exercise. Or the beginning writer can decide that here is the place to start it all, to begin appearing in print. One cannot merely wish to become a reviewer, and have it happen. There are steps to be taken. One may try breaking into the review columns or Sunday page of a metropolitan newspaper, but unless one happens to have academic or other qualifications as a specialist, breaking in is not easy. If you live in or near a one-newspaper town, you might try what a writer friend of mind did once. She lived in a small town in Oregon, had written a great deal, but had never published anything. The town had one bookstore and one daily paper. She went to the owner of the bookstore and asked her whether or not she would advertise in the paper if it carried a book column. Armed with the bookseller's affirmative, the prospective reviewer called on the editor. Would he, she wanted to know, use book reviews if the bookstore advertised? He would, and she was soon launched on her career as a writer.

Books are sent out by publishers' publicity departments for the purpose of being reviewed. The fledgling reviewer becomes part of this communications chain upon succeeding in persuading a newspaper editor to review a forthcoming book. That is one way to break in. Another is to take a new book out of the library (or buy one at the bookstore) and write a review of it. Then either send the review on speculation to a magazine (like *Midstream* or one of those suggested at the end of this chapter), or send or take in your review to your local newspaper. If you are trying to persuade the editor of a regional weekly or shopping news throwaway to introduce a book column, this would be a good medium for showing what you can do, showing your readers and yourself. Armed with clippings of your reviews, you are now equipped to approach a newspaper of larger circulation, or to approach book publishers directly, in requesting copies for reviews. With your work in print, you can show that you have a place for your work to appear in, and you can demonstrate as well that you have become a qualified reviewer.

There is more than one way for an unknown to approach a literary editor. One successful reviewer recommends contributing to your newspaper's letters to the editor page. In this way your name will become familiar to the editor and to the paper's readership as well. Acting on a hint given in class, a student, a woman of means and leisure, decided to inquire about the possibility of contributing, gratis, a monthly book column to the alumni magazine of her college. Her motive was to appear in print; she had never had a career of her own but had been the wife of a foreign service officer and had lived abroad and experienced several cultures at first hand. After a lifetime of observing people and events, she took up the professional contemplation of books.

Money was not this student's motive, and it would be well to make the point here that writing book reviews is not, any more than is writing poetry, a way to make money, even a recognizable amount of mad money, through your typewriter. For appearing in small newspapers and many magazines, the reviewer's sole reward—aside from the often incomparable one of the delights of reading and discovery—is the copy of the book. One builds up a library this way, but even in these terms the compensation is small. Yet book reviewing has its distinct rewards. It is, most of all, a professional activity. Appearing in print with regularity as a book reviewer is being a writer. The experience gives one the confidence to go on to larger and less ancillary work. Again, it is writing; it is appearing in print. And, as Humpty Dumpty says, there's glory for you.

## SUGGESTED FOLLOW-UP
## FOR THIS CHAPTER

### 1. *What to read*
Read books of course—and books about books. Two recent and outstanding examples of the latter, both containing literary articles as well as book reviews, originally published in the *New York Times Book Review* and *The New Yorker* respectively, are Nona Balakian's *Critical Encounters: Literary Views and Reviews, 1953–1977* (Bobbs-Merrill, 1978); and John Updike's *Picked-Up Pieces* (Knopf, 1975). The best introduction is *Book Reviewing* (The Writer, 1978), edited by Sylvia E. Kamerman, containing chapters by reviewers and literary editors, among them four on reviewing children's books.

Read book reviews themselves, in the *New York Times* especially, but also in the quality magazines, and in any specialized magazines you come upon—this in order to acquire an idea of the wide range of interests and audiences the book review addresses.

## 2. What to write

Make it a habit to write a review of every book you read, whether you do so to keep up with your own field or for pleasure. This could be in the form of a journal entry. If you wish to check your judgments against those of the professionals, check *Book Review Digest* in your local library. A bound volume covers a year's reviews; the entries are arranged alphabetically, with their favorable or unfavorable rating (for example, 75/25 equals yes with reservations); the original views of the reviewers are represented by citation and quotation.

## 3. Where to send it

Most magazines carrying book reviews engage a regular columnist or assign books to reviewers. Yet a number of periodicals encourage the submission of book reviews by the free-lance writer. Here are a few of them:

*Arizona Quarterly* (80 percent written by free-lancers; gives annual award for best book review)

*Astrology Guide* (bimonthly; circulation 55,000)

*The Book-Mart\** (monthly tabloid; circulation 95,000; 40 percent free-lance)

*Collage\** (monthly tabloid; circulation 100,000)

*Electronics Journal\** (monthly newspaper; circulation 31,000; 15 percent free-lance; reviews books "published in the last 120 days")

*Family Pet\** (quarterly; circulation 3,000; 25 percent free-lance)

*Farmstead Magazine\** (bimonthly; circulation 50,000; 95 percent free-lance)

*Journal of Popular Culture* (quarterly; circulation 3,000; 100 percent free-lance)

*Learning: The Magazine for Creative Teaching\** (monthly during school year; circulation 225,000; 45 percent free-lance)

*Metro: The Magazine of Southeast Virginia\** (monthly; circulation 20,000; 75 percent free-lance; reviews books by Southern authors only)

*Midstream* (monthly; circulation 14,000)

*Monitor\** (quarterly; circulation 3,000; 90 percent free-lance)

*Old Cars Newspaper* (weekly tabloid; circulation 95,000; 40 percent free-lance)

*Planning\** (publication of the American Society of Planning Officials; 11 times a year; circulation 15,000; pays $25 for reviews, lengths 300–800 words)

*Reason Magazine* (monthly; circulation 20,000; 50 percent free-lance)

*San Francisco Bay Guardian* (weekly; circulation 25,000; 25 percent free-lance)

*San Francisco Review of Books* (monthly; circulation 15,000)

*Seventeen* (monthly; circulation 1,500,000)

*Spiritual Life\** (quarterly; circulation 17,000; 80 percent free-lance)

*Women: A Journal of Liberation* (quarterly; circulation 20,000)

\*These magazines will send a free sample copy on request. The addresses and names of editors for the magazines listed above may be found in *The Writer's Handbook* and *Writer's Market*. Also consult recent and current issues of *The Writer* and *Writer's Digest*.

# CHAPTER 5
# FACT IS CREATIVE

An unfortunate prejudice deeply rooted, it would appear, in the minds of many, writers and nonwriters alike, is the view that to be truly "creative" one must write fiction. A poem, nonfiction's disparagers agree, is "creative" and so is a play. A short story is undoubtedly creative, a novel eminently so. But the serviceable workhorse of prose, the magazine article or the nonfiction book, is, apparently, to be dismissed as the work of a tinsmith, a banging together of materials that are irredeemable dross. As these critics see it, no inspiration gives birth to factual prose; nothing aesthetic nourishes it; in its fashioning there is no joy. Fact is fact, they say, and fiction is fiction. They have no patience with the paradox that the reverse can also be described as true: fact is fiction, and fiction is fact.

Because nonfiction is associated with drudgery and conceived of as completely lacking in aesthetic reward, prospective writers overlook its creative possibilities. There is no denying that nonfiction has acquired a bad name. The suspicion still lingers that, despite its long and splendid history in our language, nonfiction is not "literary" enough. To quote Truman Capote slightly out of context, "That's not writing, it's typing." Young writers unquestionably tend to shun it; few would make a career in nonfiction the subject of ambition. At writers conferences nonfiction is, if indeed it is given room at all, usually subordinated. A general air of grubbiness (even financial success can seem grubby to the dedicated amateur) hangs over nonfiction; the glamour of writing attaches to fiction alone. Practitioners of nonfiction, however established their reputations, are seldom the stars of a writers conference. In the family of letters, nonfiction is regarded as an orphan.

The downgrading of nonfiction leads to an unrealistic, even absurd, state of affairs. In the hothouse climate of amateur aspiration, nonfiction may be a minor, lightly regarded discipline, but in the real world of print nonfiction has swept all before it. The short story, once dominant in both quality magazines and in family magazines of large circulation, is published far less frequently today, and then as if by sufferance. Short fiction, it is true, survives and even flourishes in the little magazines and in the literary quarterlies, but elsewhere it is preeminent no longer. To recognize the long-standing ascendancy of nonfiction is not, of course, the same thing as to establish a claim for nonfiction as an art form. Popular acceptance alone is not sufficient for that. But an awareness of the facts of publishing serves to place overly romantic evaluation of fiction in perspective. There need be no quarrel between the two. Both forms demand artistry, as the classics of nonfiction—for an example, in biography— abundantly testify.

Anyone who has attempted nonfiction knows that it, too, comes out of the resources of the creative impulse. And anyone who has written so much as the message on a postcard also knows how difficult it is to keep fact and fiction apart. "Having wonderful time. Wish you were here." Fact or fiction? The truth is, in both fact and fiction we lie a little. That is to say, we present our perceptions, and our perceptions only, of the essence, the very heart of the matter. Nonfiction cannot hope, any more than fiction can, to manifest the totality of a moment. What happens is not a literal transfer of an idea, or an emotion, or the contours of a sunset into the mind of the recipient of a communication. Whether we offer the entity of thought or image as actual or as imaginary, we lie a little. That is, we winnow, we condense, we strive to achieve emphasis, we interpret. In both fiction and nonfiction, we of necessity perform a creative shaping; this is necessary because mind and eye alike recoil from a terrain that offers neither peaks nor valleys.

Such an attempt to communicate involves the self in a fundamental way. That involvement is of its very nature creative. The commitment to communicate in language encompasses, when it succeeds, the basic, organic quality of style. "Don't worry about style," say the editors of *American Laundry Digest*. "What we want is good writing." As though the two could be separated! If anything is sure in this enterprise of committing words to paper, it is that style is not mere topping or extrinsic decoration. The implication that the presence of style always indicates "bad writing" is unfortunate. Choosing a particular verb or adverb over another is not pretension but precision. Style, after all, is the right doing of the thing done. It follows that the writer who demands the integrity of the work will participate more fully in the creative act than one who does not. The honest matching of words (style) to things (substance) leaves no question of avoiding soundness for the sake of style.

A magazine article on even the humblest subject—laundry—can become a creative exercise. Such a piece, although the writing is simple and unadorned, requires that choices of approach be made, and that even such prosaic facts as statistics and measurements be assimilated into some design for the whole. Determining the beginning, middle, and end of one's treatment of a subject, however routine, however uninspiring—the label information on a can of beans, or the time and route stipulations on a bus transfer—is an art involving choice, judgment, and the assigning of proportional values. All these are functions of the creative act. The writer in disposing of these elements is creating a new entity: a paragraph or paragraphs of related statements. Where there was nothing, there now is something. Of the most affecting poem, the most searching play, the most triumphantly revealing novel one cannot say more.

It is the nature of communication, factual as well as fictional, that every work expressed through literary form offers aesthetic challenge. The writer of magazine-length nonfiction should welcome the challenge as an opportunity to prepare himself or herself for increasingly better-paying markets. The beginning writer will, upon reflection, recognize that the encircling world of communications is one that depends primarily upon aesthetic pattern. Ours is not an age that is charmed or overwhelmed by logic. Sheer reasoning unsupported by imagery does not easily convince. Image, a logo, pattern—these are all around us. Signs not syllogisms persuade. In our domestic architecture, in the symbols advertising uses to seduce us, and in the shapes and contours of the appliances with which we surround ourselves we find and react to a streamlined world of design. Pattern defines us, manipulates our world.

A condition exists, then, that the writer can at once explore for achieving effective reader appeal and for personal gratification. Fact writing, the magazine article in particular, affords us an area for applying pattern. One of the most efficacious designs for magazine-length prose is one that is modeled after that perfect geometric figure the circle. "In my end is my beginning," as Mary Queen of Scots was supposed to have said in quite another deadline situation. The appeal is to the reader's assent to your exposition, your argument, your demonstration, when made not with circular argument but in a way that permits your final statements to echo your first.

Whatever pattern you use, you will wish to begin with a bang. You have no hope of easing your reader—and your first reader is an editor, short of time and perhaps of temper, poised, alert, and professional—into what you have to say. You are in the position of the hillman who wanted to attract his wife's attention so he shot her in the foot. What you have to do with your beginning is to shoot your editor in the foot. Attract his or her attention first, and then hold it. You do this in a sentence or two—at the most in two short paragraphs. Your opening should be a kind of verbal violence, but it must be consonant with the tone of your whole piece, and above all it must be accurate. An arresting opening statement in an essay about Jane Austen might start off: "It has not been known until now that the author of *Pride and Prejudice* was a man, George Austen, who used as pseudonym the name of his sister Jane." Arresting no doubt, but a complete falsehood, and therefore unusable.

In your search for a good opening consider current reader interest. What is there in the subject you have chosen, or been commissioned, to write about that would most strike a reader's curiosity or interest? Sometimes a sentence containing an enumeration will do it, if the figure involved is startling enough. A controversial statement (but one well chosen for its relevance to the theme of the article) is an attention getter. If you can find one short and pithy enough, a quotation (the best source is a person directly involved in your subject; a bookish quotation from someone who merely wrote *about* the subject is usually less effective) has the additional visual advantage of quotation marks to catch the reader's eye. You are sending out a message to the eye as well as the mind, to both at once.

All of this should be in proportion to the total wordage at your disposal. You cannot be continually winding up. Sooner or later, and usually the sooner the better, you must throw the ball. Your next consideration—next in execution but perhaps first when the piece is still an unwritten idea or a collection of disparate notes—has to be your audience of one, the solitary reader. He or she is both one and many, an individual and a type. Authors differ on whether or not they have a particular reader in mind as the recipient of what they write. Some say they do have such an image, and that they write as though talking to a person whom they visualize clearly. Others close off vision and turn inward; theirs is an implicit belief that they are writers because they are sensitive and accurate instruments recording the public mind. They see things as others see them; they want to talk about, instinctively, what others want to know.

The beginning writer is not likely to possess the confidence of this latter group. Common sense will produce a kind of negative knowledge that can be helpful here. One does not aim an article on geriatrics to the editors of *Seventeen* or one on historic farm implements to *Vogue*. Again, one does not attack the concept of the American family in an article bound for *Family Circle*. Beyond that there are matters of language level in writing for children (would Lewis Carroll have been able to sell "Jabberwocky" to *Humpty Dumpty*?) and specialized interests, such as the territorial ones of regional magazines. Seen in a positive way, the writer's concept of the reader being addressed is a courtesy, an attempt to speak mind to mind. In most instances, this understanding is conveyed wordlessly; that is to say, the reader is addressed and identified implicitly, not explicitly.

In terms of words expended, the body of the work clearly is the place for abundance. Here the weight, both metaphorical and actual, of the article is felt. It is for the body of the work that the article was written; it is for the body that it deserves to be read. No piece, however ingeniously introduced, with whatever arresting opening, no piece unerringly targeted to the reader, will be worth anything at all if the body of the work does not validate it. In this central position the author spreads her or his wares, displays relationships, enlivens through pertinent examples or anecdotes, pounds home the message. Given the weird lead we contrived for the Jane Austen opening, and supposing the "you" to be a reader with definite literary background and interests, we now have to produce fact and argument, demonstration and persuasion that will validate such targeted beginning.

When arresting opening, ideal reader, and the substance

of the piece have been accounted for, the ending remains. For most beginners the opening paragraphs and the concluding ones are the most difficult parts to write. They have the ideal reader in mind—perhaps themselves multiplied. And they know what their subject is; they are full of it. Even when they have solved the problem of the opening, there is still that of an effective ending. An arbitrary, hortatory—and therefore faintly hostile—ending would spoil everything. An open-ended conclusion sounds attractive, yet it too seems arbitrary. Circular pattern may come to the rescue. The backwoods preacher's formula for his sermons sums it up: "I tell them I am going to tell them; I tell them; I tell them I told them." A return to your beginning enables you to tell them you have told them.

This kind of ending is easily accomplished. Look at your arresting opening. If it is well crafted there are words or phrases you can use again, to form your concluding paragraphs. The quantity you are looking for is just the same; you must not be the reluctantly departing guest, overlong in your going. Nor do you wish to give the impression of trailing off, of fading indecisively away. You seize upon your initial phrasing, then, and ring changes on it. You have impressed pattern on your piece and, what is more important, on the mind of your reader. She or he will notice the shape and feel of what you have done; it will give him or her (as it has given you to contrive it) aesthetic satisfaction; and it will linger. It might be objected that what is being advised is redundancy. Far from it. You do not repeat yourself exactly and fully; you do so only partially. You provide not repetition but an echo.

This echo provides the reader with a sense of *déjà vu*; before he or she realizes what is happening, pattern convinces. When these words were first introduced—in your opening— they came to the reader in an abstract fashion, as a notion. As the reader (drawn by the implied "you") read on, a connection of sustained logical discourse established itself. Then came the ending, a harking back, through the use of key words or phrases—sometimes sentences slightly, subtly changed—and what was first a notion, an abstraction only, has now become concrete, is now not notion but experience. Basically the same words and the same idea have become pleasantly familiar, because of what came in between: the body of the work. This is how the circle closes, one and complete.

It is possible, of course, that an attention to aesthetic pattern and persuasion by this kind of design may be inappropriate for your subject matter. Your article may be bristling with facts that overwhelm, arguments that demand assent, anecdotes that make their point with hilarious clarity. In such a context it is conceivable that a marked attempt at a pattern would seem pretentious and out of place. The application of design could conceivably cause a grim piece to appear frivolous and weaken or even destroy your carefully built up argument. Unless pattern can appear to come out of the way your mind works and apprehends a subject, the result may not be "good writing," after all. Should that be so, kill it. Things not working out may simply be unworkable. It does not work now, for this particular piece your mind has fashioned; it may work later, for another. Perhaps what you need is the laconic advice David Dempsey gave the participants of a recent session of the Georgetown University Writers Conference: "When you have come to the end, just stop."

Another pattern useful in the organizing of one's material for a magazine-length article is the one that calls for beginning in the middle, *in medias res*. This is the news-angle beginning; you open at the point of immediate news interest. This device works well, indeed seems indispensable, when your subject is a person. You must catch your reader's eye and mind with a striking statement about who your subject is *now*. What made her or him newly prominent? Is he or she a Republican elected in a state that usually elects Democrats? There's your lead. Is he or she a newcomer who edged out the bosses' choice in a primary? Again, a lead, the shaping of which will depend on the "you," the reader. If the publication is a newspaper published in the same state, or a magazine with regional coverage, you must give some thought to making your opening seem fresh "news." If your publication is nationally circulated, and your subject is not yet a national figure, your problem is less difficult. Your subject is likely to be fresh to your readers.

With the *in medias res* beginning, the writer meets the reader halfway. No reader is eager to be informed right away where the subject of the article went to elementary school, how he delivered newspapers as a teen-ager, or won an athletic scholarship to Princeton—not if the news hook is that the subject was just nominated for governor after a bitter primary fight, or returned from Denmark after a sex change operation, or become controversial for proposing a new cure for cancer. The newsworthiness of your subject dictates the approach you should take. After you have selected the news lead, have begun with the *now* of your subject, the reader will gladly follow you chronologically. Having aroused the reader's curiosity, you are free to dip into the past, starting your *then* with your subject's first day in nursery school, if you have something pertinent to reveal about it, and continuing down the years to the present.

The same pattern is applicable to a subject other than a person, even to something as intangible as a concept. An idea exists in time and thus has a *now* and a *then*. The method is identical: begin in the middle, at the point of highest interest at the moment of writing, then go back as far in time as the subject requires and proceed chronologically from there. Often the subject susceptible to this treatment will be an old and familiar one; all the more reason for seizing it at the point of today's interest. Nobody, least of all the editor, wants to read a magazine article that starts off far back in the past and only after working up from that past, of forgotten events and concerns, arrives laboriously at the present. Such a manuscript will find its way into its return envelope shortly after appearing under the editorial eye.

These two patterns for the article must not be thought of as mutually exclusive. They may be easily combined; nothing precludes articulating the news approach with circular movement, with beginning and ending the article *in medias res.* Settling such matters of format is part of the writer's professional strategy. So also is the determination, usually decided instinctively, of the voice to be assumed in the telling. This question of narrative angle, crucial to fiction, should be considered for nonfiction as well. The choice is a simple one: between writing the article in the first person or in the third. Unlooked-for consequences often follow this choice. Try transposing something written in the third person into the first: words and phrases that sounded appropriate and sincere can now become coy and pretentious. Conversely, a first-person account rephrased in the third person can lose its immediacy and warmth. The one has become overfamiliar, the other remote and cold.

For factual writing the third person seems a sound, strategic choice. The writer's preliminary thinking, research, and purpose in writing have all been concentrated objectively, outside himself or herself. In this approach the thing measured, not the measuring instrument, is seen as primary. The beginning writer is seeking the confidence, the seeming anonymity perhaps, of considering objects outside the self. Just as the book review benefits from third-person objectivity—the "I like this book because" approach is irredeemably amateurish—the larger prose piece, the magazine article, derives support from an emphasis on the external rather than the internal.

It may be objected that the writer who follows the course of objectivity is being deprived thereby of freedom of expression. This would be a serious, indeed fatal, flaw if it were true that by embracing objectivity the writer gave up so fundamental a right. But the very opposite is true. It is a romantic fallacy to see rule or restriction as suppression. The professional knows that rules provide the means for experiment and opportunity. The use of the third-person pronoun does not involve a surrender of one's freedom—far from it.

Self-expression has more than one source, and the writer's individuality may be shown as much through the apt choice of verbs and adverbs as through the use of the first person pronoun.

The choice of the third-person pronoun would seem to provide the beginning writer with a fundamental tool for discipline in the craft of writing, that craft "so hard to learn," as Chaucer long ago discovered. Further, the excessive reliance upon the first person for nonfiction can, for the beginning writer new to publication, mean not discipline but indulgence. An acceptance or two may be followed by a series of rejection slips, and the reason may be that the "I," at the writer's present stage of development, is capable of only a very few uses. The exploration of self enjoined by the use of the first person requires a confidence in one's public identity, one's print persona, which is not easily, surely not automatically, come by. It often takes time and experience to prepare and then present a self one can publicly explore. This discovery of a usable self, inevitably involving a usable past of awarenesses and encounters, will in most instances be gradual. It is a discovery for which the writing of fiction rather than of nonfiction may be the proper response. In any case, one's choice between the two personal pronouns should be freshly made for each new article; one should not be locked into a permanent commitment to one or the other.

A random check of current periodicals will be enough to show conclusively that, with the exception of the confession group, most magazines fill their pages with articles written in the third person. This is no accident. More topics, after all, require objective analysis than they do the author's subjective self-exploration. My personal reaction to travel in outer space, to take a clear example, is unlikely, unless I am an Isaac Asimov, to attract or deserve readership. But a carefully researched and reasoned third-person recapitulation of what is now known or projected about the subject may conceivably interest others. (The rub is that Isaac Asimov has undoubtedly already written it.) The demand for information, any examination of the magazine stands will demonstrate, overwhelmingly outweighs the appetite for nuggets of personal revelation.

Yet there is a forum in magazines, narrow perhaps but deep, for the personal article. And it is a field every beginning writer should try at least once. For many of us, it is true, it is more difficult to write about ourselves than about the things we see around us. For many the self is likely to remain *terra incognita* long after other subjects have been thoroughly mapped and explored. It should be pointed out that the personal-experience article, once known as the familiar essay, need not be written in the first person only. The form does require that the person behind the piece is perceived not as an intelligence only, but as a person. Communication with a human face, as it were. And putting it that way enables us to see the enormous attractiveness such an approach contains for both reader and writer alike.

It is true that we daily encounter matters other than facts and figures from outer space. Outer space exploration may attract us to the extent that more routine matters obsess us. A warm, deeply felt piece about one's thoughts upon seeing a "falling star" has its place as well as a think piece on the farther planets. Nearer to our ken swim such matters as leaky pipes, crabgrass devouring the lawn, cats perched stubbornly in trees, or cars double-parked on narrow streets. Ponderously objective comment on any of these would be inappropriate, yet they deserve notice. The personal essay in which the writer mounts a class action, speaking on behalf of many, is the apt vehicle. Reaction not research is the chief ingredient of the formula here, the very stuff of what Marjorie Holmes calls the "creative article," persuasively arguing the case for in her book *Writing the Creative Article.*

Some beginning writers have a creative sensitivity to and

habit of observation of the furniture that nature and human ingenuity have provided as backdrop for our lives. They meet facts head on, but as material for impression, not argument. They have the powers of generalization, but they put these powers to a gentler use than that of statistical or sociological survey. They like to paint in tiny dabs and scratches, not in large, sweeping lines. Temperament and long habit have given them a perspective for the close-up, not the panorama. Poets of prose, they involve their readers intimately. "Look at me!" they cry out, and one, seeing oneself as well, responds. A recent student of mine illustrates the point; as a reaction to her responsible but somewhat mind-dulling job she has been drawing upon the fact that she is from a small town in the deep South to write and publish newspaper feature pieces on her reactions to life in Washington, D.C. It is not punditry, but highly amusing, sometimes irreverent, commentary on the pomposities of official, bureaucratic life. In one piece she attends Baptist worship to see what effect President and Mrs. Carter have on the congregation and the occasion. The result is provocative and delightful.

Life delineated with a light touch unendingly yields subject matter for the essay-article. Again, the effect is of the first person even when the third person is used. That this deft approach is not entirely frothy but a thing of substance is attested to by the success of the New Journalism. In New Journalism—perhaps the influence and image of television's "talking head" are operative here—the subject becomes subordinated to the writer's personality. Cronkite absorbs, swallows the news; Cronkite *is* the news. Something of this ingestion of subjects takes place increasingly in the daily press as newspapers struggle to keep alive in the bullying presence of television. More and more, one's daily paper reads like a magazine. Features crowd out hard news; news coverage shrinks as more and more daily journalism leaves news reportage to radio and to television. Staff writers supply much of the "soft" news of course, but expanded sections (on food, family living, and the like) allow for more "special" contributors—free-lancers.

As the bearers of news (particularly television's "talking heads") tend to become the focus of the news, replacing the makers of the news, journalism reaches out more and more to fiction for its techniques. The borrowing from the novelist's toolbox, especially by print journalism, is characteristic of what has become known as the New Journalism. The New Journalism may be described as fact-based reporting that centers upon the personality of the reporter and allows for such fictional devices as imagined scenes, action, and dialogue; in a word, "facts" are valued for their contribution to a preconceived design rather than for their literal accuracy. In the New Journalism the emphasis has shifted away from the facts and is on the writer and the quality of the writing. The range of this type of journalism is wide—all the way from the acrid and brilliant social criticism of a Tom Wolfe to the quirky humor of an Erma Bombeck.

There can be no denying that the New Journalism's admixture of the fictitious and the factual has enormously extended the reach of nonfiction. In skillful hands, nonfiction can be made lively, colorful, and flexible—almost, but not quite, to the point of nonfact. The fairness doctrine—as it applies to the reader—would seem to require that the writer issue clear signals of his or her intention. Such signals might include exaggeration so obvious that the author's true meaning cannot be mistaken. Satiric intent clearly indicated is another possibility. At any rate, what is intended only figuratively and what carries fictional embellishment should be sufficiently labeled so as not to mislead an attentive reader.

The degree to which fiction and nonfiction have borrowed from one another has increased in recent years. "I have watched," writes Theodore Solotaroff, who was for a decade editor of *American Review,* "the definition of what makes a piece of writing a short story, or even fiction, pretty much collapse before my eyes and even within my own mind." Both are approaches to reality, and ever since Herodotus, father of both history and fiction, the two have parted, coalesced, parted and coalesced again and again. At whatever stage of union or disunion, the two, existing as they do in time and space, are divisible into parts and the relationship between those parts has been the same: movement. Both forms are comprised of beginning, middle, and end; both progress from one to another.

It is through its movement that prose, like any type or form of communication, lives. At one point, before which it is not, it begins. It progresses from that point to midpoint, from midpoint to end. Aristotle observed this centuries ago in his *Poetics*; his observation has been the basis ever since of what happens in prose. The following examples of nonfiction illustrate what happens as nonfiction moves from coming into being to its final state of completeness.

Thomas Babington Macaulay in his *History of England*, opens a chapter with bold strokes:

> *The death of King Charles the Second took the nation by surprise. His frame was naturally strong, and did not appear to have suffered from excess. He had always been mindful of his health even in his pleasures; and his habits were such as promise a long life and a robust old age. Indolent as he was on all occasions which required tension of the mind, he was active and persevering in bodily exercise. He had, when young, been renowned as a tennis player, and was, even in the decline of life, an indefatigable walker. His ordinary pace was such that those who were admitted to the honour of his society found it difficult to keep up with him. He rose early, and generally passed three or four hours of the day in the open air. He might be seen, before the dew was off the grass in St. James's Park, striding among the trees, playing with his spaniels, and flinging corn to his ducks; and these*

*exhibitions endeared him to the common people, who always love to see the great unbend.*

*At length, towards the close of the year 1684, he was prevented, by a slight attack of what was supposed to be gout, from rambling as usual. He now spent his mornings in his laboratory, where he amused himself with experiments on the properties of mercury. His temper seemed to have suffered from confinement. He had no apparent cause for disquiet. His kingdom was tranquil: he was not in pressing want of money: his power was greater than it had ever been: the party which had long thwarted him had been beaten down; but the cheerfulness which had supported him against adverse fortune had vanished in this season of prosperity. A trifle now sufficed to depress those elastic spirits which had borne up against defeat, exile, and penury. His irritation frequently showed itself by looks and words such as would hardly have been expected from a man so eminently distinguished by good humour and good breeding. It was not supposed however that his constitution was seriously impaired.*

Macaulay uses the device of contrast as his principal instrument of movement. Many of the sentences are polarized; the mind of the reader engages in movement from one to the other. In some of the sentences the two terms express an agreement:"... mindful of his health... habits were such...." In other sentences the two terms express an opposition, a contrast: "Indolent as he was... he was active and persevering." With all its dualisms, the first paragraph adds up to a unity—the reasons why the king's death would be taken as a surprise. The transitional phrase "at length" allows the jump, the movement in summed-up time, from the first paragraph to the second. Contrast is at work again, in the second paragraph. One sees the reason for the vignette of King Charles playing in the grass with his dogs and feeding his ducks: in the second paragraph he is depicted as being in his laboratory, remaining indoors. As the paragraph concludes, Macaulay alludes to the king's exile at the execution of his father and of his fortitude then contrasted with his uncharacteristic petulance now.

In the following passage from *Vanishing Cornwall* Daphne du Maurier demonstrates movement, backward and forward, in time and place:

> *Some five-and thirty years ago you could still ride or drive in pony and jingle about the roads and byways of "the headland of slaughter," even in the summer, and be the one intruder. A friend and I once pitched a small tent between Cape Cornwall and Botallack Head, on an evening of great calm. I can remember now the stillness of sea and sky, the remote wash of the Atlantic against the rocks below, our only companions gulls and ravens. We cooked bacon over a furze fire, and the satisfying smell of it, with the bitter-hot tang of the white ashes, is in my nostrils now. The night came slowly, and we lay with the flap of the tent open, to watch the stars. Then, if never before or since, it seemed possible to become one with those sleepers, long dead, whose bones were ashes like the ashes of our fire, scattered beneath the tombs of West Penwith. They, as we did, must have cooked food over a furze fire, and lain awake and watched the stars. They, unlike us, would have stood sentinel upon the cliffs, awaiting, perhaps, with excitement and fear the thrusting prows of invading craft, line upon line of them, low and narrow, surging inward from the sea. Waking at dawn, the flap of the tent still open, I saw framed on the far horizon, quite motionless, the sea a glassy calm, a full-rigged ship. Whither bound, where from, we never discovered. The sight was a rare one even in those days, but the glimpse of it made perfect a moment of great beauty, never to stale with time or vanish from memory.*

The style here is marvelously nervous, darting as it does from a consideration of the immensity and wonder of nature to the contrasting domesticity of a meal still pungent in memory. Night is part of the movement, and with it comes an evocation of Cornish men and women of ancient times as they awaited "with excitement and fear" the coming of the invading Danes. The following morning (note the repeated detail on the tent flap, fixing scene), the speaker experiences another "sighting," this one real yet as ghostly as the imagined one of the "thrusting prows of invading craft." The present, the recent past, and the distant past are all three related in movement skillfully modulated and controlled.

The mind can be guided in movement through the abstract, can travel with pure concept as well as with the levels of contrast in a human life, or with the stages of a journey from place to place. The mind's journey, as it moves from consideration of one set of facts or propositions to another is, again, a use of movement. In the following chapter opening from *A New Age Now Begins: A People's History of the American Revolution* (McGraw-Hill, 1976), Page Smith uses comparison and contrast in his progress from one idea to another:

> *The story of colonial America is in large part the story of action in England and reaction in America; of periods of close attention by the British to the "plantations," followed by periods of "salutary neglect." Indeed, the colonists could not have chosen a better century in which to settle in America than the seventeenth. It was certainly one of the most turbulent in British history; whatever their intentions, the men or, more accurately, the factions that directed the affairs of England in those stormy decades had little time to devote to colonial affairs. The colonies, left largely to their own devices, flourished. But salutary neglect was not, of course, the whole story. A policy worked out laboriously by a succession of*

*governments, primarily through the Lords and then by the Board of Trade and Plantations, defined the relationship between the mother country and her American colonies. Some able men concerned themselves with the colonies in the eighteenth century, among them the great diarist Samuel Pepys and the philosopher John Locke.*

*Beyond that, the colonies followed, as closely as they could from the other side of the Atlantic, the course of events in England. And those events exerted an enormous influence on the attitudes and aspirations of the colonists themselves. What they believed they were witnessing in the homeland was nothing less than a struggle to the death between arbitrary power, in the persons of the Stuart kings, and constitutional government, represented by Parliament. The colonists were convinced that on the outcome of that struggle rested their own fate as free men under lawful authority. The great struggle of the kings against Parliament that took up almost the entire seventeenth century in England helped implant in the colonists their belief in their "rights as Englishmen"— rights that they were willing to fight to protect.*

Smith's chapter is entitled "Legacy of Liberty"; his two beginning paragraphs prepare his readers for his discussion of "political stability" in England and its effects on America. The concluding sentence of this chapter rounds out the movement begun in the passage quoted above, and in a way that echoes its ideas and phrasing: "So the English colonies grew greatly in numbers during that tumultuous century, and they learned, perhaps better than the British themselves, whatever lessons the events of that era were capable of teaching to attentive students on the other side of the Atlantic."

As a final example of movement, consider this passage, a single paragraph from *The Education of Henry Adams*:

*One had heard and read a great deal about death, and
even seen a little of it, and knew by heart the thousand
commonplaces of religion and poetry which seemed to
deaden one's senses and veil the horror. Society being
immortal, could put on immortality at will. Adams being
mortal, felt only the mortality. Death took features
altogether new to him, in these rich and sensuous
surroundings. Nature enjoyed, played with it, the horror
added to her charm, she liked the torture, and smothered
her victim with caresses. Never had one seen her so
winning. The hot Italian summer brooded outside, over
the market-place and the picturesque peasants, and, in the
singular color of the Tuscan atmosphere, the hills and
vineyards of the Apennines seemed bursting with
mid-summer blood. The sick-room itself glowed with the
Italian joy of life; friends filled it; no harsh northern lights
pierced the soft shadows; even the dying woman shared
the sense of the Italian summer, the soft, velvet air, the
humor, the courage, the sensual fulness of Nature and
man. She faced death, as women mostly do, bravely and
even gaily, racked slowly to unconsciousness, but yielding
only to violence, as a soldier sabred in battle. For many
thousands of years, on these hills and plains, Nature had
gone on sabring men and women with the same air of
sensual pleasure.*

In this eloquent passage, a requiem on the death of his sister,
Adams employs contrast to build up to a climax that fuses
death and nature in a striking final image.

In spite of the linkages and mutations that tend to make
fiction and nonfiction symbiotic, the two differ markedly when
it comes to the authority each commands. Broadly put, fiction
is independent, nonfiction dependent. Fiction carries its
own verification, its own validation. A short story or a novel
presents an imaginary world that bears an ambivalent relationship to reality; it reflects the world of actuality as we

live it. But fiction's world and our world run on parallel lines, never meeting. No matter how much based upon actual life and real people a novel may be, it is still an analogously created entity, a structure of the imagination. The events in the novel may have happened, but *not in this way*. They occurred in the mind of the novelist only—*that* was their *then*. They are occurring *now*—in the same fashion—in the mind of the reader. But they never happened on the extramental plane of reality. They *could have happened*; they still *may happen*. But their existence remains after the order of imitation, and there they remain.

Fiction is separate from reality and yet accountable to it. Fiction is *not unreal*. It may be put that fiction is accountable to reality as being *able to happen*, as typifying, or allegorizing, what has happened. Fiction happens *as if*. The ambivalent relation of fiction to the real world by no means frees it of our reckonings. The responsibilities of fiction are many, and they depend to a large extent upon the order of reality. Realistic and naturalistic fiction must be evocative of reality—we must see it, hear it, smell it, touch it—in the images it presents of people and visible things. In a sense, fiction is the account of the expected and the expectable. Unlike nonfiction, it must follow probability's law. In actuality—but not in fiction— the illogical, the outrageously improbable occurs. But even in fantasy fiction, especially in fantasy, logic and consequence remain enthroned. The parallel between events in fantasy and events in life is often faint—ideational rather than representational—yet it must be palpable. Woody Allen's prize short story "The Kugelmass Episode" employs a time machine that allows the protagonist to enter the pages of *Madame Bovary* and permits Emma herself to visit New York—all with impeccable logic.

The writer of fiction, then, may be held accountable, in a large and general way, only to such notions and experiences of reality as everyday living and observation confirm. Fiction comes to us in all its vivid separation from the tabulations, the statistics, the graphs and charts—all the "visuals"), and all the footnotes that trail nonfiction. The writer of nonfiction, on the other hand, carries such encumbrances. Nonfiction involves an accountability that is specific, one that, for example, will not permit the Eiffel Tower to be moved to New York or buffalo to graze upon the White House lawn. Statements made in nonfiction can easily be looked into; they are, in Emerson's phrase for Whitman, "available for post office." But those facts that are found in fiction, although recognizable and familiar, are forever beyond our touching.

The people of nonfiction are not mythical but actual. They lived at this time or that, in this place or that. They can be tracked down in encyclopedias and other works of reference. Thus the very authority for what the nonfiction writer says, for the gestures made in language, comes not from within, from a territory of imagination untraveled by others, but from the everyday world we all inhabit. Thus the nonfiction writer is not detachable from the work in the way the author of fiction is. Nobody asks the fiction writer, "How do you come to know all this?" The short story writer's age, occupation, and educational background are matters of indifference to editor and reader alike. A mountaintop residence high in the Himalayas will not call the novelist's bona fides to write about urban America automatically into question.

The identity and the credentials of the nonfiction writer —even the author of the semifictional "creative article" —can be of equal importance to what has been written. Hence the importance of the query letter and, to a slightly lesser degree, of the cover letter sent in with the completed article. The more technical the subject, of course, the more necessary it is for the free-lance writer to present credentials— showing education, employment, opportunity for experience or research in the field, and availability of experts on the subject for interview. A query letter is a proposal of an article to be written; naturally, part of the credibility of the proposal depends upon the editor's estimate of the ability of the writer to carry it out.

Obviously, care should be taken when one is deciding upon the kind and amount of personal information to be contained in the query letter. Clearly, there must be enough such information, enough and no more. An account of the writer's life story and its struggles is manifestly inappropriate. Only that biographical statement relevant to the subject of the proposed article should be included. The quarterly *Contemporary Literature*, for example, "does not encourage contributions from freelance writers without academic credentials." The writer lacking such credentials would ordinarily not consider this magazine a reasonable target. But suppose she or he happened to possess family papers or correspondence bearing on the subject or to have personal knowledge of an important contemporary writer? That being so, the query letter would be the place to mention it.

The tone of the query letter should strike the right note, somewhere between assurance and diffidence; that is the writer should be neither cocksure and know-it-all in approaching the editor, nor yet abject. Perhaps a classic (and never-to-be-imitated) example of the former is the letter Branwell Brontë, brother of Charlotte and Emily, wrote to the editor of *Blackwood's Magazine* proposing himself as a contributor to replace one who has recently died. "Read what I write," Brontë admonished the editor. "And would to heaven you could believe it true, for then you would attend and act upon it." He went on to say that he intended to write for *Blackwood's* and no other magazine, "for the idea of striving to aid another periodical is *horribly repulsive*." Give me a subject to write about, Brontë urged, I will do it. His parting admonition was: "Now, sir, do not act like a commonplace person, but like a man willing to examine for himself." This last may be the heartfelt wish of all who would contribute to magazines, but it is a wish that had better remain unspoken.

The query letter should be composed with care. Its function is to propose the writing of an article. (If the article is already written, it should be submitted at once with a cover letter which indicates your "authority.") A paragraph, not more than two, should be devoted to a précis of the article. The letter will indicate any special items of reader interest (timeliness, new developments, future projections) that the readers of this particular magazine will wish to be informed about. One should take care to write the query letter in the tone of the article—this letter is a sample of what is to come, more especially of the mind that is shaping what is to come. If you have any clippings or photocopies of previous work, these should be enclosed. List magazines you have previously sold to; if these are too modest and limited, be general (type them rather than naming them) in describing them. *Better Homes and Gardens* suggests that the query letter contain "a good stab at a title."

To the extent that the query letter gives the editor a whiff of the flavor you bring to your subject, the greater the chance the editor will be intrigued with what you propose. Nobody is likely to be as ingratiating as poor Branwell Brontë, nor should the letter sound too slick or glib. You are offering a journeyman's performance, not selling corner lots in a cactus grove. Should the response to your query letter turn out to be an affirmative one, you will of course write or finish writing the article, taking care to confine its length to the limit proposed and observing whatever deadline the editor gives you. It is important to take an affirmative response as nothing more than an indication of interest. You have been given a "go ahead," it is true, but what you have is only an invitation to carry through with your proposal. As *Columbia* puts it in its "data sheet" for writers: "No definite commitments are made in response to queries. Binding commitments are made only on receipt of the finished article."

A cover letter is appropriate for inclusion with a

manuscript written in follow up to a query. Such a letter should be brief, avoiding any presumption that your article has been accepted for publication, yet identifying it as the piece the editor and you discussed. The tone should be friendly but not' overly so. The relationship you hope to establish is a professional one. Neither acceptance nor rejection of the article need be thought of as opportunity for further correspondence on that subject. You risk boring the editor with thanks or irritating him with recriminations. It is good to remember that in this business today's enemy is tomorrow's friend; an angry response to a rejection is unproductive and unprofessional. Besides, editors in the magazine and book worlds, small communities after all, tend to move on fairly regularly; who knows around what corner you may meet next. In rare instances, the response to your piece is neither outright rejection nor acceptance. You may be offered a collaborator (definition: someone who does not have the material you have fashioned but who can write more professionally) or given an offer for your material, which will be assigned to another.

Should that happen to you, you will be called upon to choose between pride and policy. If this was to be your first time in print, your reaction of hurt pride is quite understandable. You as well as your words (and they are indistinguishable to you, naturally) have been turned down. There is another way to look at it: "Take the cash and let the credit go." Earn while you are learning. Less cynically put, if you decide to sell your material and remain momentarily anonymous, you have an opportunity to learn when the article finally appears. A comparison of your manuscript and the printed version will be a short course in revision and editing.

If the editor is patient and not pressed, you may be offered the opportunity to revise and resubmit. Should this happen, you will be given guidance; if you follow it, although again this does not imply commitment, you are likely to have your article accepted. Emily Flint, for years managing editor of *The*

*Atlantic Monthly*, once told a conference of college editors that the magazine sometimes worked over months and through several revisions with authors whose ideas and information happened to be superior to their ability to phrase them. In most such instances, the writer is an expert of some sort or one who has sole possession of or the sole right to use materials basic to the subject. Such editorial collaboration is far more likely to happen in book publishing, where deadlines, though important, are not as regular or pressing as those in the magazine world.

Just as writing nonfiction is participating in the creative act, so is the revising of one's work. The process of cutting, revising, rewriting, or rearranging passages can be as exciting and as satisfying an experience as the original writing. While revising one is up to one's elbows in language, sharpening the relationship of the signifier—the word—with the thing signified. Hidden in the Fog Count, perhaps, waiting to be freed is the entrammeled idea you originally had; or, even more gratifying, your original idea now becomes apparent to you. Suddenly, you see what all along you had, without quite knowing it, been struggling to say.

## SUGGESTED FOLLOW-UP
## FOR THIS CHAPTER

### 1. *What to read*
Read short nonfiction of course. And read magazines voraciously. If you can possibly do so, allot regular times, at least one long afternoon or evening a month (one a week would be even better) to occupying the periodical corner or room in your local public or college library. Move around from shelf to shelf; read at least one article that bores you; check it through to see why you were bored—you are in the first stages of awareness of the market; writer as reader.

As for books, perhaps these for now, one classic and one contemporary: Herbert Read's *English Prose Style* (Boston: Beacon Press 1952), which contains brilliantly analyzed samples of great prose passages; and Beatrice Schapper's *Writing the Magazine Article* (Writer's Digest, 1970), which is a kind of workbook, showing, through photographs as well as text, the stages of development of several magazine articles in their progress from original idea to printed page.

## 2. What to write

*Lists.* Make lists of things you like, things that interest you, even things that bore you. List complaints and grievances— things that don't work, things that clutter. Then arrange (combine, subordinate, and expand) the items on a single subject. Make a rough outline—it need be no more than a numerical ordering of your list. Write your article.

*Facts.* In a field that interests you, one that you know reasonably well, compile all the facts you can think of: (1) those which are generally known and accepted; (2) those little known; and (3) those in dispute. For your article, experiment with the order and relative importance of these three categories of facts. Decide what you wish to emphasize, what to subordinate—and then write.

## 3. *Where to send it*

Try newspaper Sunday sections first, or regional magazines. Make sure that you have slanted your piece appropriately, with a localized lead and locality-targeted references. If you decide to try for a magazine of national coverage and circulation, consider a specialized market first (one your subject fits) rather than a large-circulation general magazine. Your chances would seem to be better. Still, if you think that you would rather measure your work against the best there is, do so of course. Whatever you decide to do, send your manuscript out with hope and confidence. And don't haunt your mailbox; get busy on something else.

# CHAPTER 6
# SEARCH
# AND RESEARCH

Let us suppose that you have, after much trial and error, made a sale—of a newspaper feature, or perhaps a magazine article. You have seen your name in print! There it is, on the page open before you, over the article you have written and under, very probably, a title you did not choose. You have experienced your first awakening, a reminder of the immutable law that declares an author may propose but it is the editor who disposes. Writers can be found who are unkind enough to suggest that the replacing of your perfectly good title with one of his or her own selection is the editor's attempt (the only one of which he or she is capable) to be creative. Such a suspicion, it must be stated, comes close to paranoia. A far more likely explanation is that the title is the result of some in-house requirement. It may simply have been that the title you submitted was too close to one used for an article in a previous issue. The likeliest reason for the adjustment is that the original title would not, in the type point selected, fit the allotted space.

Your words are in print at last, and as you contemplate the pages before you, your eye encounters phrases you wish that you had put differently; you think of points you should have made, but did not. In mounting disquiet you read on, only to meet with misprints. Perhaps even a pied line leaps out at you. The guilt was not yours, the fault is not yours to mend. It is rare for the author to be given the privilege of reading and correcting magazine copy (book publishers demand the author's proofing) and even then one may merely be joining co-conspirators in error. Katherine Anne Porter once privately complained about the efforts of magazine proofreaders to "improve" her copy by means of arbitrary revisions, all changes resulting from misinterpretations of her intention. She found the process comparable to the carelessness of the laundry that returns the wrong things. Lamentable as the practice is, nothing can be done after the fact; one is wise to pass over such tribulations in silence.

Now let us suppose that you have appeared in print, and you feel that your struggles are over. But they are not. Your labors, if you hope to find yourself in print with any regularity, have only begun. Do not waste your time with either recriminations or self-congratulation. You have won only a single battle, not a war. You may publish soon again, even the next time out, or you may discover a gap between your first and second acceptances equal to that between first acceptance and the time you started seriously to write. A concurrence of factors over which no writer, however often published, can exercise control, or can even guess at, may have led to the acceptance of your article. To observe this is not to reflect unfavorably on your first success. A piece of equal or greater merit might have been rejected if it had happened to arrive over the transom at the wrong time. Your contribution may have been accepted partly—in addition to its intrinsic merit—because the editor's inventory in that particular category was temporarily low. At another time an even better piece of work may be returned to you because an editor found himself momentarily overstocked.

You are to be congratulated that you have broken the silence barrier, that chilling wall between the aspiring writer and the published one. You may of course prefer to retire from the fray, as Thoreau did from making pencils after he proved with a single pencil that he could do it. It is much more probable that you will wish to try again—and again. Like travel, appearing in print is habit-forming. You will, then, seek to sustain the momentum that has been started by your initial acceptance. You may have other ideas for other articles. In your gratitude and zeal, you may press these on the editor who sent you your first check. But the editor may not find them compelling enough, or may simply not wish to use your work again so soon. The editor may choose to avoid setting up a dependence restrictive to both sides. You must not lose faith in yourself at this point; there are other markets.

Your present problem is how to introduce system into what has been hit or miss up to now—many misses and finally one hit. The situation calls for looking around you, for trying to bring order to bear upon what must seem at first a bewildering morass, infirm and slippery underfoot. Markets for your work exist, many more than you would suppose. It is important for you to find them, not only for the articles you have on hand or in mind, but also, and especially, for the fact that an exact awareness of these outlets will expand your notions of subjects you can write about. For every beginning writer who has demonstrated competence by achieving print there are easily dozens of markets whose standards of coverage and competence she or he can meet right now. It well may be that the magazines where, at this early stage, you have the best chances for welcome are not those which can be found on the average newsstand or at the supermarket. The public library will offer a much more varied selection, especially of magazines of modest circulation as well as of magazines that circulate only through subscription. In the metropolitan library of a large city or in a university library, the possibility of finding a wide range of periodicals is obviously greatest.

The widest range of all may be discovered through the two annuals published by the monthly magazines *The Writer* and *Writer's Digest*. The listings in these manuals and the current market and special-market listings in the two magazines will provide you with an enormous mass of information on many hundreds of magazines and on what their editors are looking for. To write without consulting these sources, preferably before but also after the piece is written, is a serious and crippling blunder. Your search for what to write as well as your search for where to send it should originate from here. This is the way to become productive and professional. The amateur, along with Walt Whitman, loafs and invites his soul; the professional locates targets, sets attainable goals.

No doubt you will have completed a second article. In a wave of euphoria you rushed ahead, not pausing to query. Then your article was returned to you, with exemplary dispatch, by "your" editor. Deciding not to bury it in a folder, you determine to send it out again. Your success in selling your earlier article has persuaded you, rightly, that this is a sensible decision. Indeed, you should submit it at least two dozen times before banishing it to the back of your files. Checking the magazines by category, you work out your list of magazines that in subject, length, and treatment your article seems to fit. You arrange your magazines in order of their rate of payment, placing those which pay on acceptance ahead of any paying on publication. (If you wait until publication to be paid, it could take months.)

You will have noticed on checking through, say, the *Writer's Market* that some magazines allow for simultaneous and photocopied submissions; others accept photocopied submissions but not simultaneous ones. A few will consider photocopied and previous submissions. Most magazines will make none of these exceptions; they insist upon being the only ones to be looking at the manuscript, and they will read ribbon copy only. When they see photocopy or carbon copy they take it to mean that some other editor or editors may be considering the material at the same time. They are interested only in exclusives.

Most editors are still firmly opposed to simultaneous submission, and they are inclined to look upon the affair as a matter of ethics. Similarly, land powers regard sea blockade as heinous; sea powers do not. To the editor's objection that he or she is being asked to purchase something that will not be his or hers alone, the contributor can justly complain that if she or he approaches markets one by one everything with a news hook can be outdated in the weeks and sometimes months nonsimultaneous submission entails. A few years back a much-publicized contributor to business magazines solved the dilemma in spectacular fashion. He would send his article to five magazines at once. With each copy went a form letter that parceled out the following five weeks. Magazine A was given the first week to consider buying, magazine B had the second week, and so on. The odd thing is it worked, again and again. The writer was aggressive and overbearing, but he happened to be one of the outstanding writers in his field. Obviously, no beginning writer—indeed few well-known writers—could possibly succeed with such a high-handed approach to publishing. For most writers the dilemma of single-approach offering and consequent delay remains.

When you mail an article, or story or poem, to a magazine, you are offering what are known as first North American serial rights. (Hence the objection by editors to simultaneous offering to several of what can only be given to one.) In this context "North American" includes Canada but (because of the language difference) excludes Mexico. Theoretically, one is free to offer the identical piece to a magazine in New York and one published in London; the language is the same, but the circulation areas do not conflict. Unless you specify otherwise, you are offering first rights in the act of submission. Some magazines insist upon purchasing "all rights" but will assign reprint rights to the author after first publication.

Implied in your submission is the magazine's prerogative, upon acceptance, to be the first to publish your material for mass distribution in a periodical (serial). The magazine may reprint your piece in whole or in part at a later time. The magazine may offer reprint rights elsewhere, dividing the compensation equally with the author. It sometimes happens that, even though receiving only half the amount paid, the author will receive more money for the reprint than for the original appearance. Certain understandings also obtain with first acceptance. "It is understood," runs the warranty for the magazine *Marriage and Family Living*, "that you will not offer other rights, for example, pamphlet or radio rights, until after publication by us. It is also understood that, should you subsequently offer this work to any other media whose audience conflicts with that of the original publisher, you will note on the first page of your manuscript that the first North American serial rights have been sold to *Marriage*."

Some magazines do not copyright their contents; one contributes to these with the knowledge that with publication one loses the right to one's words; they become public domain. Such publication has its benevolent side; it may mean that your material will be taken for school use. Many magazines do not pay at all, or only in contributor's copies. These are mostly literary or "little" magazines, many with a circulation of five hundred or under. Is appearing in one of these a subtle way of not really being published? Not at all. Many of these magazines confer prestige upon their contributors; some help the writer obtain professional preferment or academic promotion. And most important for the young writer who has ambition to be a literary artist, such magazines are scouted by book publishers. It should be said that nonfiction has a more difficult time here. These magazines are more hospitable to short stories and poems from newcomers; their articles are usually written by experts and upon assignment.

In outlining the requirements for their magazines, editors reveal much about themselves and their interests. When an editor is quoted as saying that the prospective contributor should query first, this remark should not be taken as a covert invitation to send the complete manuscript with a cover letter. Editors of magazines based on college campuses, as are the majority of quarterlies, are equally serious when they state that they do not read manuscripts (or answer their mail either) in June, July, and August. The campus shuts down, and so does the magazine. Similarly, when the editor of *Columbia* advises that "articles without ample illustrative material are not given consideration," he means it. Another editor may observe that the submission of "b & w [black and white] photos, as appropriate, with mss. enhances publication probability." *TV Guide*, on the other hand, provides its own photographs and photography to illustrate free-lance material. The editor of *Pastoral Life* requests "a few lines of personal data" accompanying the manuscript; in other words, in the cover letter.

Editors may sometimes sound crotchety in describing their requirements—a possible hint to the prospective contributor that an off-beat query letter and manuscript may go over well with them. "Spend five years reading books about archeology" before attempting to contribute, the editor of *Art and Archaeology Newsletter* advises, only half humorously. The editors of *Modern Bride* are conciliatory: "We edit everything but don't rewrite without permission." *Redbook* is genial: "Please don't hesitate to send it because you think your spelling or punctuation may be a bit rusty." *McCall's* is equally friendly, pointing to the monthly newsletter section "Right Now" as a likely place for a beginner. "Read the magazine closely for style," says *House and Garden* with a touch of asperity, "and avoid things we've already done. We get too many free-lancers sending us material on subjects for which the crest has already passed."

Editor-contributor relations can range, as we have seen, from cordial to testy (never quite from ardent to Zoilean); the relationship, although almost always impersonal and perhaps better kept so, is subject to the limitations, irritations, and contradictions of any other human enterprise. The free-lancer will do well to be wary yet not given to suspicion—editor and writer do not occupy an adversary position. The amateur finding himself or herself with a returned manuscript and another rejection slip and then discovering that a few issues later the magazine has published a piece on the same subject is sure that foul play has occurred. ("The editor stole my idea!") The facts may be otherwise. Perhaps the writer happened to send in a piece on a subject the editor had already commissioned someone else to do, or perhaps the piece was in the composing room at the very time the writer's piece, unsolicited, came in the mail. Besides, ideas cannot be held exclusively; hence they cannot be stolen. The putting of ideas into words is another matter, capable of plagiarism.

It is well for the beginning writer, then, to send in his or her manuscripts with an attitude of trust. There is a need, nonetheless, for a more equitable arrangement in general between editors and contributors. A tradition of trust based upon a set of fair standards should be set up to eliminate misunderstandings and, in some cases, injustices. Such is the opinion of PEN, the international organization of published authors. PEN sent to the membership of its American center the following standards to serve as the basis of working arrangements between writers and editors, standards to apply to both solicited and unsolicited manuscripts: articles, fiction, and poetry. In a memorandum to its members PEN recommends the following:

**1.** That there be a letter of agreement from the editor to the writer after an oral agreement on an assignment, or an accepted article proposal, specifying: a. the number of words; b. the deadline; c. the fee to be paid; d. either a guarantee ("kill fee") or a clear understanding that the work is to be submitted on speculation; e. the nature and limit of expenses to be reimbursed by the magazine; f. any special instructions as to subject, treatment, or style.

**2.** That payment be made to the writer within 10 days of the *acceptance* (not publication) of an article; that full payment be made if a commissioned article is killed through no fault of the writer's, as when a magazine changes hands or editorial decisions are changed after an article is completed; that the writer be allowed to resell an article if it is killed, even if a kill fee is paid; and that payment be made for any subsequent use in a different form of the original ideas and phrases of a killed article.

**3.** That the editor give the writer a decision on acceptance or rejection of a commissioned article within at most four weeks of receiving it, preferably sooner; that the magazine print an accepted article as soon as possible within the magazine's schedule, but no more than a year after acceptance, except by mutual agreement; and that if an article is not printed within a year the writer may reclaim and resell it, without returning any payment.

**4.** That the editor consult with the writer before making *any* substantive changes in the writer's copy; that the editor also send galley proofs to the writer in time to make any corrections; and that, in the extraordinary cases where time pressures don't permit sending out galleys, any changes be read to the writer over the phone.

**5.** That the editor not do violence to the intent and spirit of an article through the use of headlines, cover-lines, subheads, break heads, illustrations, captions, identification boxes, and the like; that writers make known to the editor their feelings, and request consultation, about any of these production procedures; and that editors recognize an obligation to respond to these feelings insofar as the mechanics of production permit.

**6.** That publications purchase first North American serial rights *only*, all other rights (for foreign sales, anthologies, reprints, etc.) being reserved to the writer unless a specific prior agreement states otherwise; that copyright be assigned to the writer by the publication 30 days after the article appears; and that all requests for reprint rights at any time be referred, and all payments made, to the writer.

One could be dismissive and conclude from the above merely that the seller's lot was ever thus in a buyer's market. But such cynicism would be unbecoming in a beginner; what is at stake is nothing less than the existence of a healthy context for creativity.

The prospective contributor can best foster amicable relations and increased understanding between buyer and seller by becoming thoroughly familiar with the magazines themselves. Everyone who hopes to sell to the magazine market should have an in-depth knowledge of a dozen or so magazines. These should include the magazines that are a reasonable target for now and also magazines that, when one can show bolstering clips and credits, will offer the next step up. Nearly one hundred American periodicals will send a free sample copy to the inquiring writer on request; an equal number will supply a copy upon payment of the single issue price. Most public libraries subscribe to a variety of magazines of several categories, allowing a back-up study of the issues of the previous six months.

Magazine editors, unlike book publishers, have a precise image of the readers they have or would like to have. "*Northern Virginian*," says the editor, "commands a largely suburban readership. Most earn family incomes in the upper twenties, are college-educated, are in their forties—with at least one child under seventeen, and are highly interested in dining out, travel, and entertainment, as well as in historical subjects. Many are intensely aware of current events, career developments, home affairs, and travel, as indicated by important other periodicals read. Most pursue professional or semiprofessional occupations." No potential contributor can hope to arrive at such detailed conjecture—"at least one child under seventeen" is a master touch—yet there are ways through which a serviceable thumbnail profile of a magazine can be drawn.

The first thing to take into account in such an informal survey is the level of sophistication of the magazine's format.

The level of the quality of the artwork, the typography, the photographic and other illustration, and the general design will unmistakably indicate the level of sophistication (and income) of the magazine's readership. Gloss and obvious expense in such matters inevitably point to the level of sophistication expected of contributors. One does not find sleazy writing in such surroundings. The level of sleekness in luxury-targeted advertising will serve as another signpost. Nonluxury advertising ("Build your own wet bar") will normally be an indicator in the opposite direction. Utilitarian advertising, anything "how to," will be paralleled by utilitarian copy commanding fairly low rates per word. Institutional advertising by Ma Bell and others will be found in the literary quarterlies—an indicator of indirect subsidization and of the sad fact that although quality writing will be expected, quality recompense will not be forthcoming.

If the periodical under examination contains a "Letters to the Editor" column, the contents should be examined with meticulous care. These letters offer the most direct evidence available to the nonstaffer of the interests of the magazine's readers. The amount of unfavorable comment the editor permits, and the degree of defensiveness with which the editor responds to criticism, will also prove revealing and may be helpful in directing the prospective contributor what to put in a query letter, and what to leave out. The magazine's regular departments—it may take the study of several issues to identify these—will be most helpful. Usually these are staff-written or are assigned to outside regulars; the professional quality of the writing and the amount of expertise these departments show can provide illuminating evidence of standards for the free-lancer to measure his or her work by.

The nondepartmental letterpress itself, the magazine's main content of contributed articles, fiction, and poetry, will reward the most minute attention and analysis. Comparisons between magazines, in their paragraph lengths, in such apparatus as subheads and picture captions, and in their contributor's column, will yield valuable inferences. The contents will, to the careful analyst, speak two languages: the open language directed to the magazine's reader and the arcane language of technique which reveals the professionalism in choice of language levels and other strategic dispositions. A comparison of an issue or two from the sixties with current issues of the same magazine would reveal, instructively, changes in approach, tone, and subject matter. Such an examination would doubtless demonstrate with immediacy contemporary patterns in thought and idiom.

Over one hundred and fifty magazines will send guidelines to prospective contributors upon request. Among these magazines are literary magazines, regional magazines, trade journals, children's magazines, religious magazines, specialist magazines, and large-circulation family and general magazines. Still more rely upon free-lance contributors for 50 percent or more of their contents. They are all reasonable targets for the beginning writer who has something to say and has already acquired or is commencing to acquire professional skill in saying it. For many the requirements are those of modest craftsmanship, nor are they to be despised for that. The need for clear, concise information is pressing; and industry supported by talent will not go long unrewarded if the beginner's search for markets is sincerely, intelligently made.

Many magazines provide guidelines to assist the free-lance writer in the search for markets. *Chicago*, for example, a monthly magazine 80 percent of whose articles are written by free-lancers, and with a sophisticated audience interested in the arts, dining, and the good life, carefully outlines the steps the writer should consider in working on a "story," a reportorial article:

1. The story should attempt to answer a single, simple question. Posing it may help you to craft a coherent well-organized

article. Once you have done the initial research, you and your articles editor should have enough information to formulate that question; the answer will be the core of your story.

2. By the time you have completed your research, you should have established a point of view. Don't merely present all sides of an issue and hope that the reader will discern the truth. On the other hand, don't force a point of view that is unsubstantiated by your research, or tailor your research to validate a preconception.

3. A good magazine story is a good *story*. Merely describing a state of affairs does not constitute a good story. Relate how that state of affairs came to be and why, who was instrumental in bringing it about, how it has evolved, what it means to the reader, and what the future holds. When appropriate, use the devices of the novelist to capture and hold your readers' attention: description, narrative, anecdote, dialogue, specific detail. If the story is intrinsically interesting and if the situation has consequences that do or might affect our readers, then the story is potentially a good one. If either of these elements is missing, your story may not be appropriate for *Chicago* magazine.

4. A good story should focus on individuals, not institutions. Although institutional structures have an impact on how decisions are made and shaped, it is ultimately individuals who act and whose lives are affected by those actions. Most stories can be made more vivid, more interesting, and more truthful by concentrating on the people involved: their personalities, backgrounds, motives, on what they stood to gain or lose, and how they fared.

5. A good story is almost always the product of several drafts. Our readers' time is limited; your writing should be a distilled and improved version of the original. Remember: We don't pay by the word.

**6.** Above all, a good magazine story is credible and fair. Any individual or institution whose character or actions have been impugned by the author or by anyone quoted in the article has a right to rebut those charges within the article. Should that individual or institution decline comment, say so in your story. *Chicago* magazine's libel insurance does not cover freelance writers.

The editors of *Chicago* exempt fiction, reminiscences, humor, and service features from these suggested rules, and add that "it is your responsibility to discuss with your editor how they should be applied to individual assignments." The editor of *Rhode Islander* is even more receptive to new writers: "If your stuff is really good, we'll buy it if it comes in by pony express."

America, it has often been observed, is a country of magazine readers. A study of the market, at whatever level of intensity, will convince the free-lancer that this is so; the opportunities for publication will be seen to be many and varied. Even a hobbyist in a narrow area, who might be expected to be already familiar with his or her specialty, may find new sources of publication in that field of interest. A magazine survey should widen one's concept of new approaches for article material already at one's fingertips. A search among the magazines themselves and among the guidelines their editors send out will indicate the needs of the market. The next step for the prospective contributor is to find ways to satisfy those needs.

An ability to communicate is essential to success as a free-lancer; contributing to this ability are inborn talent, the habit of observation, and training, whether self-directed or otherwise. This is the *how*. But there still remains the *what*, the problem of what to write about, of what gives solidity and persuasion to the thing said. Here the beginning writer, particularly the young writer, is at a disadvantage. The young writer seldom comes equipped with long experience (rare is the

Mozart among writers, embarking upon a career in early childhood), with intimate knowledge of a special field, or with stored-up anecdotes and instances gleaned from wide reading. A thoughtful search of the markets may increase one's knowledge of places to send one's work and provide the needed incentive for a free-lancer to become not only a published writer but also a writer whom editors can depend upon as a regular and frequent contributor.

Awareness of the markets and of the incentives that come from such knowledge will not of themselves provide the writer with something to say. For this reason search must be succeeded and confirmed by research. Research, not as it is used for academic or scholarly purposes, bristling with bibliography and footnotes, is the foundation for the article writer's sustained effectiveness. It is at the basis of the writer's knowledge of a subject and also the source of the article's structural development. Research anchors reportorial articles in authority. Initial research on a subject provides the backbone of the query letter and of the editor's response to it. A query letter that asks, in effect, that the editor suggest what is to be done with the subject will inevitably be met with a frigid response, much like the one given to Branwell Brontë. His query letter has remained in the files of *Blackwood's Magazine* for nearly a century and a half.

A free-lancer's research for an article in a popular magazine requires a responsibility to accuracy, logic, and the rules of fairness in quotation and citation by providing objective context. An accurate quotation used out of context is unfair to your source and to your reader. These requirements do not differ from those imposed by an academic journal or other scholarly publication. A free-lance writer's research differs from a scholar's primarily in the fact that in the completed work the evidence for the former's research is included within the text itself. Instead of the appended apparatus of footnotes and bibliography, documentation in the popular article is submerged in the text, implicit rather than explicit. That the article is based upon exact knowledge is clearly implied, even though its facts or discoveries are not attributed to the page of the original documentary source or the date and place of the interview.

The free-lance writer must, of course, make careful notation of sources in the process of taking notes for and writing early drafts of the article. This documentation should be in finished enough form to submit to the editor immediately upon request. Such a request can be anticipated by supplying a summary of these sources in the query or cover letter. In a general way, the article itself will possess, through confident quotation and citation, an air of authenticity that will give the editor confidence in the research done; it will be palpable. There may be reasons, at times, why the editor will take the precaution of having your article checked for possible legal repercussions, whenever it contains comments that may be considered unfair or libelous. Some magazines, notably *Reader's Digest*, employ a staff team especially to research all the facts in the material they buy. Research, it can be seen, is not just frosting on the top, but flavor that runs throughout. The professional writer can employ research for more than one purpose. Such research tools as statistics, graphs, and charts can be used to support an argument already arrived at. The writer determines what line to take, then goes about in search of supporting evidence. This method is perfectly valid for the "creative article," for in this type of piece the author's witty commentary on the "facts" is the main point. The article's "truth" is one of personal perspective, not hard evidence. In this kind of writing, the writer and the reader are in on the secret from the start; they proceed in tacit agreement that the topic is to be subjected to a light, deft, humorous point of view. Fact, opinions, quotations and supportive anecdotes all come together in a unity controlled by persuasive technique.

The other method of research is like that utilized by the scholar in his or her study or laboratory. Here reliance is not based primarily upon intuition, or generalized powers of perception, but on step-by-step elucidation. For the scholar the subject begins not with conviction but with hypothesis. The role of research in this way of arriving at a conclusion is the provision of means for testing the hypothetical case the writer has put. Will the facts, will the opinion of experts, will the observed phenomena support the writer's original hypothesis, or fail to support it? Should the results be negative or inconclusive, a new hypothesis must be formulated. Usually the result is to refine and qualify the original hypothesis.

Generally, the article that intends to present a personal slant on a subject containing no controversy or one whose conclusion unaided common sense will arrive at, can be made more piquant or striking when facts now forgotten but once generally known are resurrected. The article of this nature can be developed by supportive research that bolsters what reasonable people would have been able to arrive at on their own. Research of this kind, research used for this purpose, is not to be derided, but the writer ought to make it clear to himself or herself and to the reader that this is precisely what is happening.

Research that tests hypotheses would mean overkill if applied to many articles and purposes. Nonetheless, it should not be thought of as a method or procedure for scholars and experts only, exclusively the tool of the specialist and not capable of use by the generalist. This kind of research is preeminently the method of investigative reporting. Its conclusions are not foregone but hard won. The free-lance writer willing to do the detecting, clue-following footwork (often in the literal sense) of the investigative reporter will enjoy the experience of seeing his or her subject grow in importance and complexity and, after a time, present some single thread, some overwhelmingly directive evidence leading to a conclusion. This conclusion may turn out to be the very opposite of the tentative idea that first suggested the subject. Even a 180-degree turn, if honestly arrived at through following the trail of facts can offer satisfaction and reward.

The object of investigative research is either the furthering or the fresh discovery of knowledge.

Research may be conducted in the field or in the library, among people or among books. The free-lancer's research will normally begin in a library, proceed to the field—in interview, observation, or experience—and return to the library for in-depth exploration of what has been directly learned. The place to begin one's library research is in the reference section, with a good encyclopedia. The encyclopedia entry on one's subject will (1) identify it, (2) give its history and periods of development, (3) suggest its current relevance and problems, and (4) predict its future. The entry will usually list two or three books that are the most authoritative. (Here the date of the encyclopedia is important; in many developing subjects no book written more than five years before the date of consultation is completely up-to-date.) Each of the books listed at the end of the entry will probably contain a bibliography of two hundred or more titles, of magazine articles as well as books. Then the game, as Sherlock Holmes liked to put it, is afoot.

One's first notes are likely to be those taken from the encyclopedia article, the source of important names and dates. It is well to read the entry with a sense of the currency of the subject. Do people regard the subject differently now than they did a generation ago? A decade ago? This is a good acid test for ecological questions. Are there schools of thought about the subject, whether it be physics, modern art, or medicine? If the research subject is a historical personage—England's Queen Emma, for instance—is there any reason why she should be recalled today, because of an anniversary of her birth or death, or because of recent documentary discoveries about her life or period? Or take another minor historical figure, King Louis Philippe of France, whose journals have recently been published. He lived in the United States in his years of exile, in various places, thus offering a subject for treatment in a newspaper Sunday supplement or in a regional magazine. All sorts of tangents suggest themselves—his story might lead into a treatment of French cuisine or one of domestic architecture and furnishings of his period.

With subjects such as the above one might think no field research is possible. Although it is likely, for Emma and Louis Philippe, to remain a matter of digging in books and periodicals, it is possible to extend the investigation through field research, correspondence with experts, visits to museums and special libraries, even trips abroad. Corresponding with those who possess inside knowledge or access to files or documents may become a valuable early stage in a writer's research. Although the writer's share of the correspondence is obviously a search for information, it should not proceed from total ignorance of the subject. The relevance and timeliness of the questions you ask will indicate your own level of familiarity with the subject and will go far toward shaping a generous and apposite response. The act of writing to the U.S. Department of Agriculture or the California Highway Patrol or the Library of Congress Geography and Map Division is a form of research when the information sought is unavailable elsewhere and when the right questions are asked.

The research for many subjects may properly begin in a newspaper's clippings library (now called the morgue only on late, late TV). The next step for the researcher, in cases for which documentation has not reached the stage of books or even magazine articles, may be to interview people: public officials, academic experts cited in the news stories, or even the famed man in the street. The writer may be surprised to find that a number of people are willing to extend help in both the field and the library. The cooperation of the librarian is to be cultivated as one of the most valuable sources of aid the free-lancer will ever have. If the writer is prepared with a basic knowledge of the subject, people whose careers and livelihoods revolve around it will usually be found extraordinarily generous with their time and assistance. Among those whose assistance is to be accepted with caution but without crippling suspicion are information officers and publicity people. The researcher willingly receives what they have to contribute, carefully aware that it is based upon advocacy not objectivity.

The free-lancer is fortunate when he or she can turn to an academic expert as a source of information and opinion. This source is likely to be objective and also thoroughly informed of the latest trends and findings. Often a university's information bureau will offer its services in setting up the time and place of the interview. Interviews with experts in medicine, law, politics, pharmacy, philosophy, and other fields are available through a university, and of course these interview opportunities are excellent "story" sources for the writer of researched articles. Like most experts, university professors and administrators are likely to be fired with enthusiasm for their subjects and in a single interview to throw off more ideas and suggestions than can be used in a dozen articles.

Whether your subject is unemployment insurance, the new sources of food to be found in krill and plankton, the common fears of first pregnancy, or the "pistol personality and trigger temperament" that leads to violence, there is a university department that can serve as a source of theory or of information providing background for what you write. Consider the possibilities in the following story suggestion from a university publicity office:

PREPARING FOR THAT SECOND CHILD. *When the second child comes along, special problems may come with him, says Dr. Edward Sheridan, a child psychiatrist. "Expect and accept a mixture of feelings in the first child," he says. "Many parents burden the first child with the obligation that he must feel all love for baby. Then the hurt goes underground and remains unexpressed." The second child, too, may over-identify with the first child, helping him to protect his No. 1 status. Most important, however, parents should accept a mixture of responses in their children. "All too often," says Dr. Sheridan, "our responses to children's behavior aren't as varied as the children themselves. Even if you have identical twins, each will have a different mother and father because each views parents through different lenses."*

Here is the basis for an article of either the "creative" or objective type; research through interview can expand the writer's grasp and insight and provide substance for either.

The newspaper is a research tool even nearer at hand. The alert free-lancer will scan daily and weekly papers for items in the news that may serve as germs for research projects. How better to learn what is timely? Local news can be as vaulable as statewide or national news, often more so; it can lend human dimensions to an abstraction or generalization. A wire story carrying an out-of-town dateline may well stimulate the interviewing of a local authority on the subject. Take, for example, a national celebrity quoted as deploring the idea that the beginning of life is the time to start preparing female children for the "change of life." Can you find a local authority to agree or disagree? "The family that eats together stays together, historically and traditionally," a newspaper quotes a sociologist as declaring. The statement immediately suggests research into the history of the American family. Was the family table, now largely deserted for junk meals at the fast-food counter, really the cement of yesterday's family? What traditions of togetherness, now apparently weakened or lacking, supported family cohesion in the past? Questions, clues, and deductions will get the writer started.

After preliminary reading and checking, the researcher is ready to arrange for an interview. A query letter, often a telephone call, will be sufficient to set time and place. If the writer is doing the article on speculation and not under an editor's assignment, the query should, without overemphasis, make that fact clear. The relationship between the writer and the person who consents to be interviewed should be one of trust and openness, one without unreasonable expectations on either side. Permission to tape the interview should always be obtained in advance or at the beginning of the interview. The writer should be prepared to use the reporter's traditional pad and pencil if so requested. Use of a recorder carries with it the advantage of guarantee against misquotation. This advantage can be lessened if the procedure makes the subject uneasy, diffident, or stilted. For many persons under interview the absence of both recorder and pencil is the most unnerving apparatus of all.

The person under interview may reasonably expect that the writer avoid wasting time by being unprepared to the point of lacking even threshold knowledge of the subject; that the atmosphere set up by the questioning be friendly, efficient, and pertinent. The writer cannot be expected to know as much about the subject as the expert; if that were so, there would be no need for the interview. The expert has a right not to be entrapped; the relationship between the two should be cooperative, not adversary. The interviewer, on the other hand, has a right to expect more than offhand answers to questions that have pertinence, to follow up unexpected leads opened up in the conversation. Courtesy should be taken for granted, but it may be well to draw certain lines in reference to colleagues and personal considerations. No have-you-stopped-beating-your-wife? questions.

What expectations that might arise from interviewing could be considered unreasonable? The writer has no right to hector or bully; the information he or she seeks is not legal to obtain, at least not from a private person. The writer may note evasion and decide to supplement this interview by interviewing other experts; he or she may, through correspondence and telephoning the subject's peers, determine the regard his or her subject is held in. It is also permissible to ask for translation from jargon to layman's language, and to inquire whether or not his or her version adequately presents the sense of the technical language he or she has been given. The interviewer may, of course, rephrase questions; it is more important to be accurate than it is to fear appearing incompetent. A certain thickness of skin is required for all writing that takes you out of the study or library and into the unquiet and disordered world.

The subject of the interview has a right to be correctly quoted, but does she or he have the right to make certain that the writer has done so in the manuscript? If a recorder is used, it would seem unnecessary to demand to see the quotation as it is to appear in print. But what if the expert has second thoughts? Suppose she or he has come to a view of the matter that contradicts in a major way the information given out to the writer? Two possibilities exist here. If the demand for change is based upon the discovery of previously neglected or newly discovered facts—fresh laboratory test results, for example— then the request for change is reasonable. If the consulted expert would, let us say, merely like to phrase the matter differently in order to appear more polished in delivery, then the request for change is unreasonable.

A more serious consideration is that of the scheme and content of the article. A reasonable stand on the matter would seem to be this: the expert is just that, an expert, and has a right not to be misquoted or misrepresented; but the writer is responsible for the rhetoric, for the context in which the quoted material appears. The expert may not responsibly demand that she or he be quoted in the beginning of the article, or in the conclusion, that no other experts be cited or quoted, that what she or he said in the interview be summarized rather than directly quoted, or that the expert be the one to determine which parts will be quoted directly and which only para-phrased. These determinations belong to the writer, who must not surrender them. The beginning, unpublished writer has equal privileges here with the writer who has been pub-lished. The principle is the same for both: the writer, not the expert interviewed, is the expert when it comes to writing. Any surrender of the writer's authority where the writer should have authority is nothing less than an attack on the integrity of the work itself. After all, the writer, the beginning writer especially, is not likely to interview the world's sole authority on the subject. There are other experts.

The problem of quotation occurs in library research as well. Publishers allow, to a sharply limited extent, direct quotation for the purpose of writing a review when the book first comes out. Use of material for quotation, even in the same limited amount as permitted to the reviewer, for purposes other than critical evaluation upon first publication is forbidden without written permission and, usually, royalty payment. Current literature, whether in periodicals or in books, comes under that prohibition. (The new copyright laws favor the original author, extending copyright protection from the previous period of fifty-four years from the date of original publication to the length of the author's lifetime plus fifty years.) Material in the public domain (whose copyright has run out), most U.S. government documents and publications, and uncopyrighted materials such as handouts, briefing documents, and news releases may be quoted freely, that is without payment or request for permission. The acknowledgment of the source of uncopyrighted material should, nonetheless, always be given. Citation or paraphrase of copyright material carries the obligation of acknowledgment but not of permission; in this instance the ideas come from others, but the words are yours.

The physical act of taking quotation notes under library research conditions is much more convenient now than it used to be. Photocopying has removed all the drudgery formerly involved; hours of hand copying have been replaced by mere minutes under the photocopier button. Yet the basic need for decision on what to place on the note cards remains. It makes no more sense now, even with mechanical assistance, than it ever did to reproduce page after page in the hope that somehow the material that would prove useful will appear on the reproduced page. Notes should be taken of all facts and opinions intended for use in the finished article, but not everything should be quoted. As a general rule, material that is not strikingly put, that the writer can equal when in possession of the relevant facts, should be paraphrased, not directly quoted.

Pages or passages in your sources that contain definitions—legal, scientific, etymological—should be copied exactly, either by hand or by machine. These definitions will be touchstones for every stage of the writing. Material that through the passage of time has become distinctive because of spelling, punctuation, or phraseology, should also be recorded for exact quotation. A chance to spell public *publick* should not be passed up; anything that lends authentic flavor and attracts the reader's eye is too valuable to be ignored. Sometimes the material may be contemporary but because the source is, say, British, the idiom will be just different enough from the American to stand out. Therefore it will have a piquancy of flavor and be worth quoting. A passage translated from another language rendered with some slight change in the expected word order will again be worth direct quotation rather than paraphrase.

Well-chosen quotations, whether derived from field research or from the resources of a library, lend both flavor and substance to an article. They are almost as obligatory for nonfiction as scene is for fiction, and for somewhat the same reason—they contribute the sparkle of life. Equally important to the presence of quotations is their placing. They can be used to pace the middle of an article; when they come from an interview they will usually be numerous enough to appear in a developmental sequence. But the problem sometimes comes when one hesitates about using a quotation at the beginning or saving the same quotation for the end, both crucial positions for the article's rhetorical effectiveness. Consider the following statement by a professor of medicine: "Cold and cough remedies on the market today are a shotgun arsenal." Would this be more effective for an ending or for the beginning? If it comes at the end as a kind of climax, what can have preceded it? Surely the shock effect of the image will be stronger if the quotation is used as the lead.

The purpose of research is for use. For the free-lance writer at least, research is always a means, never an end. It is a tactical and strategic mistake for the writer to consider research as a thing apart from the actual writing, as though writing could begin only when the process of research left off. Rightly conducted, research *is* writing; the quotations and paraphrases hammered out in the course of the writer's learning about the subject often turn up unchanged in the final piece. A good paraphrase may often be the source of paragraphs, pages even. And there comes a time when one must be done with research, when an increase of information will only contribute clutter not enlightenment. At that point books and fieldwork are useful no longer; the writing itself must be faced and finished.

Research begins in questions and it ends in answers. Its purpose is the focusing of exact knowledge through the act of communication, whether or not this knowledge has been acquired laboriously, through the researcher's pouring over books or exploring in more literal ways. When Mark Twain complained about James Fenimore Cooper's "literary lapses" because of the woodenness of Cooper's Indians and their tendency to snap twigs in defiance of nature and of probability, he was criticizing Cooper's research. Cooper was writing erroneous nonsense about matters he should have instinctively known, or, in the absence of a country boyhood, should have had both the wit and the humility to look up.

## SUGGESTED FOLLOW-UP
## FOR THIS CHAPTER

### 1. *What to read*
For a thoroughly knowledgeable introduction to the book business and to the opportunities for free-lance jobs in copy

editing, proofreading, indexing, and the like, see the aptly titled *The Complete Guide to Editorial Freelancing* (Dodd, Mead, 1974) by Carol L. O'Neill and Avima Ruder. The book contains a countrywide guide to book publishers who offer employment to editorial free-lancers in such areas as copy editing, indexing, research, manuscript reading, and jacket-copy writing.

In *Supertalk* (Doubleday, 1974), Digby Diehl presents, with appropriate comment, the interviews (in question-and-answer format) he conducted with celebrities as different from one another in background and achievement as seismologist Charles Richter, Gloria Steinem, Melvin Belli, and Norman Lear. Diehl distinguishes between the interview and the profile in his introduction. As an *exercise* choose one of Diehl's subjects, preferably from those familiar to you from television or other exposure, and write a profile based on one of Diehl's interviews. (For weekly examples of short profiles see *TV Guide*, of long ones see *The New Yorker*.)

## 2. *What to write*

Are you wondering how to combine research and travel? The monthly *Journal of Genealogy* stands in need of "good articles on researching in foreign countries."

Look around you for subject matter for the interview article, for people, unknown or celebrated, whom you can call upon to interview. Perhaps this will be the oldest inhabitant who remembers local historical events or has colorful memories of now vanished landmarks. Or there may be current economic, medical, or legal issues of national scope on which the opinions and findings of a local authority can be brought to bear.

Examine the market directory immediately following, for inspiration and suggestions on subjects to write about. The interview article, like the book review, is a form that provides a solution to the beginner's search for something to write about.

## 3. *Where to send it*

The interview article market is wide and varied; it offers the beginning writer a reasonably attainable first market. The editor of *Movie Stars*, for example, considers the interview a good entry level piece. She writes: "Submit an interview with a secondary character on a popular TV series, or a featured actor in several films, whose face has become known to the public. It is best if you query first, presenting your interview idea and including some personal information about yourself—a resume and some previously published material, for example."

Listed below are some of the markets to be studied for publication in this field:

### Health and Medical

*Contemporary Surgery:* monthly, free writer's guidelines
*Dental Economics*; monthly; 60 percent written by freelancers
*The Dispensing Optician*; 11 times a year; 50 percent free-lance
*Health Care Week*; free sample copy
*Lab World*; 50 percent free-lance
*Modern Veterinary Practice*; 75 percent free-lance
*Physician's Life*; bimonthly tabloid; 50 percent free-lance

### Large Circulation
### (over 200,000)

*Cavalier*; monthly
*Chatelaine*; monthly; Canadian; women; free sample copy and
    writer's guidelines
*Chic*; monthly; "for affluent men;" writer's guidelines for
    S.A.S.E.
*Dude*; monthly; 80 percent free-lance
*Ms. Magazine*; monthly
*Quest/78*; free writer's guidelines
*Yankee*; monthly; free sample copy and writer's guidelines

## Literature and performing arts

*Blackberry*; quarterly; interviews with writers and poets
*Book Forum*; quarterly
*Cue Magazine*; biweekly; New York City coverage; free
    sample copy

## Musical

*Clavier*; 9 times a year; free sample copy
*Paid My Dues*; *Journal of Women and Music*; free writer's
    guidelines
*Music City News*; monthly tabloid; free sample copy
*Music Journal*; 10 times a year; 70 percent free-lance
*Opera News*; weekly (monthly in summer)
*Triad Magazine*; monthly 100 percent free-lance Chicago
    coverage

## Newspapers

*Indianapolis Star Magazine*; weekly magazine section; state-
    wide coverage
*Midland Reporter Telegram*; daily; material related to the oil
    business or West Texas
*Midwest Roto*; circulates in 150 Midwestern newspapers;
    emphasizes "hometown" people and values
*Seattle Times Magazine*; weekly supplement; free sample copy
    and writer's guidelines

## Regional

*Adirondack Life*; bimonthly; interview Adirondack personali-
    ties
*Broward Life*; monthly; Florida leisure world; 50 percent
    free-lance
*Chesapeake Bay Magazine*; monthly; 45 percent free-lance;
    writer's guidelines for S.A.S.E.

*Chicago*; monthly; 80 percent free-lance; sample copy and writer's guidelines

*The County Magazine*; 50 percent free-lance; free writer's guidelines

*Kansas City Magazine*; monthly; 85 percent free-lance; local area

*New England Magazine*; weekly; 40 percent free-lance

*Pennsylvania Illustrated*; bimonthly; 50 percent free-lance; free writer's guidelines

*Philadelphia Magazine*; monthly; 50 percent freelance written; "Philadelphia focus"; free writer's guidelines for S.A.S.E

*Southern Exposure*; 70 percent free-lance; free sample copy

*Valley Monthly Magazine*; monthly; free sample copy and writer's guidelines

*Westchester Magazine*; monthly

## Religious

*Lutheran Journal*; quarterly; free sample copy

*St. Anthony Messenger*; monthly, free sample copy and writer's guidelines

## Special interest

*Alaska Woman Magazine*; bimonthly

*American Cinematographer*; monthly; free sample copy

*Arise*; monthly; coverage, mentally and physically handicapped; free sample copy and writer's guidelines

*The Black Collegian*; bimonthly during school year; 55 percent free-lance; free sample copy and writer's guidelines

*Graphic Arts Monthly*; free sample copy and writer's guidelines

*Modern Maturity*; bimonthly; 75 percent free-lance; free sample copy and writer's guidelines

*Popular Photography*; monthly

*Sierra*; 10 times a year; 30 percent free-lance; free sample copy and writer's guidelines

*V.F.W. Magazine*; monthly; 50 percent free-lance; free writer's guidelines

## Sports and outdoor

*Appalachian Trailway News*; bimonthly; 90 percent free-lance; free writer's guidelines

*Backpacker*; bimonthly; 80 percent free-lance; writer's guidelines for S.A.S.E.

*Black Belt*; bimonthly; free sample copy

*Bowhunter Magazine*; bimonthly; writer's guidelines

*Diver*; 8 times a year; 45 percent free-lance

*National Fisherman*; monthly tabloid; 65 percent free-lance; free sample and writer's guidelines

*Outdoors Today*; weekly newspaper tabloid; free sample copy

*Runner's World Magazine*; monthly; 70 percent free-lance; free sample copy and writer's guidelines

*The Sports Informer*; biweekly tabloid; 90 percent free-lance; free sample copy

## Trade journals

*Area Development Magazine*; monthly; 50 percent free-lance; free sample copy and writer's guidelines

*Creative Computing*; bimonthly

*Employee Relations Bulletin*; semimonthly; 50 percent free-lance; free sample copy and writer's guidelines

*Muffler Digest*; monthly; free sample copy

*The Peanut Farmer*; 8 times a year; free sample copy

*Snack Food*; monthly; 15 percent free-lance; free sample copy and writer's guidelines

*Today's Education*; quarterly, free writer's guidelines

*Today's Secretary*; monthly, October–May; 75 percent free-lance; free sample copy and writer's guidelines

*Today's Transport International/Transporte Moderne*; bi-monthly; 100 percent free-lance; free sample copy and writer's guidelines

The periodicals listed above do not exhaust the interview article market. They have been chosen to illustrate the range of this market and the variety of subjects open to the free-lancer who becomes skilled at interviewing—the art of allowing others to reveal their knowledge and themselves. You may consult your local library for such specific information as addresses.

# CHAPTER 7
# TWO PINCHES
# OF SALT

Let us assume that you have published three or four articles in the Sunday feature sections of your newspaper. Your by-line is becoming familiar. An article of yours, pummeled into shape after consultation with the editor, has appeared in a national magazine of five-figure circulation. You are correct in thinking that you have made a kind of quantum jump here. Magazine articles must hold up (as they may not appear for weeks, even months, after acceptance) for a longer period than newspaper articles; this is the basic difference between them. You have even enjoyed the experience of watching an amateur group perform your one-act play. It follows that you are ready for instant success in fiction. That much is obvious. All you need do is seal up the manuscript, along with the S.A.S.E. (self-addressed stamped envelope), and drop it in the mailbox. This will not work. Success in nonfiction has, quite reasonably, given you confidence: you *can* write. You can probably write good fiction as well, but it will take redoubled effort—and a new kind of effort—to do so.

   If it is any consolation (and it should be), you are exactly where playwright Neil Simon would be if he was engaged in writing his first novel. Also beside you at the starting gate would be humorous essayist Erma Bombeck, if she were planning her first short story. For a complex set of reasons, the transfer of skills achieved in one literary form to success in another is by no means automatic. Some celebrated examples of writers of genius serve to make the point. Playwright George Bernard Shaw began his career with spectacular lack of success—as a novelist. Even when two forms are closer than plays and novels, obviously a case of apples and oranges, equal success in more than one form is rare. Skill with the short story does not predispose to success with the novel. Flannery O'Connor was singularly powerful as a writer of short stories, yet her two novels lack the authority and impact of her short fiction. The prolific Irish short story writer Frank O'Connor wrote only one novel, stillborn.

The challenge to diversify remains, nonetheless, for every writer. If one wrote nothing but nonfiction, one might never truly "find oneself." Perhaps the core of discovery of self is to be sought only in fiction and in verse, where language is used emotively as well as cognitively. Like the man who climbed the mountain because it was there, the writer, through continuing experience with form, realizes that it is through form and form alone that the self can be expressed. Forms not yet attempted appear on a writer's landscape as objects still to be conquered. This realization leads to constant experiment, to the trial and error approach to the discovery of oneself and one's feelings, of one's concerns, and of the external world. Experiment gives scope to fortuitous discovery, to the happy accident that can point out where we should have been going but would perhaps never consciously have set out for. As Thoreau puts it, we arrive at the best things by accident; the "memorable thought, the happy expression, the admirable deed are only partly ours."

A devotion to form and to the excitement and satisfactions that the act of writing can instill is reason enough for attempting short fiction. Considering today's market, a strong monetary motive would be misplaced. "Don't even think of writing short stories," Larry McMurtry told the participants of the Georgetown University Writers Conference. The gist of his remark was that the short story is no longer a means by which one may attain even modest compensation. The market keeps shrinking, it is true. Magazines that once prided themselves on offering the best in American short fiction, that in a sense created it through their encouragement, are now defunct or have sharply constricted the space they allow to fiction. *Story*, under the gallant editorship of Whit Burnett, the classic showcase for two generations of American fiction—it was the first to publish Saroyan, Mailer, Bradbury, Capote, McCullers, and others—is no more. *Esquire*, once a force in our literature through the fiction it printed, now all too seldom functions as a vehicle for the discovery of new talent. *The Atlantic Monthly*, however, still stands out among the quality magazines as openly hospitable, with its "*Atlantic* Firsts," to the beginning writer of the short story.

Many readers—but apparently not enough of them— complain that fiction is hard to find in popular magazines of large circulation. In some magazines, however, notably *Redbook*, fiction is far from being made peripheral to the magazine's monthly fare. And if in the past fiction in popular magazines was too fatuously devoted to stories about "happy people with happy problems," nobody can seriously argue that "slick"—so called after the coated paper used by such periodicals—magazines now refuse to face contemporary problems, often at their grimmest. Consciousness-raising in many fields and for many purposes has become part of the role popular fiction plays in large-circulation magazines today.

The market for fiction, it could be argued, is more elusive than that for nonfiction, and one hears that many professionals have turned away from fiction altogether, often with regret, to write articles and book-length nonfiction. Oddly enough, today's uncertain climate for the short story, which no longer commands the prices that gained a fortune for F. Scott Fitzgerald—his heyday turned out to be the heyday of the commercial short story—works to the disadvantage of the career writer but to the advantage of the beginner. The two kinds of short stories—the commercial and the literary—are still being written for two kinds of markets. Fitzgerald was the only American writer of stature who wrote and published both kinds of stories. He wrote his "cheap" stories in a week or weekend and was paid handsomely for them; stories like the classic "The Diamond as Big as the Ritz," which took three weeks to write, sold to H. L. Mencken for a fraction of the price *The Saturday Evening Post* paid for such pieces of fluff as "Bernice Bobs Her Hair." The temptation to emulate Fitzgerald in writing for both cash and credit has been removed. The cash market has been almost wiped out; the other market flourishes, but it pays abysmally less than Mencken's *Smart Set* ever did.

The magazines providing a market for popular fiction, though fewer than they once were, have not disappeared entirely. Two of the most significant are *Redbook* and *Seventeen*. Both of these mass-circulation magazines welcome the new contributor; both publish stories which, at least in contrast to the fiction published in the literary quarterlies, can be described as popular, even relatively happy and upbeat. These markets, although cordial, are fiercely competitive. The beginner may well choose to work his or her way up to their standards by publishing fiction in family, religious, and fraternal magazines. These minor markets do not welcome shoddy work; but as they serve a relatively unsophisticated readership they are somewhat more receptive to the beginner. Their rates of payment are modest; their editors say they would publish more fiction if they could. Demand exists; the problem is one of supply.

Minor markets such as those provided by religious and fraternal magazines would not be enough to keep the short story viable, as they offer neither sufficient financial nor aesthetic incentive. The survival of the short story form now seems to depend upon the "little" magazine as it is called, and upon the literary quarterly. For the past few years the editors of our two annuals, *The Best American Short Stories...*and

*Prize Stories . . . : The O. Henry Awards*, have gone to these magazines for their annual selections almost exclusively. The beginning writer with literary ambitions that extend beyond publication will find examination of these annuals indispensable. Year by year they record and further the progress of the short story as an art form. Current themes, the reach of technical experimentation, and fiction's new directions are all exemplified and projected in their pages.

The short story, then, is alive and well, if you know where to look for it. Fiction that has no purpose beyond light entertainment is being published in magazines that welcome, indeed depend upon, the free-lancer; so is serious fiction. Both kinds invite the writer who would explore dimensions of reality that nonfiction, which remains anchored in the world of the actual, cannot enter. Fiction is worth attempting, if only for the reach it gives, even to the writer who turns from it back to nonfiction. (He or she returns strengthened by solving cognate problems, for one thing, in handling dialogue and anecdote, in acquiring ease in transitions.) Different as they are, one form assists another. The magazine article, for example, expands the reach of the newspaper feature, liberating fact from exactness in times and places—"Five o'clock yesterday at Fifth and Main"—rendering the particular no less accurately yet at the same time giving it the larger air of the general. "Yesterday" becomes "recently." Fiction carries the process further: it universalizes. "Recently" becomes "always." Fact is freed from this time and this place to become all times and all places.

The freedom fiction confers, of course, is not to be equated with freedom from all responsibility. The authority of fiction differs from the authority required of nonfiction. The latter is external; fiction's authority requires an inner logic, an integrating consistency. Marianne Moore's famous definition of poetry applies: "imaginary gardens with real toads in them." Facts remain facts. As a writer of fiction you cannot place Arizona on the Eastern seaboard—not even in fantasy—and have your Arizona bear any resemblance to the Arizona we know of, or the Eastern seaboard be where and what it is. In dream sequence, or a madman's rhapsody, Arizona can be placed just south of the Rhone and its inhabitants can be made to speak French. (The measure of the dream and of the rhapsody will be the reader's knowledge of the actual Arizona.) In science fiction set in a future age, erosion may account for Arizona's being east and seaboard: such a placement will be seen as in response to new geographic facts. But short of cataclysm such as this, the Arizona of today's geography and the Arizona of the mind must remain where and what they are now.

People who cannot bear to read fiction, much less write it, sometimes possess the complacent and superior conviction that the world of fiction escapes rather than penetrates fact. Nothing could be further from the truth. Even light fiction—like light verse—illuminates life, if only fitfully. Serious fiction, the fitting of the freshly minted word to the moment experienced, the thing observed, records a reality no less true because it is not actual. Sometimes the reality of fiction, its responsibility to actual events as they unfold, is even greater than the reality nonfiction represents. Even nonfiction is not the thing itself, but signs and images— words only—about the thing. And when one considers that nonfiction is the vehicle of press releases, government hand-outs, and advertising copy, it must be admitted that language is as frequently used to conceal harsh reality as it is to reveal it.

It sometimes happens that news events of some scope and importance come to us, through nonfiction, with distortion. Marquis Childs, the news commentator and columnist, has told in two different ways the revealing story of his handling of an important international conference: as a journalist he was officially present and accredited to cover the event; and, later, he wrote a novel about it. Contrary to what one might expect, Marquis Childs as novelist was able to tell more of the truth, a rounder truth, of what goes on at a conference than Marquis

Childs could do as a reporter. His explanation of how that could come about makes for a revealing commentary on the nature of the truth of fact and the truth of fiction. As a reporter Childs attended a Geneva conference in his professional role of competent observer and commentator; he had done his homework, and he was present for all conference sessions. But neither he nor any other news correspondent was permitted to be in the room with those around the baize table. Like the others, he was briefed.

But the person who briefed the reporters covering the conference and told them what went on during the sessions had not been present either; he had himself been briefed by someone who had been there. Hence the press was getting its facts at two removes. What Childs and the others filed went under the name of *non*fiction. Yet these reporters all knew more of the full story of unfolding events than they could reveal. They had all had the benefit of "backgrounders," for example, material not for attribution which would enable them to place what they were able to reveal in some kind of context. Thus at the time of the conference they all knew—from social gatherings with its principals at the end of the business day, for example—more than they could pass on to their readers. So the truth, the reality that they reported was partial.

Some months after the conference was all over, Marquis Childs went over the same ground—this time as a novelist. Equipped with a fictional crisis, he could now openly interview the chief participants and pass on what they told him, not in a press dispatch but in the pages of fiction. Knowing the personalities and the politics of those who had sat around the table and conferred, he could convincingly model his fictional characters on them. He could report now on maneuvers engaged in and the conclusions reached, this time in terms of how and why they were arrived at. He could be—in fiction!—at once more specific and less speculative. This time Child's Geneva was an atmosphere, a presence, not a mere dateline. The concrete touches that fiction can encompass even more fully than those the most author-centered New Journalism permits, were able to lend a vibrancy and a conviction that no amount of brilliance in factual reporting could achieve by itself. The result in the pages of Marquis Child's novel *The Peacemakers* (1961), as so often happens with fiction, is a reality that adds dimension to fact without in any way diminishing actuality.

A classic instance wherein fiction enhances fact occurs in two contemporary versions of the tragic sinking of the *Commodore* in 1897 off the Florida coast. Aboard was Stephen Crane, already famous as the author of *The Red Badge of Courage* and as a correspondent, on his way to Cuba to report the insurgency there against Spanish rule. The vessel, carrying a cargo of guns and ammunition for the Cuban rebels, went down some twenty miles off Mosquito Inlet. Crane's experiences in the sinking served as the basis for his news report filed with a New York City daily and for one of his greatest short stories, "The Open Boat." Both his news story and his fiction are, after their own modes, "true." Yet, as always happens, each version embodies a truth that the other omits. This comes about because the author in his search for significance and verisimilitude at the same time pares away the irrelevant. In this instance, Crane omitted any reference to his own heroic actions. One might say that personal modesty dictated this decision for the news story; the artist's quest for the universal required the same judgment for fiction.

For an examination of the two truths we begin with an episode of the incident as reported anonymously in the Florida press:

> *The mate's boat, containing nine Americans, was smashed and the mate, two engineers, six firemen and sailors were lashed to a raft which Captain Murphy attempted to tow ashore twenty miles away, but the terrible sea and northeast gale swept them away.*

> *The dinghy, occupied by the captain and companions, was twenty-seven hours at sea, Montgomery and Crane holding Captain Murphy's overcoat as a sail until the beach was sighted. High seas were breaking a half mile from shore. Montgomery, Crane and Murphy were washed onto the beach where citizens provided them with medical attendance. Higgins was killed at the overturning of the boat which made ten Americans and six Cubans lost.*

The above is taken from a page-one news story for 5 January, 1897. The following is taken from the deposition by Captain Murphy, as reported in a page-6 news story in the same issue:

> *John Getchell, one of nature's noblemen, who lives upon the beach, saw our dreadful predicament. He stripped to the skin and plunged into the surf and helped the steward and Mr. Crane in. I was safe in shallow water. I then saw Higgins' body on the wet sand. We rolled him and made every effort to bring him to life, but unfortunately failed. Poor fellow, he was brave and did his duty faithfully.*
>
> *We had not been on the beach long before the good women of the town came to us with hot coffee and all kinds of restoratives. Their attentions warmed a man's heart to the appreciation of human charity. Not one of these women came to us without some present of food, clothing, and all with offers of shelter.*

What has been quoted above is, it would appear, in the best tradition of journalism: accurate and clear. The account contains no nuances, no shades of meaning. Captain Murphy reveals himself as the sturdy, prosaic fellow he undoubtedly was. He is the stuff of which fiction can be made, but he appears before us in another light, no less wonderful: the glaring light of factual day.

Stephen Crane's report appeared in the New York *Press*, datelined Jacksonville, January 6. His news coverage of the event concludes with the following:

*The lighthouse of Mosquito Inlet stuck up above the horizon like the point of a pin. We turned our dingy toward the shore.*

*The history of life in an open boat for thirty hours would no doubt be instructive for the young, but none is to be told here and now. For my part I would prefer to tell the story at once, because from it would shine the splendid manhood of Captain Edward Murphy and of William Higgins, the oiler, but let it suffice at this time to say that when we were swamped in the surf and making the best of our way toward the shore the captain gave orders amid the wildness of the breakers as clearly as if he had been on the quarter deck of a battleship.*

*John Kitchell of Daytona came running down the beach, and as he ran the air was filled with clothes. If he had pulled a single lever and undressed, even as the fire horses harness, he could not seem to me to have stripped with more speed. He dashed into the water and dragged the cook. Then he went after the captain, but the captain sent him to me, and then it was that he saw Billy Higgins lying with his forehead on sand that was clear of the water, and he was dead.*

Crane is factual, although he is in error, perhaps, about the name of the running man; Captain Murphy said it was Getchell. Crane does not fictionalize here, but he does call upon simile and reaches for more vivid imagery ("the air filled with clothes") than does the other reporter; and his sentences have more careful cadences. Most important of all, he recognizes that the incident contains an "instructive" story not to be told until later.

Crane told that story in "The Open Boat," a short story bearing the subtitle; "A Tale Intended to be after the Fact: Being the Experience of Four Men from the Sunk Steamer *Commodore*." The short story opens with the memorable line "None of them knew the color of the sky" and concludes with this passage:

*Presently he saw a man running along the shore. He was undressing with most remarkable speed. Coat, trousers, shirt, everything flew magically off him.*

*"Come to the boat!" called the captain.*

*"All right, Captain." As the correspondent paddled, he saw the captain let himself down to the bottom and leave the boat. Then the correspondent performed his one little marvel of the voyage. A large wave caught him and flung him with ease and supreme speed completely over the boat and far beyond it. It struck him even then as an event in gymnastics and a true miracle of the sea. An overturned boat in the surf is not a plaything to a swimming man.*

*The correspondent arrived in water that reached only to his waist, but his condition did not allow him to stand for more than a moment. Each wave knocked him into a heap, and the undertow pulled at him.*

*Then he saw the man who had been running and undressing, and undressing and running, come bounding into the water. He dragged ashore the cook, and then waded toward the captain; but the captain waved him away and sent him to the correspondent. He was naked—naked as a tree in winter; but a halo was about his head, and he shone like a saint. He gave a strong pull, and a long drag, and a bully heave at the correspondent's hand. The correspondent, schooled in the minor formulae, said, "Thanks, old man." But suddenly the man cried, "What's that?" He pointed a swift finger. The correspondent said, "Go."*

*In the shallows, face downward, lay the oiler. His forehead touched sand that was periodically, between each wave, clear of the sea.*

*The correspondent did not know all that transpired afterward. When he achieved safe ground he fell, striking the sand with each particular part of his body. It*

*was as if he had dropped from a roof, but the thud was
grateful to him.*

*It seemed that instantly the beach was populated
with men with blankets, clothes, and flasks, and women
with coffee pots and all the remedies sacred to their
minds. The welcome of the land to the men from the sea
was warm and generous; but a still and dripping shape
was carried slowly up the beach, and the land's welcome
for it could only be the different and sinister hospitality of
the grave.*

*When it came night, the white waves paced to and
fro in the moonlight, and the wind brought the sound of
the great sea's voice to the men on the shore, and they felt
that they could then be interpreters.*

First, we might note what happens in three of the
accounts of the assistance the survivors received when they
reached the shore. From the first press report we learn that
"citizens provided them with medical attendance." In this
instance, nonfiction provides abstract statement. Captain
Murphy makes the point more graphically: "The good women
of the town came to us with hot coffee and all kinds of
restoratives." "Hot coffee" presents the concrete, but "all kinds
of restoratives" is formal and vague. Crane omits reference to
the incident in his news story, but in his fiction he places the
incident at the beginning of the final interpretative movement.
Note the striking effect of "populated." Instead of the captain's
platitude on "human charity," Crane supplies the highly individual, somewhat patronizing phrase "all the remedies
sacred to their minds." As this is fiction writing, not news
reporting, objectivity is no longer sought.

Even more striking is the more extensive attention given
to "one of nature's noblemen," as Captain Murphy put it.
Murphy says simply that the man "stripped to the skin."
Interestingly enough, Crane's news report initiates his image of

the air "filled with clothes" and contains his fireman's horse in harness image, later dropped. In its place is the more striking—and certainly less dated—image of the man as being "naked as a tree in winter." Crane divides "The Open Boat" into seven sections, and in the sixth he introduces its most extended metaphor. There the correspondent, frightened and hallucinating throughout a "dismal night" in the dinghy, suddenly remembers a verse beginning

*A soldier of the Legion lay dying in Algiers*

and he begins to see the soldier:

> *The correspondent plainly saw the soldier. He lay on the sand with his feet out straight and still. While his pale left hand was upon his chest in an attempt to thwart the going of his life, the blood came between his fingers. In the far Algerian distance, a city of low square forms was set against a sky that was faint with the last sunset hues. The correspondent, plying the oars and dreaming of the slow and slower movements of the lips of the soldier, was moved by a profound and perfectly impersonal comprehension. He was sorry for the soldier of the Legion who lay dying in Algiers.*

Here is a compelling example of fiction's extension of the real. The passage about the soldier in Algiers is obviously after-the-fact invention, a brilliant use of the device of contrast to explore and heighten meaning. "The Open Boat" is indeed "after the fact" in ways that deepen and illuminate the real.

The truth of fiction, like the truth in all the arts, is arrived at through a form of make-believe; that is its paradox. Each art form must be approached through acceptance of an appropriate convention. Everything depends upon the beholder's "willing suspension of disbelief." As art is an imitiation of life, art is real on these terms: imitation is an order of reality, the right real thing. Nobody expects a sculptured dog to bark, nor complains that a Breughel village is a trick of perspective on two-dimensional canvas. One accepts the simulated movement on film as more than an illusion of optics, agrees with opera that people communicate with each other by singing. In the theater, life behind the proscenium arch includes doors that open to a real outdoors. Theater's missing fourth wall allows us to see the secret life that goes on between painted boundaries.

Fictional narrative has its convention also, its price for being permitted to be caught up in its particular magic. Just as drama must be allowed its missing fourth wall, through which the audience observes the action and accepts as truths such palpable lies as those asserting plywood doors lead directly to bedrooms or balconies or rugged woodlands, fiction in its own way tempts reason. Fiction too builds a frail defense against being ignored. Anyone can stop fiction in its tracks by refusing belief. Dr. Johnson dismissed *Gulliver's Travels* with the offhand remark that once somebody thought up little people and big people, the rest was easy. "You're nothing but a pack of cards," says Alice, and the intricate edifice comes tumbling down. Most theater goers stay fixed in their seats after disbelief comes, but it is easy to turn away from the pages of a book. A story is, after all, only the alphabet combined and recombined, endlessly tricked out. There are all sorts of ways to stare down a barkless dog.

Fiction's convention is, quite properly, a conjurer's act, a magician's make-believe. What the reader must do to enter fiction's world is stand attentive to a person mounted on a wall. This person is proclaiming to all who will listen what is going on behind the wall. This is the device the reader must accept. Whereas the playwright sweeps aside the curtain and displays three-dimensional beings, the narrator lacks the objects themselves and can use only the signs and symbols of objects to display wonders. The novelist and short story writer occupy a position on the wall; their office is to portray an unseen action. Think of the person on the wall, the teller of fiction, as a juggler, constantly tossing three objects in the air. These are the three ingredients of narrative. They are description, summary, and scene. There is no other. The entire art of narrative, considered from the aspect of what goes to make it up, consists of keeping these ingredients in motion.

By *description* we mean words used to present to the mind concrete images of the shape, texture, and color of things; the words that allow the imagination to "see." Description may be of two kinds: static or dynamic. In *static* description everything else is halted for a head to toe account, a top to bottom cataloguing. Sir Walter Scott wrote hundreds upon hundreds of pages of this kind of description. Here is a sample from his novel of Crusader days, *The Talisman:*

> *The Frank seemed a powerful man, built after the ancient Gothic cast of form, with light brown hair, which, on the removal of his helmet, was seen to curl thick and profusely over his head. His features had acquired, from the hot climate, a hue much darker than those parts of his neck which were less frequently exposed to view, or than was warranted by his full and well-opened blue eye, the colour of his hair, and of the mustachios which thickly shaded his upper lip, while his chin was carefully divested of beard, after the Norman fashion. His nose was Grecian and well formed; his mouth rather large in proportion, but filled with well-set, strong, and beautifully white teeth; his head small, and set upon the neck with much grace. His age could not exceed thirty, but, if the effects of toil and climate were allowed for, might be three or four years under that period. His form was tall, powerful, and athletic, like that of a man whose strength might, in later life, become unwieldy, but which was hitherto united with lightness and activity. His hands, when he withdrew the mailed gloves, were long, fair, and well proportioned; the wrist-bones peculiarly large and strong, and the arms remarkably well shaped and brawny.*

All action stops for the picture taking, a still picture. Scott's pages are fecund with these sorts of descriptions, not lacking in precision and power but painfully slowing down the action, particularly for the impatient modern reader. The modern reader has been conditioned by Hemingway's sparing use of description, particularly in such early stories as "The Killers" and "Hills Like White Elephants."

*Dynamic* description substitutes the part for the whole (the Frank's "full and well-opened blue eye" caught in a moment of exertion, in battle perhaps) and places it within a context of action and emotion. The following passage from Conrad's "The Secret Sharer" illustrates physical description of objects spliced into the flow of narrative:

> *I paced a turn or two on the poop and saw him take up his position face forward with his elbow in the ratlines of the mizzen rigging before I went below. The mate's faint snoring was still going on peacefully. The cuddy lamp was burning over the table on which stood a vase with flowers, a polite attention from the ship's provision merchant— the last flowers we should see for the next three months at the very least. Two bunches of bananas hung from the beam symmetrically, one on each side of the rudder casing. Everything was as before in the ship—except that two of her captain's sleeping suits were simultaneously in use, one motionless in the cuddy, the other keeping very still in the captain's stateroom.*
>
> *It must be explained here that my cabin had the form of the capital letter L, the door being within the angle and opening into the short part of the letter. A couch was to the left, the bed place to the right; my writing desk and the chronometer's table faced the door. But anyone opening it, unless he stepped right inside, had no view of what I call the long (or vertical) part of the letter. It contained some lockers surmounted by a bookcase; and a few clothes, a thick jacket or two, caps, oilskin coat, and*

*such like, hung on hooks. There was at the bottom of that part a door opening into my bathroom, which could be entered also directly from the saloon. But that way was never used.*

*The mysterious arrival had discovered the advantage of this particular shape. Entering my room, lighted strongly by a big bulkhead lamp swung on gimbals above my writing desk, I did not see him anywhere till he stepped out quietly from behind the coats hung in the recessed part.*

*"I heard somebody moving about, and went in there at once," he whispered.*

*I, too, spoke under my breath.*

*"Nobody is likely to come in here without knocking and getting permission."*

*He nodded. His face was thin and the sunburn faded, as though he had been ill. And no wonder. He had been, I heard presently, kept under arrest in his cabin for nearly seven weeks. But there was nothing sickly in his eyes or in his expression. He was not a bit like me, really; yet, as we stood leaning over my bed place, whispering side by side, with our dark heads together and our backs to the door, anybody bold enough to open it stealthily would have been treated to the uncanny sight of a double captain busy talking in whispers with his other self.*

In the passage above the physical description is parceled out, given to us only at those points and in those quantities that make it part of the suspenseful flow of the action. A generation accustomed to the device of close-up on film expects description to be part of the dynamism of the story's onward movement.

Description, then, presents images, directs the eye to the story's visual elements, projects on our mind's eye the shades of hue of the Crusader's neck and the size and color of his teeth; and the objects of the captain's cabin. The second ingredient of narrative, *summary,* presents not concrete image but abstract statement. Summary is the great expository device at the disposal of our person on the wall, the narrator. Through the use of summary the narrator gives us background information, presents a time switch, changes the places of the action, and telescopes time and place to convey a habitual action. Summary is narrative's great and subtle servant; it introduces; it articulates; and it identifies the characters and their relationships. It introduces characters, theme, places. It carries the story along; it skips; it takes broad jumps in time and place. It elucidates knotty matters. It comments; it utters confidences. It summarizes.

Often the initial note of the entire narrative is struck by summary. This is a device favored by Jane Austen. Her novel *Emma* begins with this summarizing paragraph:

> *Emma Woodhouse, handsome, clever, and rich, with a comfortable home and happy disposition, seemed to unite some of the best blessings of existence; and had lived nearly twenty-one years in the world with very little to distress or vex her.*

Note the abstractions: "clever," "happy," "existence," "distress": much for the mind to take in, but nothing for the eye to light upon. *Pride and Prejudice* begins even more pithily: "It is a truth universally acknowledged, that a single man in possession of a good fortune must be in want of a wife." That is Jane Austen's opening paragraph—and opening shot as well. Here is Henry James, in an early short story, using summary for background:

> *I have no intention of following Lieutenant Ford to the seat of war. The exploits of his campaign are recorded in the public journals of the day, where the curious may still peruse them. My own taste has always been for unwritten history, and my present business is with the reverse of the picture.*

*After Jack went off, the two ladies resumed their old homely life. But the homeliest life had now ceased to be repulsive to Elizabeth. Her common duties were no longer wearisome: for the first time, she experienced the delicious companionship of thought. Her chief task was to sit by the window knitting soldiers' socks; but even Mrs. Ford could not help owning that she worked with much greater diligence, yawned, rubbed her eyes, gazed up and down the road less, and indeed produced a much more comely article.*

Hawthorne initiates the action of his story "Rappacini's Daughter" with this paragraph of summary:

*A young man, named Giovanni Guasconti, came, very long ago, from the more southern region of Italy, to pursue his studies at the University of Padua. Giovanni, who had but a scanty supply of gold ducats in his pocket, took lodgings in a high and gloomy chamber of an old edifice which looked not unworthy to have been the palace of a Paduan noble, and which, in fact, exhibited over its entrance the armorial bearings of a family long since extinct. The young stranger, who was not unstudied in the great poem of his country, recollected that one of the ancestors of this family, and perhaps an occupant of this very mansion, had been pictured by Dante as a partaker of the immortal agonies of his Inferno. These reminiscences and associations, together with the tendency to heartbreak natural to a young man for the first time out of his native sphere, caused Giovanni to sigh heavily as he looked around the desolate and ill-furnished apartment.*

Scott frequently used summary to shift scenes and to move from one set of characters to another, as in the following examples from *Ivanhoe*:

*While these measures were taking in behalf of Cedric and his companions, the armed men by whom the latter had been seized hurried their captives along towards the place of security where they intended to imprison them.*

*Leaving the Saxon chiefs to return to their banquet as soon as their ungratified curiosity should permit them to attend to the calls of their half-satiated appetite, we have to look in upon the yet more severe imprisonment of Isaac of York.*

We may call this the "meanwhile back at the ranch" device.

In *The Red Badge of Courage* Stephen Crane uses summary far more efficiently and subtly than Scott, blending physical and psychological movement—motion in place and in feeling:

*He accepted new environment and circumstance with great coolness, eating from his haversack at every opportunity. On the march he went along with the stride of a hunter, objecting to neither gait nor distance. And he had not raised his voice when he had been ordered away from three little protective piles of earth and stone, each one of which had been an engineering feat worthy of being made sacred to the name of his grandmother.*

Washington Irving concludes his classic yarn "Rip Van Winkle" with the device of summary, here used to account for habitual action:

*He used to tell his story to every stranger that arrived at Mr. Doolittle's hotel. He was observed, at first, to vary on some points every time he told it, which was, doubtless, owing to his having so recently awaked. It at last settled down precisely to the tale I have related, and not a man, woman, or child in the neighborhood but knew it by heart. Some always pretended to doubt the reality of it, and insisted that Rip had been out of his head, and that this was one point on which he always remained flighty. The old Dutch inhabitants, however, almost universally gave it full credit. Even to this day they never hear a thunderstorm of a summer afternoon about the Kaatskill, but they say Hendrick Hudson and his crew are at their game of ninepins; and it is a common wish of all hen-pecked husbands in the neighborhood, when life hangs heavy on their hands, that they might have a quieting draught out of Rip Van Winkle's flagon.*

More often, of course, the summary device is serviceable as the vehicle of ongoing action, as in this passage from "The Last of the Valerii" by Henry James:

*One morning it seemed to me that I had been hearing for half an hour a livelier movement of voices than usual; but as I was preoccupied with a puzzling bit of work, I made no inquiries. Suddenly a shadow fell across my canvas, and I turned round. The little explorer stood beside me, with a glittering eye, cap in hand, his forehead bathed in perspiration. Resting in the hollow of his arm was an earth-stained fragment of marble. In answer to my questioning glance he held it up to me, and I saw it was a woman's shapely hand. "Come!" he simply said, and led the way to the excavation.*

In ordinary conversation, people speak of describing when summarizing is what is meant: for example, "She described the baseball game to him." Actually there may not have been a single element of visual description in her account of nine innings of play; it may all have been abstract, all summary. The two ingredients are nonetheless related; together description and summary make up the narrative voice.

The final ingredient of narrative is *scene*; by itself scene comprises the narrator's dramatic voice. Scene cannot be equated with narrative (or it would be indistinguishable from drama—story would be play), but without scene there is no fiction. Nonfiction employs description and summary at will and in varying degrees. Summary is the structure of most essays, most magazine articles. Description will enter into the piece depending upon the subject matter; it can play either a major or an exceedingly minor role. Thus the narrative voice is a property of the historical essay, the treatise in philosophy or economics, the scientific analysis, the legal brief. It is story that brings events to life, drama that reveals actors who exist or have existed. The use of anecdote, as in nonfiction, is not enough to constitute story. It is true that anecdote presents people and dialogue, but only as illustrative of a theme, not as happening.

Scene is people in a place (or places) and acting in a continuing time. Scene is not to be confused with setting, which is background merely, the place where things happen. Scene involves action, scene happens. The two ingredients of description and summary individually or together function to *tell*. Scene *shows*. The reader is conscious that someone is responsible for the information conveyed by description or summary. The Frank's nose is Grecian. A swinging lamp lights up the captain's cabin. The narrator is telling us these things. But when the characters take over, when they move or speak on the pages of fiction, it is as though they were as three-dimensional and alive as the actors on a stage. The effect of a play is that the playwright has disappeared; the lines that have been written are his or hers no more. They seem to originate in the minds and issue forth independently from the mouths of the persons in the play. That is scene. In a short story or novel the *as if* effect is the same. The writer has created a living stage in the reader's mind: the characters are alive and in motion, and time is moving in successive waves. And that too is scene.

In the beginning paragraphs of "Young Goodman Brown" Hawthorne makes our minds his stage:

*Young Goodman Brown came forth at sunset into the street of Salem village; but put his head back, after crossing the threshold, to exchange a parting kiss with his young wife. And Faith, as the wife was aptly named, thrust her own pretty head into the street, letting the wind play with the pink ribbons of her cap while she called to Goodman Brown.*

*"Dearest heart," whispered she, softly and rather sadly, when her lips were close to his ear, "prithee put off your journey until sunrise and sleep in your own bed to-night. A lone woman is troubled with dreams and such thoughts that she's afeared of herself sometimes. Pray tarry with me this night, dear husband, of all nights of the year."*

*"My love and my Faith," replied young Goodman Brown, "of all nights in the year, this one night I must tarry away from thee. My journey, as thou callest it, forth and back again, must needs be done 'twixt now and sunrise. What, my sweet, pretty wife, dost thou doubt me already, and we but three months married?"*

*"Then God bless you!" said Faith, with the pink ribbons, "and may you find all well when you come back."*

*"Amen!" cried Goodman Brown. "Say thy prayers, dear Faith, and go to bed at dusk, and no harm will come to thee."*

*So they parted; and the young man pursued his way until, being about to turn the corner by the meeting-house, he looked back and saw the head of Faith still peeping after him with a melancholy air, in spite of her pink ribbons.*

With the merest touch of description—Faith's pink ribbons—Hawthorne sets up his scene in a brief paragraph of summary. He frames the scene at its end with an even briefer summary paragraph. Far from being static, summary is dynamically moved along by Hawthorne's choice of verbs: "came forth," "put...back," "thrust." In another kind of dynamism and with deft economy, Hawthorne introduces two of his three chief characters and, his most important achievement, he introduces the conflict that separates them. In three hundred words the author has established two characters, a place, a time—sunset and continuing time from "Dearest heart" to "no harm will come to thee"—and an action, the words and the physical movement of departure. Unquestionably, it "plays."

The presence of scene distinguishes fictional narrative from all other forms of prose discourse. Scene gives such narrative its singular triumph. To be able to enter the mind of another and create within that mind a reality, a living entity, which can be experienced immediately and afterward recreated in memory is to be able to enjoy the creative act fully and truly. The writer of fiction by creating scene achieves with gradual steps—the progress is linear, word by word and line by line—what the playwright can do easily and instantly—simply by pulling back the curtain. (There, three-dimensionally, the playwright's people and furniture stand before us. With similar ease, the playwright can dispose of description. A hint or two to the set and costume designers will suffice. For the description of characters, much can be conveyed by little. The playbill need only note, for example, "Mabel, 35, overweight, discontented." The casting director will take care of the rest.)

It is with summary that the narrative artist, the short story writer and the novelist, will enjoy a distinct advantage over the playwright. The reader of fiction accepts summary straight and uncut. Not so the theatergoer. For one thing, unless the play is farce or theater of the absurd, direct summary, or exposition, is itself absurd. No actor realistically can say to another: "Charles, you are my brother. I am three years your senior. I was born in Detroit, whereas you, upon the moving of our family to Atlanta, were Georgia-born." Straight farce. But narrative summary can directly inform the reader: "Charles and Dennis were brothers. Charles, the elder by three years, was born..." This is not brilliant narrative, perhaps, but perfectly acceptable.

Thus far we have been looking through the wrong end of the telescope, making things small. To see narrative's structural components we must take the longer view and examine the three stages of movement that together comprise narrative action. These states of motion are the *complication*, the *climax* (or *crisis*), and the *resolution*. Although equally indispensable to narrative, the three components account for unequal quantities of words expended. Complication is by far the longest; the length of the other two is confined to the tasks of bringing matters to a climax and bringing them smartly to the ending. As Poe demanded, economy—there must be no extraneous word, no word that does not tend to singleness of effect—must rule throughout; but the latter two components must be especially "cost effective."

The normal proportions of narrative's three components may be represented by a scalene triangle, thus:

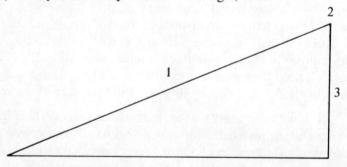

Angle 1 represents the complication; angle 2, the climax, the point of meeting of angles 1 and 3; and angle 3, the resolution. This is the normal schema for story, whether "slick" or literary. Narrative imbalance occurs, as it often does with Hawthorne, when the action can be accurately graphed by an equilateral triangle:

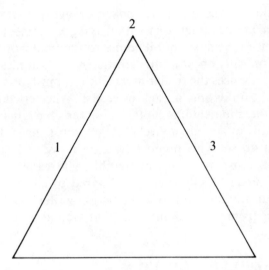

In such stories as "The Minister's Black Veil" and "The Gentle Boy" Hawthorne is overlong in coming to his resolution; the triangular configuration is equilateral. The ideal development of a play may be symbolized by a scalene triangle also. The traditional labels for the three legs are (1) rising action, (2) climax, and (3) falling action.

The territory of complication runs from the opening word of the narrative, story or novel, to the moment of climax, the whole length of leg 1 of the triangle. Within this portion the chief character meets with all sorts of successes and reverses, with each success leading to another problem to be solved. New options remain to be chosen. Then the moment comes when there are no more options. This is the moment the narrative has all along been moving toward. The chief character, the protagonist, the hero or heroine, makes the final determinative choice (or sometimes evades choice for the final time) and the story is over. Nothing more is left to be shown in dialogue or other action about that character.

Fiction moves in time and space, dragging characters and situations, taking along story with it as it goes. It must never be at rest, once it begins, until it comes to the final word. Yet all that motion will appear as mere restlessness, as aimless action, unless it convinces the reader of its truth. It must, above all, be believed. "You're only a pack of cards!" Alice cried, and the skeptic, the momentary captive another's imagination has invaded, always ready to echo Alice, must never be given license to do so. This preposterous business, this conjurer's shell game, must at all times be credible. The reader comes to it with one pinch of salt already, prepared to climb back into disbelief at any moment. It is the fiction writer's task to keep the reader from ever reaching for that second pinch.

## SUGGESTED FOLLOW-UP
## FOR THIS CHAPTER

### 1. *What to read*
Fiction, fiction, fiction—short and long. Among novels read both the classics and your contemporaries. And do not scorn first novels; rather, cultivate them. You have much to learn from first novelists, particularly how to identify and avoid their errors, taking your cues from the reviewers. Every time you pick up a magazine containing fiction, do not put it down until you have read all the fiction in that issue. The two popular magazines particularly hospitable to the new writer are *Seventeen* and *Redbook*. Devour them regularly.

Each year for well over half a century, two American publishers, Doubleday and Houghton Mifflin, have been bringing out annuals of the short story, anthologies of "best" stories. Anyone with a serious interest in the short story and where it is going should read both these anthologies every year. For the past several years William Abrahams has been bringing out *Prize Stories...: The O. Henry Awards* (Doubleday). The late Martha Foley for almost forty years edited *The Best American Short Stories...* (Houghton Mifflin); she is to be succeeded by a different editor each year. The latter volume includes an annual list of one hundred distinguished stories of the year in addition to those included in the volume. Both books contain names and addresses of magazines publishing short stories.

## 2. *What to write*

Begin perhaps with finger exercises. Get in the habit of keeping a notebook (always have pen and paper handy) for recording what you overhear, observe, or encounter. Make lists. Jot down things you like, notes on people you like. Do the same for things and people you dislike. For every item on your lists write a sentence or short paragraph. Describe yourself—your hand as you accidentally catch sight of it, your facial expression caught in passing. Describe yourself from the outside. Now from the inside. You know them both; have you caught the essence of this person?

## 3. *Where to send it*

It makes sense, when you are aiming for the nonfiction market, to study listings and back and current issues of magazines that interest you, and then decide what to write. With fiction, the opposite procedure seems the more sensible: Write your story first, and then look around for a place to send *that* story. It is more than a piece on a subject; it is a miniature universe.

# CHAPTER 8
# THE FRICTION
# IN FICTION

Labels are not essences. A writer might, for example, use the narrative voice, and use it well, without being aware of the term itself. What we have been calling the ingredients and the larger components of narrative are not merely conveniences of nomenclature. There is no further ingredient, nothing which cannot be identified as one of the conjurer's three. Similarly, there is no phase of the structure of a work of fiction that does not admit of a place in the action: at its complicating rise, at its moment of highest tension, or at that time of falling action which redeems and resolves all that has gone before.

In these matters the writer of fiction cannot exercise choice. However experimental the writer might be with conventions of language or the observed data of experience, the words used will act to describe, to summarize, or to set the scene. Stand logic on its head, begin at the end, end at the beginning, leave out the middle—perform what stunt you may, nothing will change the nature of narrative. What is made out of words will extend in time and space. Words move to fill the space of the book or magazine page; and it takes time to proceed from one word to the next. The word's unfolding is not instantaneous, with the immediacy of theater, but gradual and linear. These are things the writer does not choose.

Yet choice does enter in, and in a way that gives the writer creative command. The writer's freedom of choice comes with the selection of the angle of narration. This is the choice that gives decisive shape to story, decrees the form in which it will enter the reader's mind and linger there. The choice to be made is simply this: which perspective will the narrator on the wall assume in telling the story? Will it be the first person, or the third? Whichever is chosen, there are disadvantages as well as advantages to consider. There is the second-person angle, of course, but this is almost never used. The second person would seem to be all disadvantages. It draws the reader into the story: "You saw the tall, cadaverous man move forward..." The reader becomes a character in the story, drawn into events and conflicts not understood, set down in places unfamiliar, asked to encounter people never met before. The process of reading such a narrative is rather like experiencing a protracted, irritating, mystifying dream. Only a professional could succeed with something like this; the beginning writer will do well to eschew it entirely.

The first person seems a more sensible choice. It suggests itself as the inevitable approach to story. After all, this is the person familiar from writing one's letters, speaking to friends, thinking aloud: "I did this, I said that, I went here, I was there..." What could be more natural? Indeed, there is much to say for this intimate angle of narration. It seems an easy move from letters to one's friends to composing, in Robert Frost's phrase, "love letters to the world." Precedent is ample. The first person is the narrative angle chosen by many celebrated writers, among them Sherwood Anderson, who brought realism and immediacy of impact to the American short story in the early years of this century. The beginning writer, conscious of emotions and experiences to be mined for fiction, readily sees in the first-peraon angle of narration an extension of a device already familiar.

For many stories the first-person angle is an obvious

choice. The young writer, especially, commands untapped resources, with all the quick reactions and all the vocabulary of freshness. The authority of such experience invigorates; it is a wine that travels. But the first-person angle is a device with limitations. It provides a choice within a choice, however; the first-person narrator may be the major character, or merely an observer, the "I" whose narrative is about others. The advantages accruing to the first-person approach are clear; the disadvantages of this approach may not be so readily apparent. When the first-person narrator is the major character, when it is "my" story being told, there is the grave danger that, although the narrative may be credible enough, the "I" character can destroy reader interest. If the story's "I' is a bore, attracting unfavorable attention and promoting reader weariness, story suffers, often fatally.

The rightness of choice of first-person narrator in one instance and the choice of third person in another can best be illustrated by considering what happens in Mark Twain's two famous novels, *The Adventures of Huckleberry Finn* and *The Adventures of Tom Sawyer*. In both instances Mark Twain made the right choice. *Huckleberry Finn*, it will be recalled, is a first-person narrative. Huck Finn tells the story; he is the "I." Huck is constantly refreshing; he is unconventional and unpredictable enough never to weary. The reader can identify with Huck's "agin' the government" attitude; Huck's unique combination of naïveté and brashness never wearies. *Tom Sawyer*, on the other hand, is a third-person narrative. Tom's high-flown, bragging style would soon prove tiresome if transmitted as "I," "I," "I." Further, Tom Sawyer is highly romantic, given to vainglorious statements and deeds. His account, given in the first person, could not be relied upon; a first-person Tom would not for a moment be believed.

Often, the minor character who serves as first-person narrator is the most credible. The problem of the braggart is removed; this narrator is telling the story of someone else, not of the "I". Here the narrator is a modest observer, the spokesperson for an interested group, or for the reader. This angle of narration can be serviceable in many stories, reserving the spotlight for the chief character and yet retaining an intimacy and the conviction that springs from intimacy and from shared confidences. Henry James used this angle often, sometimes overcoming its inherent difficulties, sometimes not. The problem with the minor character "I" narrator is that this angle of narration requires the "I" to be always and everywhere present. How can "I" tell you what is going on if "I" am absent?

Often the writer is forced into incredible contortions in order to have the minor "I" where the action is, when plausibility would have him or her elsewhere. The problem becomes more complicated in a novel than in a short story, since in the former, ordinarily, a greater time extent and a greater number of single incidents are to be accounted for. The minor character who is the person on the wall acting as "I" will be involved in nearly inextricable situations. This character will have to account for events and lengthy conversations taking place at times when he or she was not present. F. Scott Fitzgerald has this problem in his long story "The Rich Boy," and Graham Greene becomes hopelessly entangled in it in *The Third Man*. Muriel Spark achieves the seemingly impossible in her short story "The Portobello Road." The narrator is murdered before the story is finished; she goes right on narrating it—as a ghost! Henry James usually brought it off, although not without introducing a further difficulty. In his story "The Last of the Valerii," the narrator, the "I," is the conscientious godfather of the chief female character, an American girl who has married an Italian count. The anonymous narrator, a landscape painter, enjoys the privilege of setting up his easel any time he wishes on the grounds of the count's Roman villa. Thus he is conveniently at hand to tell us the unfolding story of the discovery of an ancient statue of Juno dug up in the villa gardens. As an artist he is competent to react professionally to the value of the discovery and to interpret its meaning, for himself and the other characters.

Similarly, in the brilliant short story "'Europe'" the narrator, another unnamed "I," is able to relate the story from the vantage point of a privileged onlooker. Unfortunately he becomes more than that; impatient to see things happen, he begins to manipulate the other characters, to set them against one another so that he will have something to observe. There is perhaps nothing wrong with this, yet the intervention of the narrator tends to make him a major "I" rather than a minor one. His position relative to the major characters—the "she" and the "he" and the "they"—warps the story's structure. In "'Europe'" the narrator calls himself a "student of the case" as he observes a selfish old woman living on and on, sucking the vitality out of the lives of her three daughters, themselves already old women. The narrator delights in the ironies inherent in the situation—as he comes upon it in intervals when he visits the town of "Brookbridge" (obviously a combination of the names of the Boston suburbs of Brookline and Cambridge). The ending is brilliant, brilliantly manipulated, but manipulated nonetheless.

The first-person minor character angle of narration, all the same, recommends itself to the beginning writer. By making your "I" minor rather than major, you avoid putting yourself in the story too much. Frankly, you avoid what is an understandable but nonetheless inexcusable tendency to make too much of yourself, to treat yourself too affectionately, to romanticize, to sentimentalize this character of yours—yourself seen in the most benign possible light. Reader resistance is likely to be strong. The situation is tempered somewhat when the object of the writer's clearly expressed affection is turned into a "she" or "he." The reader is now more likely to share your concealed self-admiration rather than to resent it. Besides, the situation of an "I" discovering the personality of someone else, or puzzling over the difficulties and dangers of another is more socially acceptable; in real life it less often has to be concealed or apologized for. Grace Paley's improvement on the caution to write about what you know fits here. "Write about what you don't know in what you know," she advises.

The third-person angle is employed far more often than is the first, in both the short story and the novel. "Look at them!" the narrator on the wall seems to be saying, annihilating self. This too is a natural perspective. It is the way we ordinarily perceive life. The narrator over the bridge table, in the bar, or at poolside is more likely to gain welcome if the story is about "them." In such conversational gambits the speaker's self seems to have disappeared, but actually the narrator is everywhere present, nudging the listener, shaping response. The third-person narrator acts not as a personality to be looked at and in that way taken into account, but as an invisible intelligence, telling all, fashioning all, interpreting all. Readers today are too sophisticated (in both psychology and literary technique) to identify with the characters in fiction. A child watching a cowboy film on television leaves the room a cowboy; the identification is complete. For the mature reader identification with fiction is likely to be much more subtle than that; the identification is with the intelligence behind the story.

The pervasive presence of mind invisibly in control is best manifested in third-person narrative. Here that linkage of words of associated meanings recommended by Poe (who was a master of first-person narrative as well), the singleness of effect, can be given powerful utterance. The inherent danger is, of course, that the narrator will become a puppeteer, the events arbitrary and full of coincidence, and the story's characters mere puppets. For the story wherein event is intended to overmaster character, as in the mystery novel, no harm is done. Quite the contrary. In stories where a pitiless irony, as in the Hardy universe, is the effect to be achieved, the third-person omniscient point of view would seem to be mandatory. The narrator on the wall is all-knowing, all-seeing, all-encompassing. Nothing is outside the narrator's ken, or escapes the narrator's unsparing notice; not characters' thoughts, not pasts, not futures.

Beside´such a presence individual character withers. All characters become puppets, a condition to which the reader, also manipulated by the puppeteer—through the skillful juggling of narrative elements—gives hypnotized assent. Such an obliteration of individuality is sometimes mandatory, as with the murder victim or victims in a mystery story. It is fatal to allow the reader to come to like a character who, for the purposes of plot, is not going to be around long. The reader will resent that character's departure and tend to read on in growing resentment. If the character is eliminated early enough, and is sufficiently depersonalized while living, the reader will greet the hasty going with composure. The murder victim may be individualized posthumously. The point of the detection may well be in reconstruction of a vivid and complex personality. If the author has done his or her work fairly and well, resentment will be directed at the murderer.

Of all the available angles, direct or indirect, in which to couch narrative that of the viewpoint character is the most flexible and by far the most rewarding to work with. This angle fuses the best of the first person (the immediacy, the intimacy) with the best of the third person (the objectivity, the perspective). The viewpoint character angle carries the authority of everyone's life experience with it. The psychological rightness of the viewpoint character approach derives from the fact that it reproduces awareness exactly as we know it; subjectively and objectively at the same time. The "I" and the object are part of the same apprehension: I see myself seeing. The phenomenon is at once individual and universal; unique and shared.

Through the use of the viewpoint character a writer brings life and technique strikingly together. The viewpoint character in a narrative is the only one whose thoughts *as thoughts* are known. Consider the naturalness of it. *You* are the only person, all your life, who is a viewpoint character to you. *I* am the only viewpoint character I shall ever know. Friends, family, lovers, children—all are strangers to us. You are the only person in the world who knows exactly what you were thinking at eleven o'clock this morning. Unless by word or gesture, by body language or external action you indicated your thought, it remains within, arcane to others. One dies alone—*on mourra seul*—said Pascal; but even more mysteriously, more poignantly, one lives alone. Thinking that thought, uttering it, we are at the core of literature.

To be able to present a character inside *and* out—what an advantage! If the reader identifies with any character in your story or novel, it will be with this one. Let us suppose that you have written a story with five important characters in it. Four are men; one is a woman. The woman is your viewpoint character. Her thoughts are known. Her attitudes, her emotions shape the story. She is Doris, she is "she" and not "I"; the story is "hers" and not "mine." Nonetheless, it is she who estimates the motives, considers the actions of the others. She is the character the reader gets to know. If the minds of the other characters are not entered, their actions remain uninterpreted, even unjustified. Thus the viewpoint character towers over them easily in the reader's sympathies.

The use of a viewpoint character in your story allows the reader to enter your story in a particular way. Through sharing the character's insights, the reader can be on the inside looking in. Something quite similar happens in a play. Two characters are on stage, discussing George, who is about to join them. "I'll tell you something about George," says one. "He can be counted on to say the same thing every time he walks in the door." "I don't believe you," the other counters. "I'm willing to bet," says the first, "that the minute he walks in this room he'll say, 'Hey, gang, let's go to Clancy's for a few brews.'" The other laughs his disbelief. George enters. The audience is in on the joke, anticipating. What is the first thing George says? "Hey, gang, let's go to Clancy's . . ." The audience is happy to be in on the joke about George, flattered to know what he could not, that one of his friends predicted exactly what he would say.

The viewpoint character device enables the writer of

narrative to enjoy the playwright's prerogative of inviting participation. The other characters are not aware of the thoughts of the viewpoint character, but the reader is aware of them. The reader knows what other characters do not know. Here is a crude example of how it works:

Mabel is in the room alone arranging flowers in a vase. George enters. We pick up the narrative:

> George came toward her smiling that crooked smile of his. "Mabel!" he said. "You're looking wonderful. Is the dress new?" When will she learn, he thought, that red is not her color.
>
> "George!" Mabel replied, coming toward him. "You say the nicest things."

Who is the viewpoint character? George, obviously. The reader shares a superior knowledge, George's thought, and Mabel is the victim of both George's thought and the reader's awareness.

Viewpoint characterization can be a pleasure to work with; it can also be a subtle and powerful tool. In the hands of a master like Jane Austen this device can be used to double narrative dimension. In *Emma*, for example, she enters Emma Woodhouse's consciousness to share Emma's thoughts with us, and then moves outside Emma's thoughts in order to judge her dispassionately. Thus we have two evaluations of Emma: her own and the author's. First-person narrative can provide only one. In the following passage we see Emma handled externally and then another character (unlike Emma not a viewpoint character) in the act of thinking:

> "Nonsense, errant nonsense as ever was talked!" cried Mr. Knightley. "Robert Martin's manners have sense, sincerity, and good-humor to recommend them; and his mind has more true gentility than Harriet Smith could understand."

*Emma made no answer, and tried to look cheer-
fully unconcerned, but was really feeling uncomfort-
able and wanting him very much to be gone. She did not
repent what she had done; she still thought herself a better
judge of such a point of female right and refinement than
he could be; but yet she had a sort of habitual respect for
his judgment in general, which made her dislike having it
so loudly against her; and to have him sitting just opposite
to her in angry state, was very disagreeable. Some minutes
passed in this unpleasant silence, with only one attempt
on Emma's side to talk of the weather, but he made no
answer. He was thinking. The result of his thoughts
appeared at last in these words.*

*"Robert Martin has no great loss—if he can but
think so; and I hope it will not be long before he does.
Your views for Harriet are best known to yourself; but as
you make no secret of your love of match-making, it is fair
to suppose that views, and plans, and projects you have;
and as a friend I shall just hint to you that if Elton is the
man, I think it will be all labour in vain."*

The angle of narration in *Emma* is third person, limited,
not omniscient. The author, it will be noted, refrains from
entering Mr. Knightley's mind. "He was thinking." The
sentence is pure summary. Fidelity to the concept of a single
viewpoint character prevented the author from switching from
Emma's mind to George Knightley's. The result is a stronger
narrative. Like all technical devices, the viewpoint character
can be overused or treated merely as a gimmick. Clearly, it
would be unwise to employ more than one viewpoint character
in a short story. The result would be a kind of literary vertigo.
Being asked to enter more than one mind would distract,
and, more seriously, divide, the reader's attention. The same
objection does not necessarily hold for a novel, where characters are less likely to occupy one another's space. Elizabeth

Janeway's novel *Accident* is an example of long narrative built around multiple viewpoints, introducing a new viewpoint with each new section. In *Accident* the same scene is repeated from more than one point of view; thus a character will be viewpoint in one chapter and not viewpoint in another.

Now let us assume that your choice of the angle of narration has been made. Presumably the decision has been based on your judgment of which angle will best bring out the particular situation and conflicts that your characters find themselves in. For one story the most appropriate angle may be that of third-person omniscience, for another first-person minor character may be the most fitting. When angle is decided, the direction in which the story will move is logically the next problem to be taken up. The story's movement from initial complication to the final words of resolution may be called the plot. Even the plotless story, so called, requires plot. If one defines plot as movement, the movement of events in sequence tempered by suspense, it can be seen that even the almost eventless story has a plot.

Some writers take to plotting more easily than others do. The more logical-minded, the puzzle-fanciers, have little difficulty setting relationships in geometrical fashion. For the impressionistic, plotting comes with difficulty until the discovery is made that there can be impressionistic plotting as well. The stories of Katherine Mansfield are classics of the plotless short story, as are the stories of the great Russian, Anton Chekhov. It would be easy to say, as many have done, that in the stories of Mansfield and Chekhov "nothing happens." Actually, in terms of what is revealed about the human heart in moments of loneliness, of betrayal, and of despair so much happens in the plotless stories of these writers that heavily plotted stories of intricate action and external dangers seem drab, stilted, motionless even, in comparison.

In Mansfield's "Miss Brill" the only thing that happens is that the title character is seen seated on a park bench before returning to her drab room with a slice of cake (perhaps this time it will include an almond) she will have with her tea as a Sunday treat. She overhears a young girl, brushing aside a boy's attempt to kiss her in public, exclaim, "Not here!" and describe Miss Brill as a silly old thing. This is the sole event of the story, that is the moment of its climax, the point at which Miss Brill's existence of loveless nights and lonely days is crystallized; from that moment of revelation there is quick descent to resolution. The reader knows that the innocent folly of Miss Brill's happiness can never be restored. The progression of the narrative from the introduction of Miss Brill and the deft indication of the restricted quality of her life to the incident in the park and her reaction to it—that is plot.

Virtually all the stories one reads in the literary quarterlies descend from Chekhov and Mansfield. For many years now the stories selected for the annual O. Henry Awards have been of the plotless type that O. Henry, the master of plotting, would have fled from in horror. In its early years the volume carried stories by O. Henry's most considerable successor, Wilbur Daniel Steele, whose stories had more literary substance to them than O. Henry's but were as rigorously blueprinted and plotted. But for some time, in magazines as well as in book collections, the heavily plotted story, strong in external events, peopled by characters given to overt action, to violent, punitive, warlike movement, seems to no longer be in vogue. This kind of story may be due for a return, but today it has almost no market and it is entirely lacking in prestige.

Much more fashionable is a kind of anemic story wherein people are more likely to fall apart, from inward weakness, than to act. The protagonist needs no enemies, finding his worst enemy within. The short story protagonist, says Frank O'Connor, is a member of a "submerged population group," meaning an oppressed nationality like the Irish. But depression of spirit is international, and O'Connor's phrase describes the typical figure in international fiction. For some time the concept of character based upon free will—freedom to perform mightily for either good or evil—has been succeeded by the

Hamlet  Walter Mitty concept of the hero whose characteristic action is some form of debilitating inaction. A story based on such a concept is, like modern nonrepresentational painting, seemingly easy to do. But success with it is infernally hard to come by.

A story that has a definite plot is correspondingly difficult to construct. It will, unlike "Miss Brill," be predicated on a more complex relationship between characters and actions than the simple, fortuitous event of one character overhearing a chance remark by another. The plot short story, and that far more frequent phenomenon, the plot novel, will seek their movement from point to point through logically drawn relationships and a calculus of people driven by conflicting motives. The beginning writer will not neglect plotting, if for no other reason than that a plot can be counted on to provide one's story with a middle. Too many stories are short vignettes, beginning well, often strikingly, and ending effectively, consistent with the mood pronounced at the beginning. But what of the middle? How can the required pages be filled without padding? One way is to learn to plot. Think of a character, think of difficulties for that character, think of why the character can solve the difficulties. That is plot.

An incident taken from an actual event may prove illustrative. Some years ago a news story about a domestic tragedy in the American Southwest appeared throughout the country's newspapers. A young woman of twenty-one was being punished by her parents by being required to shoot her pet dog. She was driven out into the desert and there she turned the gun on herself. There is a story, but not yet a plot. Plot must answer the question why? For such a sad incident to have happened the way it did is enough to get it on the news wires. It is not enough to form a story. The motives of the young woman and her parents have to be probed and shown before we have a story. Here we come upon the first rule of fiction: *Invent the facts.* Fiction is invention in the root sense of the word: *invenio* "I find." Fiction is not reportage; it does not interview the actual persons of a tragedy; it takes the merest suggestion and universalizes. It discovers not what happend in a single instance, but what universally happens.

Acting on a suggestion submitted by life (and newspaper accounts abound in preplots of fiction), the writer of fiction begins to "invent," to make findings, by asking questions about people, about motives. First what was the offense that set off the chain of events leading to the daughter's death? On reflection, you will see that will not be a very rewarding starting point. Different people react differently; they do not have the same flash point. Better think about the people a little more. Accepting the newspaper's account of the victim's age, let us give some thought to the ages of the parents. (Not the actual parents, but the parents of our imagination). Should there be a difference in the ages of the parents? Only if it turns out to have relevance to our story, if an age difference will "work" for us. Are there other children? Again, not if their presence is going to be irrelevant or somehow restrictive of our story line. A brother nearly the same age would present a problem: Where was he on the day of the tragedy? Why did he fail to intervene?

A convincing answer to the last question might be that he is a paraplegic, in a wheelchair. Good invention. Only now we have endangered the story, given it to the brother. Not that this is a bad idea; one might write a story based on the helplessness, for physical reasons, of a character to intervene in a situation where intervention is desperately needed. Should that idea engage your imagination, jettison the original idea and characters and follow the new lead. Henry James speaks of "life at its messy work"; in the process of tidying up life the writer of fiction comes upon ideal images and ideal situations which he or she must follow. The tyranny of fact has no place, wields no power, in fiction.

Fictional invention will require a close look at the parents—the fictional parents—in this story. Is one dominant and the other passive, and if so which one? Try each alternative and then think it through to the consequences. A bullying father and a frightened mother will set up one set of allegiances and loyalties; an overbearing mother and a compliant or irresponsible father will set up quite another. When the writer decides which parent will be the dominant one, then it may be time to look at the incident that generated the idea of punishment. For the dominant parent as now conceived what would be the last straw? The character of the daughter is one that provides the most fascinating puzzle. You make her timid, even cringing. Very well, but then you have a problem making an offense against her parents credible. Make her rebellious, defiant, then, you must find an explanation for the fact that she has not run away from home or defied her parents in some other way before becoming twenty-one.

A version, a "truth" of this situation may result from the idea that the daughter agreed with her parents, that she passed the verdict of guilty upon herself. Here is a possibility worth developing. There is nothing in the society in which the incident happened that would explain, in time and place, the draconian measures the parents felt called upon to take. No contemporary stereotypes—the young woman was, after all, twenty-one—would explain or lend verisimilitude to what happened. In contrast is the ambience from which one of the classic French tales, Prosper Mérimée's "Mateo Falcone" derives the power, that of a Corsican village where the code of honor permits a father to kill his son who betrayed a man to the authorities. But there is nothing in the American Southwest environment of the news story that explains what happened.

Plotting can be seen as the application of movement to static situations and static people; it bears the relationship to them that film does to still photgraphy. We tend to think of motion as forward motion, but there is motion backward in time, from present to past as well. In narrative fiction the device known as *flashback* is an attractive means of foreshortening time sequence. When it is not overdone, not treated as a mere gimmick, the device of flashback can be a powerful aid to narrative impact. Through flashback one's characters can literally go backward in time. Flashback is not time remembered (while now remains now), or a past time remembered in a present dream or fantasy. With the flashback a past time becomes the present. One can move from the narrative now—a day in March, let us say—to a past time, the previous November, which becomes the now. Time starts running in consecutive seconds in this past November, which is now; the flashback runs until there is a leap to the now of March with which the story began.

Let us suppose that the main events of a short story we are writing concern a young woman—call her Mabel again—as she enters her thirtieth year. We have decided that what she does, or fails to do, will be the result of an experience she had on the evening of her high school graduation—when she was seventeen. This is to be a short story. Obviously, we cannot open with the high school scene and take her through the years until she becomes thirty. Even a novel would not allow enough room to do that. We begin, then, with Mabel at thirty, about to face a crisis, perhaps to encounter someone she had not seen or heard from since high school days. This is the now we begin with. Then the scene turns to the high school gym; the then becomes now. After the scene or scenes in that time frame, we end the flashback. The years have been erased and elliptically accounted for.

Ordinarily the time saved by flashback is a matter of years, or months at least. Flannery O'Connor's short story "Good Country People" is unusual in offering a brilliant use of flashback to account for but a single day. One of the earliest employments of the flashback technique occurs in Ambrose Bierce's story "An Occurrence at Owl Creek Bridge." In this instance, flashback *is* the story. Bierce's narrative opens with a dramatic "now": Peyton Farquhar is being hanged as a Confederate spy. At the end of the first of the story's three numbered divisions the sentence is carried out with the words; "The sergeant stepped aside." In the second section Bierce gives us a scene in which, at an unspecified previous time Farquhar and his wife, seated on a rustic bench on their plantation, are accosted by "a grey-clad soldier." The final section opens with this sentence: "As Peyton Farquhar fell straight downward through the bridge, he lost consciousness and was as one already dead." Compellingly, Bierce moves from this point to the story's resolution.

In the central panel of his story Bierce introduces his protagonist, Farquhar, by means of summary before presenting his flashback scene. Through using numbered divisions, Bierce provides a deft division between his "nows." But numerical divisions are less frequently met with today ("An Occurrence at Owl Creek Bridge," modern though it is in technique, was first published in 1891).

Slipping into a flashback and out again can be awkward. Sometimes the perfect tense is used—"she had said"—to indicate a past time. Often the word *now* is awkwardly introduced to indicate that we are back from flashback, back in the original time frame. Just as multiple viewpoint characterization should be avoided in a short story and used only temperately in a longer narrative, the flashback should be treated with respect and employed frugally. It should be noted that the flashback may be made part of the structure of both the literary short story and the popular story of "happy people with happy problems."

Related to the writer's problem of when, where, and how often to use the flashback device is the even more fundamental problem of the choice of summary or scene to move the story forward. In his amusing story "Wakefield," Hawthorne tells the tale of a man who on a whim walked out of his house one October evening and twenty years later and on an equal whim walked back in again. Hawthorne treats the story in laboratory fashion, pondering how to write it, how to choose the pieces and fit them together. "What sort of a man was Wakefield?" he asks, and then answers, "We are free to shape out our own idea, and call it by his name." The next paragraph begins: "Let us now imagine Wakefield bidding adieu to his wife." One would expect a scene to follow, but instead we are given summary, extended over several paragraphs. Hawthorne is not writing a story, as he is well aware, but a "meditation" on how a story might be written.

"Wakefield" is a first-person narrative, told by a minor observer, and yet the viewpoint is that of omniscience. Hawthorne turns the narrator on the wall into a moralist, addressing his protagonist directly: "Poor Wakefield! Little knowest thou thine own insignificance in this great world! No mortal eye but mine has traced thee. Go quietly to thy bed, foolish man; and, on the morrow, if thou wilt be wise, get thee home to good Mrs. Wakefield." About midpoint in the narrative, Hawthorne declares, "Now for a scene," but he gives us a squinting one. Wordlessly Wakefield meets his wife—we are told, not shown—ten years after his disappearance. Their eyes meet, but she does not recognize him. Then after more meditating on Wakefield's folly—living alone in a small apartment—Hawthorne tells us that Wakefield, on a whim and to evade a sudden shower, walks back into his house after an absence of twenty years.

"We will not," Hawthorne tells us irritatingly, "follow our friend across the threshold." If ever there was an obligatory scene, this would be it. Mrs. Wakefield is on the other side of that door, and we deserve to meet her, to share the action of her words to her husband on their reunion. In a fully embodied story, not a mere workshop experiment such as Hawthorne has given us, a scene between Mrs. Wakefield and her husband would be mandatory. A writer who leads us as far as this and then walks out of his obligation deserves dismembering. Hawthorne's refusal to write the reunion scene—while fully aware of its necessity—provides a witty parallel to Wakefield's own indecision; in that sense, "Wakefield" is a story after all.

In "The Crop," one of her early stories, Flannery O'Connor writes what amounts to a cautionary tale about writing a story. Her protagonist, Miss Willerton, submits resentfully to being bullied by other members of the household; she seeks fastidious escape by being a writer of stories. She plans her stories as she crumbs the breakfast table.

> *Crumbing the table gave one time to think, and if Miss Willerton were going to write a story, she had to think about it first. She could usually think best sitting in front of her typewriter, but this would do for the time being. First; she had to think of a subject to write a story about. There were so many subjects to write stories about that Miss Willerton could never think of one. That was always the hardest part of writing a story, she always said. She spent more time thinking of something to write about than she did writing. Sometimes she discarded subject after subject and it usually took her a week or two to decide finally on something. Miss Willerton got out the silver crumber and the crumb-catcher and started stroking the table. I wonder, she mused, if a baker would make a good subject? Foreign bakers were very picturesque, she thought. Aunt Myrtle Filmer had left her four colortints of French bakers in mushroom-looking hats. They were great tall fellows—blond and . . .*

After a time at her typewriter Miss Willerton decides that bakers will not do as subject for a story; "no social tension connected with bakers." She dismisses teachers for the same reason, then settles on sharecroppers (about whom she knows no more than she does about bakers) because that "would make as arty a subject as any." Besides, it occurred to her she could always "capitalize on the hookworm."

> *It was coming to her now! Certainly! Her fingers plinked excitedly over the keys, never touching them. Then suddenly she began typing at great speed.*
>
> *"Lot Motun," the typewriter registered, "called his dog." "Dog" was followed by an abrupt pause. Miss Willerton always did her best work on the first sentence.*

Later, after shopping for groceries, Miss Willerton returns to her typewriter and reads what she had written:

> *"That sounds awful!" Miss Willerton muttered. "It's not a good subject anyway," she decided. She needed something more colorful—more arty. Miss Willerton looked at her typewriter for a long time. Then of a sudden her fist hit the desk in several ecstatic little bounces. "The Irish!" she squealed. "The Irish!" Miss Willerton had always admired the Irish. Their brogue, she thought, was full of music; and their history—splendid! And the people, she mused, the Irish people! They were full of spirit—red-haired, with broad shoulders and great, drooping mustaches.*

The story ends with the suggestion that Miss Willerton has gone off on another hopeless tangent, planting a new "crop." The story is cautionary in that with it the author reminds herself—and us—that you must know penetratingly and thoroughly the circumstances, places, and people you attempt to put into fiction.

One of Miss Willerton's concerns is of crucial importance to the writer of fiction—the creation of character. A character is not separable from narrative in the way it is from drama. A critic can deplore a play and yet praise an actress in it: "Miss Jones was her usual pert, delightful self." No reviewer can sensibly write, "Mr. Smith's novel is, like his previous ones, a seriously flawed affair, but I cannot turn away from it without praise for its heroine, as delightful a heroine as Jane Austen's Elizabeth Bennet." The writer is responsible for everything that occurs in narrative, from creating the weather to issuing the weather reports. His or her people must be as credible as the plot and locale. Indeed, plausible characters can go far to reconcile the reader to implausibility elsewhere in the narrative.

What makes a character in fiction seem to live and stride the printed page is ultimately a mystery. Characterization is not reducible to formula, and it eludes analysis. Yet something can be attempted and achieved in the art of simulating personality in words. After all, it is largely through words that we project personality in actual life. And it is a commonplace of observation that people appear to us (and we to others) as either individuals or as types. Characters in fiction as well are perceived as either rounded individuals or as types. Although most characters in short fiction are types, for twenty-five typed pages hardly offer scope for a fully presented character, they had better not be conceived as such. As Scott Fitzgerald put it, to begin with an individual is to have created a type, but to begin with a type is to end with nothing at all.

The difference between a type and an individual is not one of kind but of degree. An individual is a former type we now know better. We are all individuals to ourselves (we know all the details), and types—in age group, occupation, degree of affluence, and so forth—to others. A few well-chosen and striking details will elevate a type to the status of individual. We think of Sherlock Holmes as an individual and believe we know him. What is he but a type of intellect and temperament slightly individualized through the choice of a few individualizing traits? And what is the test of individuality that we apply to ourselves and others? It is predictability. For example, if we know George or Mabel well, we can say with a strong degree of confidence, "He would not do this," or "She would not say that." If we can create a single character in a short story who the reader accepts as predictable, we have achieved much.

To be credible to a reader, a character in fiction must first be credible to the writer. Basing a character upon oneself or someone else one knows well, might seem to be a surefire way to achieve plausible characterization. Yet just as one does not always recognize one's own voice on tape, one is not always credible when putting oneself or someone close wholly and directly into a character. Besides, there can be inconveniences, some of them legal. Mrs. Frances Trollope, Anthony Trollope's mother and herself a prolific novelist, had a brisk solution: "You can't tell the pigs in a sausage." By this she meant the writer should take the outward appearance of one person, the mentality of another, the environment and background of another, and the dilemma of still another—hence a sausage of snippets. Hence also a fictional creation, not mere reportage.

Sinclair Lewis used an elaborate scheme for making characters real to himself. For his novels *Main Street, Babbitt,* and the others he drew up a dossier, worthy of the Paris police, for each of his characters, including the most minor. If he wished to introduce a character in *Main Street,* for example, whose sole function was to cross the street of Sauk Center on a dreary Sunday afternoon merely to look in a drugstore window, he would draw up a dossier for that person. This character would occupy part of a single paragraph of an entire novel and never be seen or heard of again. Yet there would be a dossier on him or her: name, height, weight, age, color of hair, color of eyes, place of birth, parents' names, high school attended, occupation, hobbies—everything that could be recorded about that person. This accumulated knowledge gave Lewis the confidence to introduce the character and march her or him across the street. The character was real to him; he *knew* the person. The stack of dossiers have been on exhibit at Yale; their pages piled up beside the typescript of the novels are in every instance half again as high.

Granted that Sinclair Lewis went to extremes, that his measures were excessive for a novel and certainly for a short story, yet this practice illustrates a sound principle of writing: know more about your subject than you reveal in words. For Hemingway the working image was of an iceberg. Ninety percent of any iceberg lies below the waterline; the white glistening mass we see above water is only 10 percent. For Hemingway the iceberg under the water was all he knew about the subject, whether it was war, hunting, or bullfighting—a distillation of a solid knowledge. His words, sparingly used in that laconic style of his, had the solidity and authenticity of the solid structure below. You should know your characters in this iceberg sense, even those who only cross the street to peer into a window. Writing a substory of notes, of careful "research" may be, for you, the way to achieve your iceberg.

Compiling some kind of dossier, some gathering of invented facts, however informal it might be, is one way of visualizing your people. They ought always to be clearly in your view, if not necessarily in your reader's. Even if you do not mention in your story that your heroine, let us say, has brown eyes, *you* should know this. All sorts of underwater iceberg material may accrue simply from that determination of the color of your heroine's eyes. Your mother's eyes may have been that color, or your grandmother's—and the thought of brown eyes may unlock dozens of memories. Let us suppose that you have decided upon brown eyes and memories have come, and yet the character lies inert. You remember your grandmother's eyes and you recall a striking incident in her life—and yet you have nothing. The story will not move. Try to *become* your character by means of the viewpoint character device. However sympathetically you may have heard the family story of, say, your grandmother's elopement in a blizzard, it has come to you always from the outside. Get inside your grandmother; inhabit her mind as well as live her story. It will move.

Get one character moving and there will be a kinetic reaction involving your other characters. It will be impossible for them to remain static. (If a character stays stiff and unmoving, get rid of that character.) Abrasive relationships among your people are required for a story to happen. There must always be friction in your fiction. Change, separation, loss, motion, conflict—these are the law of life. A towering iceberg, riding the waves, shimmering and majestic, is an essay. An iceberg and a great passenger liner, shrouded in mist and night, riding the waves inexorably toward one another—that is a story.

## SUGGESTED FOLLOW-UP
## FOR THIS CHAPTER

### 1. *What to read*

Read writers on writing. At first their shoptalk may mystify or even irritate you, but gradually you will become—the more you write—an insider. The book of books for the aspiring writer of fiction is *The Notebooks of Henry James* (Oxford University Press, 1947) edited by F. O. Matthiessen and Kenneth B. Murdock. With no thought that his notations would ever be seen by anyone else, James planned story after story, carefully setting out the source of his original idea and thinking his way—probing, revising, rejoicing ("I OBSERVE, I VIBRATE")—into the structure of his plots. Check the finished stories against their notebook beginnings for incomparable object lessons in how to write.

Another extremely valuable guide to writing fiction, one that affords insights into the author's intentions, is Flannery O'Connor's posthumous *Mystery and Manners* (Farrar, Straus & Giroux, 1969), edited by Sally and Robert Fitzgerald. The book is extremely helpful for Flannery O'Connor's wry comments on reader reaction to her stories and reflections on her writing methods and "the habit of art." Sally Fitzgerald has edited Flannery O'Connor's letters in *The Habit of Being* (Farrar, Straus & Giroux, 1979), an engrossing account of this author's struggle to write in her own way in spite of the efforts of editors and others to turn her into a conventional writer.

Different from the above in being intended for publication by its author and no less valuable for the tyro is Paul Horgan's *Approaches to Writing* (Farrar, Straus & Giroux, 1974). In this book Horgan, a prolific writer of distinguished fiction and equally distinguished nonfiction, talks shop, shares pithy and pertinent notebook entries, and finally contributes a sixty-page memoir on his apprenticeship as a writer, detailing the failures of his first five (unpublished) novels. His sixth won the Harper Prize competition; his book tells how the novel grew from a three-thousand-word sketch intended for *The New Yorker* to a book of one hundred and fifty thousand words.

## 2. What to write

Write fiction of course, at every inspiration and opportunity.

To extend your grasp of structure in fiction and to explore the underpinnings and logical relationships between your characters, you may wish to consider—primarily as finger exercises—the writing of one-act plays. If you find natural-sounding, realistic dialogue difficult to write in a story, experiment with the play, the form that is all dialogue. Again, if giving your narrative a substantial and satisfying middle (it may sag here and there) is a problem, the experience of play construction will prove of some value.

The transaction involved in converting summary to dialogue might feasibly begin with your reworking passages from classic short stories into dramatic form. For this purpose select passages that do not contain dialogue, then rewrite them by recasting the text as it might appear in a play. The following—the third paragraph of Stephen Crane's "The Blue Hotel," might, for example, prove instructive recast in dramatic form:

> *One morning, when a snow-crusted engine dragged its long string of freight cars and its one passenger coach to the station, Scully performed the marvel of catching three men. One was a shaky and quick-eyed Swede, with a great shining cheap valise; one was a tall bronzed cowboy, who was on his way to a ranch near the Dakota line; one was a little silent man from the East, who didn't look it, and didn't announce it. Scully practically made them prisoners. He was so nimble and merry and kindly that each probably felt it would be the height of brutality to try to escape. They trudged off over the creaking board*

*sidewalks in the wake of the eager little Irishman. He wore a heavy fur cap squeezed tightly down on his head. It caused his two red ears to stick out stiffly as if they were made of tin.*

The conversion might go something like this:

SCULLY (*bustling up to them*): A kindly welcome to you, welcome, gentlemen, one and all. (*To the Swede.*) Here now, sir, let me take that. Let me relieve you of all those rocks you have in there. (*Chuckles.*)

SWEDE (*pulling away*): No. No. It stays with me. (*Scully shrugs, laughs loudly, and turns away.*)

SCULLY (*to Easterner*): And you, sir. May I help *you*? (*The Easterner silently hands over his neat traveling bag and precisely furled umbrella.*)

COWBOY (*to nobody in particular*): Dakota, here I come! (*They all follow Scully over the creaking boards toward his hotel.*)

SCULLY: You'll love it here. It's not wild (*to the cowboy*), begging your pardon, sir, like Dakota. Sure, this place is the height of civilization! (*He laughs loudly, with his eye on the Swede.*) Man, this *is* civilization—set down just west of nowhere.

Converting from dialogue set in the form of a play to dialogue as it would appear in narrative is another workroom task you might find it profitable to try. Melville's *Moby Dick* offers an excellent chance to do this, as he put several parts of his long novel in play form. Consider the following opening of chapter 120: "The Deck Towards the End of the First Night Watch":

STARBUCK: We must send down the main top-sail yard, sir. The band is working loose, and the lee lift is half-stranded. Shall I strike, sir?

AHAB: Strike nothing; lash it. If I had sky-sail poles, I'd sway them up now.

STARBUCK: Sir?—in God's name!—sir?
AHAB: Well.
STARBUCK: The anchors are working, sir. Shall I get them
    inboard?

Try transforming the above into narrative. By means
of the device of summary, show Starbuck's agitation as
he shouts and gestures wildly. Do not revise Melville's
dialogue; incorporate it into your narrative. Contrast
Starbuck's excitement with Ahab's immobility. Starbuck
should be all movement, Ahab all rocklike passivity. Try
various ways of calling attention to Captain Ahab's wooden
leg. One way might be to depict Starbuck, in between his
frantic gestures, as staring at the leg fixedly, with Ahab aware
of what Starbuck is doing. Have Ahab show his irritation.
Sketch out various ways of doing this. He stamps his leg down
on the deck, he reaches down and strokes his calf, as though it
were flesh and blood, and so on.

For an introduction to the principles of playcraft consult
Josefina Niggli's *New Pointers on Playwriting* (The Writer,
1967). After absorbing the lucid guidelines of this delightful
book try converting a short story requiring one scene
only—Poe's "The Cask of Amontillado" or Crane's "The Open
Boat," for example—into a one-act play. The latter, particularly, presents a challenge; it contains important passages of
summary that will have to be transposed into dialogue in order
to make your play a faithful rendering of Crane's story. For a
fascinating "experiment in multimedia" see *Trilogy* by Truman
Capote, Eleanor Perry, and Frank Perry (Macmillan, 1969), a
presentation of the complete texts of three of Capote's short
stories in their original print version and in subsequent
television and film versions, with extended commentary on the
"subtle problems of cross-media translation."

Some useful approaches to the specialized art of screen-
writing, with tips on marketing, may be found in Sheldon
Tromberg's *Making Money, Making Movies* (Franklin Watts,
1979).

### 3. *Where to send it*

The proper outcome for a play, of course, is not print but production. Nonetheless, there are two outstanding periodical markets for one-act plays. They are *Plays: The Drama Magazine for Young People* and *At Rise: Magazine. Plays* publishes nearly one hundred plays a year for performance by young people from the younger grades through senior high school. *Plays* welcomes adaptations from classic stories and fables as well as originals of all types, including concept plays on such topics as good citizenship, ecology, and conversation. *At Rise* is equally open to the free-lancer. An *At Rise* editorial issues the following invitation to writers:

> *Where do we get our plays? Nearly all of them are submitted to AT RISE: by freelancers, many of whom have never published before. This is an exciting fact to us...exciting because we feel unknown authors who write well are often unable to publish their work simply because they have no previous credits, and no agent to sell the work for them. For these reasons, our editors are always willing to read any submissions from prospective playwrights. Sometimes we have to endure the boredom of plays that should never have been written, as well as the frustration of having to reject those that just miss. But our aim remains to give every playwright an opportunity, and to publish the very best new plays that are available to us. So, get that wonderful one-act out of your desk drawer, and let us take a look at it!*

# CHAPTER 9
# STIR GENTLY

In the theater and on the printed page, talk has the name of action. In a sense, plays are conversations that move. When plays are translated from stage to film, what was accepted as movement before is mere "talk" now. Yet conversation is necessary to scene—on the stage and in the pages of narrative. Without scene there is no story—and without dialogue there is no scene. Although the writer of fiction has the advantage over the playwright of being able to call upon the narrative voice (description and summary) more extensively than the former is permitted to employ exposition, the storyteller's characters cannot evade conversing with one another for long. To engage in talk while occupying time and space is, in both forms, to act.

The art of providing one's characters with lines to recite is of consequence, therefore, to the short story writer and the novelist. In the theater, conversation, whether the play is tragedy or comedy, is helped to convey its meaning through the assistance of body language, meaningful pauses in the talk, stage "business," and even sound effects. In spite of its lifelike devices, drama is more concentrated and deliberate than life. For example, no matter how realistic and natural stage dialogue is, it requires voice projection, thus adding artificiality—"stage English." The playwright's difficulties are many and special; in part they derive from the need to address the ear rather than the eye. The ear, required to keep up with what is being said at the moment, lacks the eye's power of recall. If you have difficulty with something being said on stage, you cannot ask the actor to repeat his or her earlier lines. Reading a novel, you can turn back to an earlier page for a point you find you have missed.

Film and fiction, although both lack the actual presence of living human beings, can often make the action seem more real than a stage play can. This is because cinema and story possess more realistic ways of creating the illusion of movement. On the stage, persons and objects must actually move. In a movie or book, they need only appear to move. On a stage, the actors are in one place only at any one time, occupying one small corner of the set. Their physical movement is therefore limited. A "chase" scene—vivid in a film and on paper—becomes farce on the stage. Film can show miles of highway and speeding cars; so can a story or a novel—in the reader's imagination. On the stage, the characters can only stand around and talk about that kind of action, and many other kinds as well. Yet talk is action. An actor, after all, is one who acts. And he or she performs action most, usually and normally, by speaking about it. In films and novels, too, talk is a major—but not the total—form of action. Talk is life.

The writer of narrative, however, cannot rely upon direct transcription from life; the tape recorder has not replaced labor on the typewriter. Life "at its messy work" in the memorable phrase of Henry James, affords spoken language which is tantalizingly incomplete, lacking context when exchanged between two people who know one another well or share information and assumptions. Art is needed to provide the thread to knit together such exchanges as the following:

"Tonight maybe?"
"But will Roger...?"
"Then there's that pick-up to make."

"Five o'clock!"

"Could be. I resent that fishing trip. I can't help it. I resent it."

The ingredients of conflict are already implied, embedded even, in these random words; they need only be made more explicit. A conversation overheard in a public place or one produced by an evening among friends can seldom stand by itself when seen in print. Such talk is almost always random, contradictory, and directionless.

Dialogue, then, must through the aid of artifice become lifelike. First of all, care must be taken to follow idiom. The accents of a region, the patois of a trade, the cliché of a class—these must receive faithful reflection. Flannery O'Connor once reproached students at a Southern college because in their short stories none of their characters spoke like Southerners. For her the native speech rhythms of a place made up the "manners" of region, age group, and social class. Gangsters may not be realistically portrayed as speaking like professors; nor may professors—even if some of them do—be made credible if they speak like gangsters. Nobody has a good word to say for characters that "talk like a book," and yet their discourse may not even enter a book, so to speak, if it is lacking in trust. Purposeless talk is too much like the aimlessness of life. Fiction's dialogue must not cease to be lifelike except in this: it must not dawdle.

To construct dialogue that fulfills such conflicting demands, one should sound out the words aloud as well as watch them unfold on the manuscript page. If you can hear, literally hear your characters, they cannot fail to come alive for you. As you hear their voices you will also see them, and experience them from the inside. Anything false they say will strike your ear at once. Does each speaker have an individual way of saying things, or are you momentarily confused as to who is who? Can the snarl of a character who snarls be discerned in the very syllables? Are speech patterns distinct enough—a problem that, by the way, concerned Jane Austen—to allow you occasionally to leave off the "she said," "he said" speech tags?

Many professionals advise reading aloud what your characters are saying. Patricia McGerr, author of a number of murder mysteries, of novels of romantic suspense (as gothics are now called), and of historical novels, as well as of short stories, always pronounces her dialogue aloud as she fashions it. When she was writing her Crime Club mysteries, she would not only read her dialogue aloud, she moved around the room simulating the movements of her murderers and their victims. Thus she not only uttered aloud her characters' threats and cries of terror but also measured out and paced the number of vengeful or evasive moves they were making. Even with her historical novels she recites the dialogue aloud. Further, she memorizes the speeches of her characters before reciting them. She insists upon being independent of the typed page so as to alert her ear to what her people are saying. In advising her students she recommends writing out the speaking parts of the narrative as though it were a play. This forces the imagining of the entire environment of the action.

Getting the dialogue to sound right is important, but it is only the first step. A tool of many uses, dialogue must be purposive to earn its way in narrative. In the stories of Flannery O'Connor, for example, rich idiom rolls off the tongues of the characters; that is their rightness. Further, their language individualizes these characters and identifies their roles in the developing crisis of the story. With what her characters say the author can set forth the basic situation leading to conflict, can develop the plot or display the personality of a character, or give body to the crisis. It is through dialogue more than any other single device that narrative can seem to live and move. As we read we receive ideas, those necessary notions the narrator on the wall wishes to convey obliquely; what comes to us immediately and directly is the human voice.

A master in many things, Henry James was eminently successful in voice projection onto the printed page. As a playwright, oddly enough, James was a conspicuous failure, yet again and again in his novels and stories he succeeded with dramatically effective dialogue. In the following exchange from *Washington Square*, Catherine Sloper's suitor and her father oppose one another in dialogue that demonstrates their conflicting views and moves the plot forward, all without a single wasted word:

> *"I have a great deal at stake."*
>
> *"Well, whatever it is," said the doctor, "you have lost it."*
>
> *"Are you sure of that?" asked Morris. "Are you sure your daughter will give me up?"*
>
> *"I mean, of course, you have lost it as far as I am concerned. As for Catherine's giving you up—no, I am not sure of it. But as I shall strongly recommend it, as I have a great fund of respect and affection in my daughter's mind to draw upon, and as she has the sentiment of duty developed in a very high degree, I think it extremely possible."*
>
> *Morris Townsend began to smooth his hat again. "I, too, have a fund of affection to draw upon," he observed, at last.*
>
> *The doctor at this point showed his own first symptoms of irritation. "Do you mean to defy me?"*
>
> *"Call it what you please, sir. I mean not to give your daughter up."*
>
> *The doctor shook his head. "I haven't the least fear of your pining away your life. You are made to enjoy it."*
>
> *Morris gave a laugh. "Your opposition to my marriage is all the more cruel, then. Do you intend to forbid your daughter to see me again?"*
>
> *"She is past the age at which people are forbidden, and I am not a father in an old-fashioned novel. But I shall strongly urge her to break with you."*

*"I don't think she will," said Morris Townsend.*
*"Perhaps not; but I shall have done what I could."*
*"She has gone too far—" Morris went on.*
*"To retreat? Then let her stop where she is."*
*"Too far to stop, I mean."*
*The doctor looked at him a moment; Morris had his hand on the door. "There is a great deal of impertinence in your saying it."*
*"I will say no more, sir," Morris answered; and, making his bow, he left the room.*

The role of summary in this passage should not be overlooked, scanty as it is. When it is used within scene, summary gives something for the eye to do—in this instance, to see Townsend's hat, to note his hand on the door. In narrative, summary provides focus for the eye while the ear is occupied with dialogue. It is a curious fact about dialogue that no matter how rich in idiom or even expressive in imagery it may be, it tends after a while to become abstract, to make us forget persons and places unless the eye is reminded of them. Without Townsend's hat he and Dr. Sloper might well be voices coming out of a mist; over their lengthy exchange we can hear them and our minds are entertaining concepts of conflict, but we do not *see* them.

Such passages when protracted and unrelieved by summary are as difficult to read as the script of a play. This problem is less likely to occur with the performance of a play than with a story or a novel; after all, on the stage before us we see the actors and the set. The careful placing of summary within scene, the interjection of things for the eye to notice even though the primary message is for the ear, reflects sound psychology. We tend to remember past conversations we have had if we can recall where we were, what someone else was wearing, and what could be seen on the table or out the window. For the same reason we can more thoroughly recall what we have read whenever it has been anchored in visual specification.

Like anything else, dialogue too can be overdone. It is easy, and therefore tempting, once one attains the knack, to spin out page after page of mere conversation, of frothy persiflage calculated to do little more than display the author's cleverness. James warned against relying upon dialogue overmuch, letting it negate the advancement of story, and falling into the mistake of allowing it to substitute for story. It was his conviction that a symbiotic relationship between summary and scene is necessary for story to occur. In spite of his theories, James was occasionally betrayed by his own technical dexterity, most notably in his novel *The Awkward Age*. The following passage from that novel is representative of technique hardened into mannerism:

> "'Mrs. Brook'?" *his friend echoed; staring an instant, as if literally missing the connection; but quickly after, to show he was not stupid—and indeed it seemed to show he was delightful—smiling with extravagant intelligence.* "Is that the right thing to say?"
>
> *Mitchy gave the kindest of laughs.* "Well, I dare say I oughtn't to."
>
> "Oh, I didn't mean to correct you," *his interlocutor hastened to profess;* "I meant, on the contrary, will it be right for me too?"
>
> *Mitchy's great goggle attentively fixed him.* "Try it."
> "To her?"
> "To every one."
> "To her husband?"
> "Oh, to Edward," *Mitchy laughed again,* "perfectly!"
> "And must I call him 'Edward'?"
> "Whatever you do will be right," *Mitchy returned* —"even though it happens to be sometimes what I do."

The discussion directly above, between Mr. Mitchett and another character in the book, one who does not identify himself for four more pages after these confidences, is about a Mrs. Brookenham and whether or not Mitchett's "fellow guest" may presume to use the group's familiar name for her. The passage deserves comparison with the one from *Washington Square* previously quoted. In the former, James—however much one character's speech seems to determine the form, and choice of word, used by the other speaker—does attend to the business of furthering plot complication over a crucial—indeed the central—issue. In the latter, James is unbearably arch and indulgent, down to his use of the subjunctive mode for "happen" in the last line quoted. In his preface to *The Awkward Age* James seems to be justifying a certain technical playfulness:

> *The novel, as largely practiced in English, is the perfect paradise of the loose end. The play consents to the logic of but one way, mathematically right, and with the loose end as gross as impertinence on its surface, and as grave a dishonor, as the dangle of a snippet of silk or wool on the right side of a tapestry.*

Novelists, James goes on to say, are

> *shut up wholly to cross-relations all within the action itself; no part of which is related to anything but some other part—save of course by the relation of the total to life.*

"The relation of the total to life!" There you have it, the goal that related, though varied, techniques of fiction strive for.

To show how scene and summary interact, I have reproduced in their entirety and will examine two short stories. The first is a story that has impressed me since I first read it in a small-circulation magazine, *Washington Review of the Arts*. Shirley Graves Cochrane's "Middle Distance" is told from the first-person angle of narration, one that has the effect of making the narrator a viewpoint character and of having the narrator's introspection erect a kind of constant scene. It should be noted that "Middle Distance" avoids occupying an interior landscape exclusively, of being an interior monologue given movement only through the association of ideas. Instead, it presents a vividly realized exterior landscape as well, a significant achievement for a lightly plotted first-person narrative:

> Coming out of the drugstore I half expect to find your white-heat car still there; instead, a red car is in its slot. I look up and down the street, hoping to see you driving back. Nowhere. I ask myself if anything about this morning has made any sense. The sixty-mile ride? The restaurant with the mounted fish? The snapshots with our *say-cheese* smiles? Whose idea *was* it that I accompany you 1/100 of the way? Mine? ("I can't stand to tell you good-bye, then go lonely back to bed.") Yours? ("Somehow it will be easier to say good-bye on neutral ground.")
>
> ...It began like any other excursion. We drove out of the city at dawn: me a proud child directing you; and like a child, morning-happy. We noted the "Liver and Money Orders" sign over the mom and pop market. Later, the miles of Condominiums Now Selling, the black x's still on their windows. Further on, the hay stacks shaped into giant loaves of bread. Every now and then desperation would stir in me and I would suppress it, like a stern grandma pointing to the family switch.
>
> From the tour book you chose a town "steeped in history"—some place interesting for me to be stranded in. We turned at the green-and-white sign, looped and tunneled our way onto sleeping Main Street where I now stand alone, feeling death seep in...
>
> Maybe I'm coming down with amnesia. My face in all the newspapers:

DO YOU KNOW THIS YOUNG WOMAN?
I practice my name: *Delly Osprey*. I can hear the
magistrate or police chief or head of the mental
health clinic say: "Obviously a fake name..." They
would ask my address and I would have to tell them:
"No. 11 Chansonette Apartments..." Again, they
would suspect faking. My age they would believe.

   ...At my recent 29th birthday party you served
Winston Churchill's favorite champagne. One can-
dle in a round of camembert made a birthday cake.
The apartment still looked like *us*, not just me,
although already you had started packing. And I
was leaving potted plants in laundry room, on roof
garden, beneath trash masher chute, hoping someone would adopt them. If I had to live alone, I would
live unencumbered.

   I didn't blame you for leaving; you didn't blame
me for *not* leaving. At least that was how we played
it. You had your PhD, an offer from the Midwest.
*Take it*, everyone advised, including me. And I had
just been made the assistant assistant to the dean;
given a fancy title and a respectable salary. So it
made sense for me to stay—right? I like a big-city
university; you are drawn to a small town with a
vintage college at its heart. It had been a good two
years. Things end.

   Your car, then, is not on Main Street. We said
good-bye, walked our separate ways. I ducked into a
drug store to buy some giant sun shades. I also
bought a pack of gum, a note pad, and two cheap
pens. One was for you—an excuse to run back to
your car. (You had asked to borrow a pen, I had only
the stub of an eyebrow pencil to lend you. I wanted
to send you on your way equipped for writing.) The
salesgirl, stamping prices, took her time, let you get
away.

I hold the pens now like merchandise samples and clutch my unneeded raincoat like a baby. The hurt hits me full in the belly; too much to stand. Carefully I distance it—deaden the feeling, shift into *mind*.

I cling to the drug store corner like it's home, feel myself dissolving into atoms. Across the street the courtesy bank message changes from July 24 to 8:42 to 75°. I watch the time jump to 8:44, 8:45. Will I watch the temperature rise into the 80's, then the 90's; stand zombie-like while the day shifts to July 24, 25...? *Quick*, click on the brain. *Bus station*, it tells me. Like an automaton I move down the street, mind commanding legs to walk. *This is a historic town*, some cassette inside my head begins. I look around. It isn't a bad town, caught in its pocket of time. Mostly Victorian but ghosted over with Revolutionary and Civil wars.

I pass a dark old-fashioned department store. Built into the sidewalk in front is a mosaic: the founder's name over an urn, worn by the footsteps of generations of shoppers. The store looks like the one in my grandmother's tales of childhood, where they kept the coffins in the back and the final shopping treat was: you got to lie down and pretend dead. I'll come back when the store opens at 9:30 and pretend dead. Unless, of course, I get a bus right out. Something in me wants to linger in this town, find what I'm looking for, what I've lost.

On the next corner is the restaurant where we had breakfast: the Traveller, chrome and glass brick. Picking it out (it was the only thing open) we tried to act like we were at Francois' the first day they put the tables and umbrellas out. The Traveller had orange plastic furniture, orange plaid curtains, orange and blue mounted fish. Seated, we identified the fish on the place mats. You said: "Catfish have a good flavor when cooked right." In my head I made a poem of it:

*Catfish*
*have a good flavor*
*when cooked right.*

I studied this found-poem, found no deep meaning. We discussed river pollution in the midwest. Pure prose. Where had the laughter gone? We ordered hot cakes; me sausage, you bacon.

All this I remember in perfect detail, yet I forget the features of your face. (Distancing again; phase out the important, concentrate on the unimportant.)

As we left the restaurant you got out your camera. *Which way?* you asked, *right or left?*

*Right*, I chose. The handsome federal houses in the first block gave way to shabby Victorian, then to blight. You explained what you had in mind: a square surrounded by old houses comfortably set in time-honored yards, with here and there a side-yard cottage with a to-let sign.

The houses got worse. "Should we turn back?" I wondered aloud.

"Well...no. *Here*." You found the one restored house—brick with an iron fence.

Me first. You posed me, said *smile*, then clicked. Wait one minute, watch out for acid, then zip—instant picture. You waved it dry, handed it to me. Not bad; better than life. *Miss Delly Osprey from the gree-eet stee-et of...* I could almost hear Bert Parks introducing me. Caught up in this absurd narcissism I felt you gently take the picture from me, watched you slip it into your wallet, covering over the picture of me with the lighted camembert birthday cake.

Then your turn. *Back a little*, I ordered, then: *too far*. You tried to follow my contradictory instructions: Closer...farther back; stay...go, back, back...forward a little...

(*Now* I see that all morning I had been distancing you to the point where I could bear the hurt of losing you. For I am a master of the middle distance, adjusting each experience, each sensation, to just midpoint between hurt and happiness. *Why not topple over into hurt or happiness?* I hear you ask. You *did* ask this, in fact, many times; your term, I believe, was *risk*; but part of my distancing technique is, I do not answer hard questions.)

I clicked at last. We went through the same waiting process, then birthed you from the camera. You came out anonymous—some passer-by we might have asked to pose to get the settings right. I wanted to swap: give you your picture, get mine back from you. Instead I put this smiling stranger into my bag. We walked back toward Main Street, then toward the car.

We asked a tall woman for the two sets of directions we needed to get out of town. Like a grade-school teacher she pointed you ahead, to pick up 70 going west; me back two blocks to the bus station. As firm a separation as if we'd been fifth graders caught misbehaving in the multipurpose room. We stepped into an abandoned arcade. (*Not yet, not yet!*) It wasn't much comfort, that second of clinging, trying not to cry. Then you to the car, me to the drugstore. I looked back once—you had turned back too.

...I leave the Traveller Restaurant now, walk on toward the bus station. A large overhead sign points it out, down a side street. It looks like a scaled-down

version of the old Southern RR depot in my
mother's home town. She once told me that when
she was four months pregnant with me, seeing my
daddy off to World War II that final time, she locked
herself in one of the pay toilets of the depot and cried
for an hour. I'm wondering if I might break her
record. What a lot of time women have spent
weeping after gone men!

I enter, approach a tall father-figure, caged
behind iron grillwork. It's clear he does not want to
talk to me, come like a child to pester him. I state my
destination. "No bus till 2:00," he says.

"What'll I *do*?" I wail at him.

He looks at me, penetrates the dark glasses, takes
pity. "You might take a walking tour." He hands me
a brochure. As a further kindness he suggests: "You
could buy your ticket now if you like." I count out
pennies to give him the exact change, make him
daddy-proud of me. He repeats: "2:00 p.m. sharp." I
wind my watch, walk out.

The walking tour brochure instructs me: "Follow
in the footsteps of history." There are two sets of
footprints, a man's, a woman's, weaving in and out
of a miniature street plan, stopping at every shrine.
(Two are meant to go together on this tour.) One
shrine is labeled "Court Square." I decide on that.
Back to Main Street, then up to the Traveller
Restaurant. Once again I am at the corner where you
asked *left or right*? This time the footsteps of history
lead left. One block up is Court Square.

It is a square surrounded by old houses comfortably set in time-honored yards, with here and there a
side-yard cottage. But no *to-let* signs. In every other
way, though, it fits your picture-taking specifications. (Did you fantasize that if we'd found a to-let

sign, we'd settle down together in this random town? The more I think about it, the more I think that was your fantasy.)

One side of the square is taken up with a blood-red courthouse; in front of this is a fountain, where you would surely have posed me. It is an unbelievable fountain. Painted milk-chocolate brown, it is topped by two naked boys, one pouring water from a conch shell down the back of the other. All summer long that water will splash from shoulder to buttocks, then over the clam-shell on which they stand, down to the snub-nose dolphins supporting it. Satyr heads are crudely attached to the pool's edge by heavy screws driven through chin and forehead. There is a brass plaque; rebuilt, 1965, by Ezra Sampson, Jonathan Middleton, Cyrus Feemster. *Why?* we would have asked each other. Why would Ezra Sampson, Jonathan Middleton, Cyrus Feemster have perpetuated this monstrosity? Ordered its paint from sample charts? Supervised the cleaning of pipes, the routing of water, the re-balancing of statuary?

The names of these tasteless restorers would have become a part of our joke stock: "As Cyrus Feemster said to Ezra Sampson as he propped up the fallen statue..." No fun laughing alone at private jokes.

I sit on one of the benches. Heavy metal, curlicued—a bench in a minor English park in Victoria's reign. It is painted milk-chocolate like the fountain. At first I am alone. Then, as in a theatre-in-the-round, a cast of characters begin arriving, making entrances, exits, acting out brief scenes. Politicians to the courthouse, children to Bible School, winos claiming their benches for the long drugged day. Directly across from me a sailor in a navy uniform just like the one in my daddy's last picture sits with his arm around his girl—a rerun from World War II. I feel again the withdrawal pains of love. *So don't look*, my distancing mechanism tells me.

Two women in mail-order house dresses walk by, market baskets on their arms. I hear them chatting about white sales, remember the department store; get up, follow them.

When I arrive at the department store a young man is standing in one of the display windows, bending to pick up handbags as a large lady taps on the glass—*that one, no! the one over there*. He selects, she rejects. I marvel at his patience. He sees me, smiles. He is very handsome; the barometer of my spirits rises. I smile, give him a look of sympathy.

Inside, the round message boxes that were the wonder of my early childhood shoot across walls and ceilings; extinct now, I had thought. Saleswomen introduce themselves—the Miss Betties, Miss Sophies of my grandmother's old store. They escort me to counters, literally wait on me. I play with the costume jewelry, a pair of sale sandals, then ask about potholders (as good a thing as any to buy). A Miss Betty walks me to the elevator. A sign says: "Ring three times for elevator service." I ring three times and the young man I saw in the window appears like the frog prince, already metamorphosized. "Good morning," he says, as though he had been waiting for just this moment. He helps me into the elevator cage, exactly the right size for the two of us. We ascend slowly; there is time to survey each floor through grillwork. It is a narrow store but tall, with several floors of elegant merchandise.

"I could almost say 'Good afternoon.'" The young man startles me.

"Oh?" I wonder if his words have special significance.

"Yes." He consults an old-fashioned gold watch— his denim suit has a vest, complete with watch pocket. "It's two minutes to twelve." I notice that he wears no wedding band. In this kind of town married men wear wedding bands. We come to the floor where linens are sold. "Thank you," he says, opening the grillwork.

I buy potholders and matching tea towels, then ring three times again. The elevator creaks up. Opening the cage the young man says: "*Now* I can say good afternoon."

"So it's after noon?"

"12:11." He sounds pleased with that fact.

I study him. Descendant of Our Founder? We'd have good children, he and I. Our genes would mesh, or whatever genes do.

I linger on the first floor, buy garter supports at the notion counter. Saleswomen call in urgent voices: "Mr. Price, Mr. Price!" and the young man rushes back and forth. "Missed a price, missed a price," is how their voices sound. Each time he passes he gives me the old eye. Leaving the store, I feel I should tell someone good-bye. Heat has taken over the street; merchants lower awnings. Shop owners come out, invite customers in to shop in air-conditioned comfort. I remember my lines, cribbed from my mother's girlhood: "Just looking, thank you"; or: "I'll keep that in mind."

I look for a restaurant that is not the Traveller and find one proclaiming home cooking. The hostess seats me at a table opposite a large painting done directly on the wall (the artist has even painted an ornate gilt frame around it). The inscription reads: "Court Square, *circa* 1890." I study the scene in its disguise of lavender shadows, lemon-yellow walk-ways, Easter-egg buildings. The fountain is battle-ship grey, ringed with lipstick-red tulips. There are no satyr heads—were they beyond the meager talents of the artist, or . . . no, I've *got* it! The satyr heads were purchased in Italy by the wife of Jonathan Middleton, affixed to the fountain by Cyrus Feemster's handyman as the final touch in the 1965 restoration.

In my fancy I can hear your spill of zany laughter, then your tall-tale-telling voice: "And as for the milk-chocolate brown, Ezra Sampson had a paint factory on the edge of town. One day it burned to the ground. Only the brown paint, stored near the door, was saved. So . . ." *Stop it, will you!*

The waitress takes my order, looking at me oddly. The food comes almost at once, the soup du jour so hot it melts the plastic spoon. I cool it with ice; nourish myself on Granny-soup. The potato salad has caraway seeds, the tomatoes have been skinned. The milk foams, fresh and rich, in the plastic glass. I dawdle, smoke two cigarettes, order pie and coffee.

Leaving the restaurant, I meet the young department store executive coming in. He holds the door, says, "Well *hello* there." I smile. Away from the store he looks younger; twenty-five at most. Can Delly Osprey, a twenty-nine-year-old urban spin-ster, find happiness with _____ Price, a slightly younger, small-town merchant heir. (I do not hear your spill of zany laughter.)

He enters the restaurant, keeps his eyes on me as I walk away. My watch says 1:03. His lunch hour, then, is 1:00. Tomorrow I must remember that. *Tomorrow!* I have the better part of an hour before my bus. Will I go to Court Square, stay there until 1:45, then walk back to catch the 2:00 bus? Or will I sit there till 2:30, stop by the local hotel and get a room? A hand keeps waving at the back of my brain—an answer to some question. I take out your picture. Already it is fading; stripped too soon from the camera or peeled too hastily. You are posed self-consciously, my raincoat spiked on the iron fence behind you. That hurt showing beneath your smile—why had I not seen *that*?

(It comes back now: Soon after you accepted the offer from the midwest you said to me: "Wait till I get past the time zone before you find a new man." Funny, until you said that, I had thought *I* was the wounded one. Maybe that was a misunderstanding.)

Carefully I weigh the evidence. It is conclusive: You did not want to leave anymore than I wanted you to. You kept hoping I would come with you, or else ask you to stay. I had not caught the signals. Because a practiced distancer like myself concentrates on safe middle distance, overlooking foreground. *You*—I had missed you. I missed you, I miss you, I shall miss you . . . I want to run the movie of our morning backward: see your white car come backing down the street, into the parking place; have us rush together, not apart, then flip the film until we are riding backwards down the superhighway, past the hay stacks, condominiums, the mom and pop market. The final scene: we walk backwards into our apartment.

But we cannot turn back. Both of us are moving on. Already you are the Kismet of some blonde Miss Middlewestern Corn Queen. And I? Will I stay on in this town? Marry someone like Price the Merchandising Prince? Raise water-fountain boys? I see this as though it were written in a book somewhere:

maybe so, maybe not. Carefully I distance the hurt
that marks the chapter's end.
     Here is the corner where I told you *right*
(wrongly). To the left is Court Square. I shall go
there now, maybe sit until I have safely missed my
bus. In one more second the light will change and I
can cross.
     ... Love, we should have turned *left* here, not
right.


There is so much to be said about "Middle Distance" that one
wonders where to begin. Perhaps the best place is with the
abundance of references, the specific detail. Surely the story's
numerous specifications strike the reader first. They come to
us, to be sure, from Delly Osprey's mind, but we feel that they
are really there, outside her, palpable, and not hallucinations.
It is worth noting that the lovers have chosen a place "steeped
in history" (not in *their* history, which is an ironic
counterpoint) in which to stage their parting. It is also a town
saturated in contemporary realities. We are made to see these,
both as they are and as they are clothed in the narrator's
emotions. They exist in and for themselves—like the man
behind the grillwork—and as a reproach to "I" and "you" and
their history. The town knows where it has been and where it is
going; but for Delly the images from her past are beginning to
blur, and the future is a matter of frightened, almost hysterical,
speculation.
     The controlled emotion in this story is especially notable.
What might have been an exercise in self-pity is, instead,
emotion proudly held back. In this story, mind is made to
conquer emotion. The story's intellectual core is the concept of
"distancing," the narrator-protagonist's determination to
master her grief and sense of loss. At times, of course, her
affliction is intensified by something seen or remembered;
then—suspense is at work—it is once again deflected. "Middle

Distance" contains several objective correlatives for the narrator's sorrow. Perhaps the most powerful of these is the childhood memory of the grandmother's tale of the store in which "the final shopping treat was: you got to lie down and pretend dead." This is throughout the story a half-considered option for the adult narrator.

Most instructive, as is often the case when one analyzes fiction, is a consideration of the roads not taken. The man in the story—"you"—is not seen; he is present as a ghost, felt rather than seen. Should the author have made him more tangible, do you think, giving us a clear look at him, enabled us to hear him in, say, three or four cutting speeches near the end? As one thinks about this—and in reading fiction critically one should consider the options not taken up as well as those that are—it will be seen that the impact of the narrator's isolation is considerably enhanced by the man's absence, even in memory. Mr. Price and the milk-chocolate-brown water fountain are the realities now.

The final paragraphs of "Middle Distance" are also worth noting. If there has been a kind of strategy of delay before, of the protagonist's wish to make the lover's presence last by lingering on this constantly evocative "neutral ground," now the intention is to have done with past and present too. "But we cannot turn back." These words announce a resolution and an ending. The final three paragraphs, the second shorter than the first and the last only a sentence long, give visual speed to the intention. These paragraphs also recapitulate what has gone before, after a moment of ironic speculation about the future, with a reference to the "water-fountain boys," the final of many images, and end with a deft quibble about right (wrong) and left. (If you had written the story, would you have entitled it "Middle Distance" or "Right or Left"? Why?)

It might be found useful to reread "Middle Distance" at a time you set aside for writing practice and to "take notes" on a theoretical genesis for this story. Write, if this idea appeals to you, a dossier of the "I" narrator, Delly Osprey, "inventing" an age and physical appearance for her, detailing her social and educational background, and, in a paragraph or two, giving the particulars of the length and ambience of the relationship that she has had with "you." Then, searching the original text carefully for clues, write a similar dossier for "you." Try, for a few paragraphs, and again solely as a private exercise, blocking out this same basic story as told from (1) the omniscient third-person angle of narration and (2) the third-person angle with "you" as viewpoint character.

The author of "Middle Distance" writes that the analysis of her story given above "revealed many things about the story that I myself was not fully aware of. For instance, the references to the coffins and pretending dead—I had not seen this as the symbol it so obviously is. I *was* consciously aware of the importance of father-loss in Delly Osprey's life. Her father had been killed in World War II, and this early father-loss accentuated Delly's hurt over the loss of her lover. The final line of the story I took out and put back in a dozen times. Now I feel it definitely belongs there. It is a *cri du coeur*—a last show of emotion before the middle-distancing becomes irreversible. 'Delly is a tough gal,' the editor told me, 'in a good kind of way.' I think so too. I am glad I got to know her and to share her life for a while."

To my request for comment on the story's textual history, Shirley Graves Cochrane replied: "The story was originally much longer. I am grateful to the fiction editor of *Washington Review of the Arts*, Patricia Griffith, for showing me the best ways to cut it. Sometimes I would say *ouch*, and she would let me retain that particular thing. Interestingly enough, there were some things that I took out that she wanted reinstated. I had cut the passage where the 'you' says: 'Wait till I get past the time zone before you find a new man,' but she telephoned to urge me to put it back in. I now see that these words show us Delly's need for a man and at the same time give us one of the few glimpses of the 'you'—of which there are, perhaps, too few.

Other references are: 'his spill of zany laughter,' a sample of his fantasy talk; the camembert birthday cake (showing whimsy); his reference to catfish (a certain practicality, even in stress); and his specified setting for the picture-taking (found too late). Put all these together and you have at least a rough idea of his character. Is it a defect that he is not more closely delineated? I think perhaps it is. I wish I had found a way of bringing him alive, despite the length limitations of the short story and Delly's own distancing of him. Perhaps a short but vivid physical description would have helped."

The first-person approach to narrative undoubtedly recommends itself for the ease and authority it supplies the writer. I am I, and they are they; nothing could be more natural. Certainly there are stories dwelling in our minds and notebooks that come from such intimate wells of feeling they demand to be told in the first person. When the demand is strong, when the formal requirement seems as pressing as the need to have the story told, one has a call to be obeyed. Of course there are other stories one has to tell, equally intimate, which somehow seem false if told from the first-person angle. Then one will wish to call upon another angle, to treat oneself as other. There are times when creativity demands that I *become* the other, and substitute the enigma of another personality for the enigma of self. My second demonstration of approach to narrative is one for which I can give strict genetic account; it is intended to show the third-person viewpoint character approach. Entitled "A Princess in Thrall, " it was first published in *Four Quarters*, a small-circulation magazine:

Around the time she became twelve, Helen began having the dream. Whether it came to her at night soon after she fell asleep, or in the morning just before she woke, she could never determine. But night after night for over a year now, the dream would come.

The worst of it was the silence. First, Danny would be in his little rocking chair, rocking, rocking, and only she would hear. And then, in the dream, the furniture would begin gliding.

She could never bring herself to talk about the dream, even to Danny. After, in the dream, Danny's chair stopped soundlessly rocking, there would be a pause. Then she and Danny would go hand in hand to the door of another room. The rug, elevated about two inches from the floor, would glide out, with the furniture on it. And another set of furniture would glide silently in. There would be other people, strange, silent people, in the room. This would happen to the other rooms, until there would be strange families in all the rooms but one.

In the dream Helen hated the silence, but during the daytime she dreaded noise. Her parents' angry voices, her father's slamming of the front door—it happened this morning, as on most mornings—these noises she did not mind. But the ringing of the doorbell, the summons of the telephone—these were signs of the silent people. This morning the telephone rang, and Helen, when she answered it, recognized the soft sliding voice of Mrs. McGettrick.

As she laid the receiver on the mahogany veneer table, Helen heard the thin voice talking into the table polish. "You there, Alice? It's about Jerry and that woman again."

Her mother came into the room then, wiping her hands on a square of paper towel. She let it drop to the floor. Then, motioning Helen out of the room, she picked up the receiver.

Helen waited expectantly in the kitchen, and sure enough her mother began shouting and throwing things. Crash! That must be Daddy's picture, Helen thought. It was near the telephone. Next the sound of books. School books too, probably. This would be an excuse... but she decided not to go in. Then her mother slammed the receiver down.

Helen got out of the kitchen in time. Methodically her mother was taking dishes from the shelves and breaking them one by one.

Will she stop at seven? Eight. Nine. It was fourteen the last time.

Then there was silence. Silence as shocking as the noiseless rocking in Helen's dream.

It was then that Helen had started washing the outside windows.

Helen climbed her ladder and looked into the kitchen. Her mother was on one knee, dustpan and brush in her hands. She was picking up the stalagmites and stalactites of china splintered and shimmering on the linoleum floor. To Helen, behind the window glass, her mother looked like some fairy princess who has a puzzle to work out. Fit the pieces together, and the enchantment works. The cottage turns into a castle, or the bird on the lawn becomes a prince from a far country.

Helen's mother tapped on the window with the nail of an index finger. Helen looked in. Her mother was smiling and saying something. They both tried to lift the window at the same time.

"I'll make sandwiches," her mother said when the window was up, "and then we can go."

To the river? Usually they didn't take sandwiches. It was only four blocks and not worth the trouble. "We'll eat here," her mother would say when they would be going to the river. "We're not millionaires." Still, sometimes she would put up a lunch, and they'd buy soda pop at Gormley's store only a block before you get to the river.

"You'll have to come and get dressed for it."

"The river? For the river?"

"We'll have to take the trolley. Your father has the car, of course."

They couldn't be going to the river, then. There was no trolley car to it. It wasn't but four blocks. From the roof of the garage you could almost see it. Well, honestly, it was too low to see, but you could make out the roofs of some of the houses on the far bank. They were on a hill, standing high above the railroad tracks that crossed the river and looped their way north.

"Do I tell Danny to come in yet?"

Helen's mother shook her head. Wear your blue dress. And see if your bathing suit still fits you."

"*Bathing* suit! Oh, *Mother!*"

But her mother brushed aside Helen's pleasure with a brusque hand. That was one of her unspoken rules. *I* haven't any reason to be happy, her thin, sullen mouth would signify, so why should *you* be happy? Helen had learned to crush signs of joy, but sometimes happiness was so unexpected, so exquisite.

For the next hour the grim business of "getting ready" went forward. When, out of a dining-room window, Helen saw Danny coming into the house, she waved him away. He mustn't spoil things. Not now.

Helen caught sight of Robert, Danny's turtle, moving about in his shallow pan. His water was pink with the disintegrated raw hamburger floating around in it. I'll wash Robert's pan out and put fresh water in it, she thought. Mother is upstairs. Here's my chance. Carefully, so as not to let the stones slide against the metal and give out an alarm, she carried the pan into the kitchen. Quickly she took Robert up to the sink, fencing him in with soap-powder boxes. Then she poured the soiled water into the sink. She washed all Robert's stones, one by one, dried them, and placed them back in the pan. "We're going to the beach, Robert," she said softly. Robert balefully tried to crawl to freedom.

Danny knocked at the back door. Their signal. One. Then two. Then three quick ones together.

Helen spoke to him through the closed door. "Sit on the back steps, Danny. We're going someplace. I'll call you when you're to come in."

She could hear the sounds of his retreat through the hallway. From the thump he made, she guessed he was skipping. The screen door closed after him, cautiously. Poor kid, she thought. What fun does he get out of life?

When she turned around, her mother was in the room.

"I'll get that mess up, Mother," Helen said, rushing over to the sink.

Her mother was peering over at Robert. He was still trying to escape. "He never can make it, can he, Helen?" her mother said. "No matter how often he tries. Just like your father." Helen's mother lowered one of the boxes and watched Robert try painfully for leverage. His wet, sticky legs kept waving, uncoordinated, one at a time.

"We'll put him back now, Helen. He's had his little outing."

Helen did not dare to look at her mother. The slight, half-hysterical edge to her voice was a familiar warning.

Helen turned on the faucet, and fresh water came into Robert's pan. Her mother placed the turtle into the pan with surprising gentleness. "Good work,

Helen," she said. Helen scanned her face for irony.

"It's all right to let Danny in now. And put Robert back. Set him near the window so the sun can get at him."

Helen took the pan and placed Robert on a chair in the next room. Then she went into the kitchen again and out into the hall. Please, please, she prayed, don't let her change her mind now. Make this a nice afternoon.

Danny stood up as soon as he heard her coming. Without a word he followed her into the house. They went upstairs. Helen dressed Danny, found his bathing suit for him, and left him quietly drawing in a coloring book.

A few minutes later, just as Helen finished dressing, their mother called up to them. When Helen and Danny came down together, they found their mother waiting.

They watched her gravely as she twisted her head to look up at them. She is wearing a turban again, Helen thought. How I wish she wouldn't. Her mother's mouth was a vivd red oblong, and when she smiled, Helen saw lipstick smeared on her teeth. She had on a white blouse and a peasant skirt.

"The lunch," she said, indicating the hamper beside her on the sofa. It is as though she were the child, thought Helen, hoping for our approval. Helen felt a quick desire to say, "No. No, we can't go."

"I'll check the back door," she said.

"Let me," Danny said, and darted out of the room. Their mother was already on the front porch when Danny got back. "I've got a surprise for you," Danny's secret signal to Helen said.

They had luck with the bus and streetcar. Their

mother let them sit where they wished. Even when
Danny knelt on the seat and practically hung his
head out the window, she said nothing. I can't figure
her out, Helen thought. She's smiling. Smiling to
herself. She even seems happy.

They came at last, through swamps and grassy
places, to the little wayside station for Twin Beach.
They had several yards to go through bald patches of
sand and clumps of tall grass before they came to the
steps that leveled off to the beach itself. The beach
was divided in half by a sand spit with a promontory
at the end of it. At high tide there was just one beach.

Helen and Danny turned their eyes resolutely
away when they passed the casino. It was their part
of the bargain, they both felt, not to "want"
anything.

But her mother put her hand on Helen's arm. "Get
Danny a pail and shovel," she said.

Helen took the half dollar from her mother's
hand. In a minute she was back with a pail and
shovel for Danny.

"Thank you, Mommy," Danny said, not taking
his eyes away from Helen's face. He did not reach
out for the pail. "Take it," Helen said roughly,
forcing his hand to grasp the pail handle.

"You two wait here a minute," their mother said,
and she started down to the picnic grove. Helen
watched the short, turbaned figure making its way
down the decline. Danny thrust his pail toward
Helen for inspection. Robert, his head and feet
tucked sullenly out of sight, lay like a stone in the
bottom of the pail. "She's going over to the parking
lot," Helen told Danny. "Get your feet out, you
dumb turtle," Danny said happily into the pail's
resounding hollow.

As they watched, their mother came back into

sight again. When she arrived at the picnic benches, she waved to them and sat down.

Hand in hand Helen and Danny came down the hill toward their mother. The sun was hot in the sky, and the tall grasses snapped at Helen's bare legs as she made her way doggedly down the hill.

"Will she mind if she finds out about Robert?" Danny asked, turning his pale face toward his sister. His freckles stood out like little brown coins.

"I don't know, Danny. Don't ask me. I just don't know."

But their mother was smiling at them. She didn't seem to notice Danny and his pail. Instead, she drew Helen to her after taking the lunch basket and placing it on the picnic table. Helen saw that her mother had her sunglasses on now, and that one of the bows was not over her ear but resting on the turban.

"It's M-8834, all right, Helen," her mother said. "Yes, indeedy, good old M-8834."

"That's ours," Helen said softly so Danny would not hear. "Our license plate."

"Yes." Her mother made a gay smile. "How jolly," she said.

Helen's eyes questioned her mother. But her mother bent down to Danny, who quickly put his pail behind him. "We're the three wise monkeys, aren't we, Danny boy? We don't see it, we don't hear it, we don't say it."

Helen started to open the lunch basket. "Later," her mother said. "I've changed my mind." Then she took Danny by the hand and walked down the slope to the sandy beach. Helen picked up the lunch basket and followed them. "I am a princess," she told herself. "A princess in thrall."

To Helen's surprise, her mother rented a beach

umbrella from a lifeguard. He carried the umbrella in a big barrow painted red and blue. Their mother gaily directed that the umbrella be set quite close to the water, at a spot which had a commanding view of the entire beach.

"Now you'd better go and get your suit on. We'll hold the fort, won't we, Danny?" Danny waved his shovel at Helen. Then he got busy digging a nice big hole for Robert.

Helen turned once and looked at them, and her glance took in the entire beach, twin beaches still, with its two dozen or so people, some of them racing back and forth or playing with beach balls. Most were wearing sweaters over their suits. Only a very few were in the water.

Quickly, efficiently, Helen slipped on her bathing suit in the bathhouse. She kept her dress on, as the nuns had taught her to do, and she had her bathing suit on and in place, all but for the buttoning of the straps, before she took her dress off and hung it beside her underclothes. She locked the door to the bathhouse, and then unstrapping her left shoulder strap, but not letting it fall down, she slipped the key chain around it.

While she was walking gingerly through the low pool of water separating the bathhouse runway from the beach, she noticed a tall woman in a white bathing suit a few feet ahead of her. The woman had a white towel wrapped around her head like a turban. A moment later she brushed the towel back with one hand and it fell to her shoulders. Helen was admiring the woman's beautiful red hair when the thought struck her: Why, that's Mrs. Morgan. I know her, she lives in our neighborhood.

Mrs. Morgan stepped out onto the beach. A man was standing with his back to the bathhouses, surveying the beach. He was wearing blue trunks, and he had a Panama hat on his head. Mrs. Morgan went up to the man and threw her towel at him. "Boo!" she said. The man caught the towel expertly without a backward glance.

As the couple went away together hand in hand, Helen suddenly knew that she had seen her father.

"One," she began counting. "Two," and she counted each slow step down to the gay beach umbrella thrust near the water's edge. "Twelve." She could see the two figures before her, making their way slowly to her right as they went toward the narrow sand spit leading to the rocky promontory. "Sixteen." She could ask to go home. She was feeling sick all of a sudden, she could say. One foot ahead of the other. "Twenty." She kept on, pausing occasionally while people passed by dragging their umbrellas after them and trailing deep wakes in the soft brown sand.

Her mother was standing in front of their umbrella, her eyes shaded by her hand, apparently peering at a sailboat which could be seen at the line where the sea and the sky came together.

Helen began to run. "Let's go home now, Mother," she said. "I want to go home now."

Her mother turned, and her mouth was open in a smile. But her eyes were not smiling. "You've seen them too, hey? You've seen them."

Two young men, kicking up soft sand, came between Helen and her mother on their way to the water.

"Helen," her mother said in a low voice, "I want you to look at this." Still smiling, she took Helen by the arm. "Look again. I want you to remember. Always."

"Mother, please! Please! Come away, Mother!"

"I want you always to remember it." Her mother pointed to the two figures, now quite alone as they climbed the rocky promontory. "You're never to forget it."

Helen broke away from her mother's grasp and started running toward the bathhouse. "Helen!" she heard behind her. It was Danny, rushing toward her. "Helen, it's Robert! He got away!" When she came to the place Danny pointed out to her, the turtle had already slipped out to the open sea.

Now this story is third person, and yet I myself am Helen. (I am also her mother and her brother Danny.) Helen's story came to me out of a moment of casual observation when I was a young newspaper reporter—"shore correspondent" was the descriptive title—in Connecticut. At one of my beaches I saw a young woman sitting on the sand; her two children were annoying her, one whining something I could not make out. After a second glance I passed on, and so far as I know I never saw them again. For some reason the image of that woman and her children remained with me. After some time I decided to tell that woman's story. But what was it? (Probably there was no story at all; the woman took them home and fed them or made them take a nap or something.) I could not rest until I found out the story. I would have to invent the facts.

It occurred to me to wonder where her husband was. When I asked myself that question, and answered it, I had a story. I decided that he would be present and there would be another woman with him. I had the conflict now, and with it dozens of possibilities for working it out. I could have had a melodramatic ending, a killing (something that never occurred to me until now); I could have had a tearful rejection scene; I could have had a reconciliation. But I would have had to know much more about the lives of the three adults than I really cared to know or to imagine. Then I thought of Helen. It would be told from her point of view; then what remained a mystery to me, the full characters of my three adults, could reasonably remain a mystery to her also.

Beginning with Helen, as I reconstruct it all now, allowed for another beginning. Starting the story at that point—with Helen on the morning of the visit to the beach—I was close enough to the climax of the story. I had determined that what would be a chance discovery for Helen would be an intentional one for her mother. Feeling the need of an innocent bystander, I invented Danny. Fragments of memory and autobiographical fact got into it. Helen's dream was one of my own; the turtle was a composite of many; Danny was myself, I suppose, and, surely, my brother. The beach was real; basically real, but I moved the topography around a little. Of Helen's mother (I never knew her name or surname) my wife said to me once, "That woman is a combination of me and your mother." I must admit that Robert is an odd name for a turtle. I cannot recall why I gave the turtle its name; but all the rest I recall and have been at pains to represent truly. These elements all came together and made a story; this is one way—perhaps not the best—a story can be made.

Both "Middle Distance" and "A Princess in Thrall" are examples of what is known as the literary story. Both attempt to give a faithful and precise rendering of life itself. Everything in "A Princess in Thrall" really "happened" once it became part of the fictional construct, took on an identity more real than the mere swatches of autobiography used to make up the whole cloth. In general it can be said that the literary story, the so-called, serious story, derives directly from life. Fidelity to reality is the writer's goal. There is another kind of short fiction, still published although less widely so than formerly, which is essentially a parody of life and not the real thing. It takes a sentimental, unrealistic view of everything it touches. Here, from an unpublished story, is a brief example: "She gave the impression of some gaily decorated fair balloon lightly touching ground, as lightly pulling its flags and ribbons gently upward into adjacent, familiar air." In this sentence words are calling too much attention to *themselves* and away from reality. This kind of fiction is variously designated popular, in kindly terms; and "slick," in less kindly.

The difference between the two can be most clearly seen in the use of language. Literary fiction, when it succeeds, weds language and event: the fresh, precise, unhackneyed, living word and the thing itself as it lives in nature. Popular fiction relates to life indirectly, and inflated words. It reflects words, phrases, and attitudes used many times over. It can be clever, it can amuse; but its references are to other writers, other stories—not to life. The opening paragraph of a light work of fiction of my own will serve to illustrate the "slick" approach:

> *The late summer sun commanded a cloud-edged sky. Now and then a benign breeze came up to stir the tree branches into playful motion. Shadows pencilled shafts of coolness across an expanse of ivy-bordered lawn. Somewhere near Adrian Pond and hidden under a fluted canopy of fern, a frog croaked. All was serene without being sedative; mellow, yet briskly so, not melancholy. A scene to walk through with head and purpose high.*

The intention here is to call attention to the words themselves rather than to present language as a direct transmission from life. The presence of alliteration ("serene," "sedative"; "mellow," "melancholy") provides clue enough to this intention.

Which form one prefers is largely a matter of style. For both kinds of stories the rule is inflexible: the choice of words must embody the author's intent. If the work is on the level of craftsmanship (as honorable a goal as any other), then the words must be crafted, and appear to be crafted. This requires a polish that calls attention to the words—not entirely separate from the object of course—as part of the object, and integral to the total effect. If, on the other hand, the work is to be on the level of art, the words employed must appear to sink into the object, so that it alone appears to be present. Here the communication is direct. That which has been experienced by the writer, and that alone, is being experienced by the reader. These two remain: style and event. Where event is striking, dramatic, and memorable in its nature, style may be allowed to be secondary. Event will carry the thing off, dragging style with it. But where nothing is happening, style must come, with precision and vigor, to the rescue. For both, the well making of what is made is the writer's challenge. In the task of making lies the writer's fulfillment.

## SUGGESTED FOLLOW-UP
## FOR THIS CHAPTER

### 1. *What to read*
There are a few outstanding books for beginning writers of fiction. A browser's deskbook, *Fiction Writer's Handbook* (Harper & Row, 1975) by Hallie and Whit Burnett, for many years co-editors of the landmark magazine *Story*, is full of wise observations that are not only practical but go to the philosophical heart of the creative process. Seán O'Faoláin's *The Short Story* (Devin-Adair Company, 1974), by one of the contemporary masters of the short story, contains a probing analysis of the art of fiction and is accompanied by a minianthology of eight classic short stories by writers from Chekhov to Hemingway. And Eudora Welty's *The Eye of the Story* (Random House, 1978) is a collection of illuminating essays and reviews including the essay entitled "Place in Fiction," which is a modern classic.

As for magazines, read those you hope to sell to. Also read magazine nonfiction, looking out for new themes for fiction. Newspapers are another good source of story ideas.

## 2. *What to write*

As a finger exercise, try turning "Middle Distance" into a
one-act play; experiment by casting your play both with and
without the "you" character. In one version confine the action
to one scene and set; in another, to two. Try a one-set (Helen's
house *or* the beach) treatment of "A Princess in Thrall,"
experimenting with methods of conveying what goes on in the
other place; test ways of revealing matters handled in the story
through the viewpoint character device.

After typing up the final draft of a story and before
sending it out, check for the following:

consistency in angle of narration

consistency of tone

sufficient scenic treatment—
no necessary scenes left to summary

consistency of dialogue and
clarity in who says what

appropriateness of title

## 3. *Where to send it*

Below are profiled, from guidelines sent out by their editors,
five markets for short fiction hospitable to the beginning
writer:

*The Elks Magazine*, Donald Stahl, editor. 425 West Diversey
Parkway, Chicago, Illinois 60614. Monthly; circulation 1.6
million. A general interest magazine with emphasis on family
readership. Fiction "can be mystery, drama, humor or satire.
Must be of high guality, with appeal to the entire family. Up to
2,000 words." Buys First North American Serial Rights; rates
start at ten cents a word. S.A.S.E. "a must."

*Ellery Queen's Mystery Magazine*, Eleanor Sullivan, managing editor. 360 Lexington Avenue, New York, New York 10017. Monthly: circulation 340,000. Open to new writers as well as "name" writers. "We have no editorial taboos except those of bad taste. We publish every type of mystery: the suspense story, the psychological study, the deductive puzzle—the gamut of crime and detection from the realistic (including the policeman's lot and stories of police procedure) to the more imaginative (including 'locked rooms' and 'impossible crimes'). We need private-eye stories, but do not want sex, sadism, or sensationalism-for-the-sake-of-sensationalism. We are especially interested in 'first stories'— by authors who have never published fiction professionally before—and have published more than 500 first stories." Preferred lengths: 4,000–6,000 words; short shorts 1,500–2,000 words. "Authors retain all subsidiary and supplementary rights, including movies and television (a remarkable number of stories from *EQMM* have appeared and are still appearing on TV)." Rates: three cents to eight cents a word.

*Leatherneck*, Ronald D. Lyons, editor, Box 1775, Quantico, Virginia 22134. Monthly; circulation 50,000. "We have recently entered the fiction market again, to a limited extent. Stories must have a strong Marine Corps slant and be in good taste. Humor is encouraged." Length: 1,000–3,000 words. Pays: $100–$200.

*Modern Maturity*, Hubert C. Pryor, editor. 215 Long Beach Boulevard, Long Beach, California 90802. Fiction suitable for older readers. Length: 1,000–1,500. Pays: $50 and up.

*Yankee*, Judson D. Hale, editor. Dublin, New Hampshire 03444. Monthly; circulation 750,000. Fiction "must be placed in New England either by specific location, general reference, or simply in a New England–type setting. Or, if a city, then a New England city. Prefer 3,000 word limit." Pays: $600.

Wherever you send your manuscript, check to be sure that you have the correct information on acceptable lengths. Whenever possible direct your manuscript to an individual, not an address only. After you send it, do not sit back and wait. Write another story.

# CHAPTER 10
# BRAINCHILD:
# IT'S A BOOK!

Our underlying premise, prudently qualified of course, has all along been this: You too can write. So long as your aims, in the beginning at least, are moderate, this is a defensible, arguable, even demonstrable thesis. To test this proposition somewhat, let us push it to the extreme: You too can write a book. Again, within reasonable limits, this is a responsible statement. Given the ability to write logical, coherent prose, the patience to engage in adequate and accurate research, and most of all the industry to persist against discouragement and delay, you too can write a book. Yet you may not, equally responsibly, wish to do so. Although writing a book is an enterprise that falls within your power, you may lack the time or the incentive to embark upon so demanding a project. You may quite sensibly decide that for you the cost in time and energy is far too high for the return in satisfaction and financial compensation, but that is another matter. It remains true that if you make the planning and execution of a book serious goals, you can reasonably hope to attain royalty publication of your manuscript.

More than that, it is possible to publish a book with greater surety and ease than it is to gain entrance to the top-paying, top-circulation magazine market. A statement like this, although not recklessly made, calls for some scrutiny. What am I claiming? Merely that you can write a nonfiction book meeting standards of quality and have it accepted for publication—and yet be unable to place an article on the same subject in a mass-circulation magazine? The answer, for many reasons, is yes. Not that magazine standards are superior: they are merely different. The magazine world and the book world are not the same, and their rules and usages, quite naturally, differ widely. For one thing, a magazine article is not, when it reaches publication, a whole but merely a part, one that must fit into a scheme of things not under the writer's control. Another holds the shaping hand.

The book writer enjoys a freedom from restraint and uniformity that the magazine contributor does not know. This includes a blessed freedom from the "graphics" that more and more surround, sometimes to the point of negating, the magazine writer's contribution. Try finding an article or story in a slick-paper magazine. It is all tricked out with illustrations and typography. Magazine editors, it is notorious, dread a "gray page"—all words and no embellishments. A book is nothing, happily, but one gray page after another. Most of all—and this is a significant consideration for the beginner— the book writer has no close-up competition (none of the pages in the book are by another), no regular contributors or contributing editors, no "name" writers to be measured against, as inevitably happens with submission to a national magazine.

To place these matters in perspective, the writing of a nonfiction book is, as it has always been, a branch of journalism and not automatically, at least not notably, an intended contribution to literature. What is being fashioned, usually, is not art but something equally useful and, it must be admitted, something even more eagerly sought: information. Just as it is the aspiration of art to be permanent, it is the nature of information to be replaceable. Book journalism differs from newspaper journalism only in enjoying a somewhat longer period of relevance. The free-lancer benefits from society's constant need for updated information or for new contexts for information already available. Fact, unlike fiction, requires constant rewriting. Therefore books to fill the communications gap between the originator and the consumer of information will always be in demand.

The same kind of subject that attracts the writer as being potential material for an article is likely to be a subject that can also readily yield a book. The same bump of curiosity, the pressing, personally felt "need to know" that often initiates a magazine article can be sufficient motive for writing a book—particularly a how-to, or self-help type of book. Leo Rosten, in characterizing himself, vividly identifies the ideal receptivity of the nonfiction book writer: "I am a hopeless *naïf*, spellbound by the history of the umbrella or the floating lanterns of Japan." Of his anthology of wit and wisdom drawn from a half century of reading, *Infinite Riches* (McGraw-Hill, 1979), he grandly, pertinently observes: "It is *exactly* the bedside reader I so often wished someone would give me on my birthday."

Writers of informative nonfiction are continually saying, in conversation and in print: "I wrote this book because I was looking for information on the subject and could not find a book that contained it. What information was available was partial, and scattered all over the place. So I started looking around, and I began to dig." Self-serving as this may sound, it does not misrepresent what frequently happens. A point to consider is that the writer of nonfiction, far more than that profitable dreamer, the writer of fiction, is a compulsive reader. He or she lives by soaking up information, tentacles always out and waving for the elusive fact, the explanatory theory. The constant search for information, the hospitality to fact, will inevitably lead the alert writer to a sense of a general need, to an awareness of what is in the air, to the topic everyone has questions about—and no answers. The result may well be the decision to attempt to fill that need with a book.

Obviously, a dart-board approach is not what is called for. The beginning writer, particularly, will be misguided to pick a subject for a book totally at random or as the consequence of casual observation of its frequency in the headlines. There should be a natural affinity between the book and its writer, even when the book is not spontaneous, not the product of compulsion a book of poems or a novel might conceivably be, but a willed object. There comes a time, and it arrives early, in the note-taking stage when you and the subject are one. You have formed an alliance, often through a hobby, or it could be a curiosity that has been repeatedly excited, or a strong intellectual or emotional interest of long standing.

Several categories of how-to books would seem to be already overcrowded, and perhaps one should not contemplate adding to their number unless one's inner drive is overwhelming. The supply of cookbooks, for example, would appear to be an instance of glut. No publisher's list seems complete without a cookbook on it, and the uninitiated might be tempted to think that writing a cookbook would be ridiculously easy. Something new in a cookbook would take not only a knowledge of how to cook but a fat file of attractive recipes, collected no doubt through inheritance and years of research; it would also require a witty approach. Given these factors, a new cookbook could make its way. Novelist Hallie Burnett proves the point. Two of her many books are cookbooks; they are titled *The Daughter-in-Law Cookbook* and *Millionaire's Cookbook*. Relying upon far more than a memorable title, each of these books succeeded because of focus and concept. Their author had an idea that was precise, fresh, and original. And best, the idea was fully executed.

A survey of recent (1979) publishers' catalogs reveals a variety of titles which would seem to be giving subjects their first book-length treatment. Adrianne Marcus, who has published several books of poetry, entered the nonfiction lists with *The Chocolate Bible* (Putnam's), a guide to chocolate-making in the United States, Canada, and Europe, in what the publisher calls "an exquisite chocolate bonbon of a book." The book is something of a surprise in these calorie-conscious times. From Houghton Mifflin comes a self-help book written by a writer whose previous books are in another field, gardening: Frances Tenenbaum's *Over 55 Is Not Illegal: A Resource Book for Active Older People*. Many will agree that here is an idea whose time has come. *Everything You Wanted to Know About Your Husband's Money ... and Need to Know Before Your Divorce*, by Shelley Eichenhorn and Gerson Geltner, is billed by the publisher, Thomas Crowell, as "the first book" to deal with the "financial breakup of a marriage, and the future security of the wife."

Books of the type we have been discussing come from two sources: special ideas and special experiences (although even the "idea" books have their origin in experience). Two examples of the former are Edward Trapunski's *Special When Lit: A Visual and Anecdotal History of Pinball* (Doubleday), a subject that might not occur to most people, and Donald Carroll's *Dear Sir, Drop Dead!* (Macmillan) a selection of hate mail through the ages, a book item that might possibly occur to many. From long experience—here the idea for a book was presumably long in coming—*College Knowledge* by Michael Edelhart, a paperback original from Doubleday, presents "everything you need to know about every conceivable subject—studying, sex, parents, work and travel opportunities, motorcycles, plants, drugs and booze, living on or off-campus, self-image, entertainment, exercise, and preparing for the big job hunt." This is the first book of an editor and free-lance journalist. Again, *Make Your Own Convenience Foods* by Don and Joan German (Macmillan) is the result of eighteen years of home cooking in preparing their own "fast foods."

Subjects for books, it is clear, are all around you. You may not need to journey beyond the room you work in to find a fitting subject, one that engages your interest and imagination. The subject may be facing you in the morning's mail (a practical book on how to avoid recieving junk mail, or how to turn it into a source of energy might attract a wide public). Your subject may leap out at you from your newspaper or television set, or arise out of a comment made on your doorstep. A book may result from idle curiosity (no curiosity is truly idle for the writer), or from a painful personal experience. Your motive for writing it may be to inform others about a pleasant discovery, or you may write to inform or warn others about problems of health or personal safety. You may undertake to write a book because you feel that you must, are impelled to share a hurtful or tragic experience—to give help and comfort to others.

A striking, original idea is the first requisite for the making of a book that will inform, entertain, or inspire. The second requirement is a commitment that subordinates everything else to it, which will eat up many months, even some years, of exhaustive and exhausting work. Extensive library and field research may form the next sobering step after the heady exhilaration of being visited by the germ idea for a book. "More than three years have passed," writes Nan Tillson Birmingham in her preface to *Store* (Putnam's, 1979), "since my cousin, Nancy Adams Holliday, and I reminisced about stores we had loved and shopping trips we had taken and she said, 'Someone ought to write a book....' Since that California summer evening in 1975 I have traveled thousands of miles throughout the United States. I've toured stores, practically lived in many, attended store promotions and openings, and interviewed hundreds of people in merchandising, fashion, design, architecture, and city planning. I was fortunate enough to be able to gather further information relating to American retailing and fashion in England, France, Italy, Scandinavia, and India."

The preface of *Store* goes on to acknowledge—with an eloquence that suggests relief over a project finally completed—the author's indebtedness to many people and research sources. Among the library sources acknowledged are those of the microfilm section of the New York Public Library and the resources of the Museum of the City of New York, the Metropolitan Museum Costume Institute, and the University of California Oral History Department. "The one thing that almost brought this project to a total halt," the author tells us, "was the enormity of the subject that I had undertaken to write about." As often happens, the making of hard decisions turned out to be a crucial part of the writing process. "The most painful job for me," Nan Tillson Birmingham writes, "was the elimination of material. I alone made the decisions about what is included in this book." The author's resolution to embark upon her book was doubtless taken lightly at first, and probably—no writer, however experienced, really anticipates all that a book project will entail—without any notion that her book would require extensive travel and a bibliography of fifty-eight titles, and would take years to research and write.

A fresh idea, like the one behind *Store*, is the first requisite for entering upon a book-writing enterprise intended to inform, entertain, or inspire. A large public exists—we all form part of it at time—harboring all sorts of half-formed notions about what others are experiencing, or talking about, or forming decisions on. It was a favorite saying of Will Rogers that we "are all ignorant, only on different subjects." Just as having to teach a subject organizes one's ideas about that subject, undertaking a book is another direct way—like learning to swim by jumping off the dock—of acquiring knowledge. The prospective book writer, if inspiration does not strike, should think about subjects for which he or she has at least minimal skill, a curiosity that comes from incomplete knowledge rather than a total lack of knowledge (in the case of the latter how would one know where to look, how to proceed?) and a desire to learn more about the subject. One's public or university librarian can be of enormous help in discovering subjects frequently inquired about—and in which subjects there are no books recent enough to be useful.

Books have a way of begetting books; the bookshelf is the first place to look. You need access to a good library, one that has a card catalog and *Books in Print*, to help you research the subject that has piqued your curiosity or, suggested itself to you in casual conversation. Suppose you find that there has not been a new book on your subject in, say, fifteen years. This is an excellent sign. You are already off to a good start. Unless you happen to be the only person in the world who is interested in your topic, it seems reasonable to conclude that you have come upon a good subject for a book, especially if it contains what is currently considered useful knowledge. Ask yourself whether others in some way apply your subject—with their hands, in their daily life or work, or for leisure?

The knowledge explosion in some subjects, particularly scientific ones, is currently so great that facts and even concepts grow obsolescent within a decade, or even sooner. A sound journalistic instinct (which can be self-taught through trial and error) is even more important than a scientific background in exploiting the opportunity such subjects afford. A good writer can interview scientists and scholars, acquiring a formidable knowledge of a subject, and produce a book. Someone with all the learning in the world who lacks the ability to write cannot hope to produce a book, surely not a popular book with wide appeal. And the need for what the French call "high vulgarization"—the popularization of difficult specialties for the intelligent lay generalist (for you and me)—was never greater than it is today.

The writer of book-length nonfiction may or may not be an investigative reporter at the start of an enterprise, although the instinct for digging will undoubtedly be present. Yet the obligation to detail for even the slightest book is such that the writer can scarcely avoid becoming a fact detective, at an early stage of gathering the evidence. Uncovered fact leads to the uncovering of further facts. The interviewing of A will often not stand by itself without the interviewing of B, and so on. Research in the field may turn out to be more time-consuming than research in the library; indeed, work in the field may be necessitated by a lack of documentation, itself an indication that your book may become a frequently consulted source. Your going to and actually viewing the places where certain events happened, or have left traces; the tactile assurance that can only come from your physically handling the actual objects of your study; the echo of your own footfall, literally as well as figuratively, may be called upon to share in the venture that is your first book. Perhaps only when you can look back on it, can see the book as itself a shadow-casting object, will its worth to you as well as to others be revealed.

Nonfiction is topical, "about something." A vast and seemingly growing field of fiction is conjecture rather than imagination; it is fiction about something. Such fiction may be shrugged off as still another branch of journalism, as nonmainstream, as *roman à clef*; but it exists, and exists in abundance. The topical novel, the subject novel, the content novel—call it what you will—may not rise to the level of art; it seldom does. But nothing need prevent its being the product of careful craftmanship, of the same level of deliberation and purpose as topical nonfiction. It may be that the reading publics for both genres overlap, that a similar hunger for information is fed by both. Such subgenres as the gothic, the western, the juvenile, suspense and mystery fiction, and the historical novel, all forms of fiction, are often vehicles of heavily researched fact lightly disguised. For fiction such as this the generating impulse is not, in the strictest sense, literary. These books are hybrids, products of calculation rather than imagination. They are, nonetheless, legitimate offspring of the writer's mind, born as they are of research and of the technique proper to fiction—they bear the shape of story.

"If I wanted to publish a novel about the hosiery business," a vice-president of a leading book firm once said to the shocked participants of a writers conference, "would I look around for a novelist? No, I wouldn't. I'd get me the best damn hosiery salesman in the country and put him to work. We'd take care of making it into a novel back at the shop." Admittedly, this is an extreme view, and, one would hope, a rare house formula for the process by which a novel, even one "about" something, is made. Accident and the shock of recognition would seem more likely progenitors of fiction, with or without a cause. According to his publisher, William Morrow and Company, Allan Topol, author of the *The Fourth of July War*, (1979) a novel projecting a future oil shortage, first thought of writing his book when, as he puts it, "one cold and dark morning in the fall of 1973, I waited in a long gasoline line during the 1973 Arab oil shortage." Novels have often had mysterious and sudden origins, as Dickens acknowledged when he explained the genesis of one of his: "I thought of Pickwick."

The idea for a novel might come in a thunderclap, but the current-topic or the historical novel can seldom be written without a protracted period of research often exceeding the time required by the actual writing itself. It might be assumed that research for a strictly contemporary novel might be unnecessary, that information would be constantly invading one's very pores, that one would be breathing in facts. For several reasons, such automatic research is too much to hope for; one reason is that the "now" of the day of writing page the first has become a faraway "then." Another good reason is that one does not know at the moment of receiving information what will be useful and what will not. Was the twelfth of this month two years ago a Monday or a Tuesday? Was there a full moon on the night of the twenty-seventh? What were the popular tunes a year ago this date? When was the microwave oven introduced? (You had better not have a character use one before they were invented.)

Henry James had a theory, and a firm practice, that a novelist should not write about a period historically anterior to what he called the "visitable past." For him that meant the Battle of Waterloo; anything before that was untouchable, prehistoric as far as he was concerned. He picked that time only partly arbitrarily; in his day a living person might have been briefly the contemporary of one who was born the year of Waterloo. Such diffidence is seldom part of the equipment of the historical novelist. Sir Walter Scott clearly saw the times of the Crusades with his eighteenth-century eyes. Scott's own period is so fashionable nowadays that we have a recognizable subgenre known as the Regency novel. It is true that we have resources today more formidable than those available to Scott, although he was himself a conscientious and meticulous researcher. Abbotsford, the baronial home built with his royalties, is full of weapons and other objects from the past he wrote about. The chief problem with engaging in enormous amounts of research is in digesting one's learning and not drowning the story and its characters in details about how to shoot a harquebus or dig a pond for bream.

The difficulty, it must be admitted, is only aesthetic and technical. Undigested research does not stand in the way of the enjoyment of many readers; one might even say that for them the story is in danger of getting in the way of research. Otherwise how can we explain the enormous popularity of the novels of Frances Parkinson Keyes and F. Van Wyck Mason in their day, and of James A. Michener in ours? There can be no question that many readers are delighted, even flattered, when presented with miniature encyclopedias of information, and the beginning writer might think that here is the formula for a best-seller. Only after having published a novel or two can a writer afford the indulgence of using the novel as a manual of macramé or a thesis on TM. As James T. Farrell said once, "It takes genius to be dull for forty consecutive pages."

The encyclopedic content of informational novels—Michener's *Hawaii* will tell you more than you could conceivably wish to know about how nature builds a coral reef—is almost always responsible and accurate. Frances Parkinson Keyes captured hundreds of thousands of readers with her historical novels, and she never misused a fact in any of them. If a certain type of hurricane lamp, for example, had not been introduced into northern Louisiana until 1830, and she had established her characters there in 1829, she would not allow them to possess one, even though by then such a lamp was in use in New Orleans. Other writers might be tempted to waffle a minor fact, but never Frances Parkinson Keyes. She could be relied upon to make her characters, and her readers, wait until in her story the time became 1830. Her readers knew that they could rely upon her for such scrupulous accuracy, and they loved her for it.

With their love went forgiveness. They forgave her, as they forgave F. Van Wyck Mason, and apparently forgive Michener, for presenting action that is occasionally glacial and characters that are inevitably wooden. One would think that it is the duty of the historical novelist to delineate men and manners with equal attention and skill, but the portrayal of manners, when it comes to fiction about the past, seems for many readers to be enough. And perhaps their indulgence, though not aesthetically defensible, can be forgiven on the grounds that much is gained whenever a writer can make the past come even partly alive. How many of us, after all, first learned about the French Revolution in the pages of *A Tale of Two Cities*, one of Dickens's lesser novels which fell far short of being definitive as an account of that cataclysm? Yet for anyone who first came to the Revolution through Dickens, its events bear the indelible stamp not of the historical Danton or Robespierre but of the fictional Sydney Carton and Madame Defarge.

The historical novel presents both opportunity and challenge to the untried writer with a dual taste for history and for storytelling. The line between historical fact and historical fiction has always been recognized as a thin one, a boundary more than a barrier. Yet the fabricator of fiction must acknowledge some limits; history may be bent here and there but not falsified. No novelist will consider portraying Napoleon as a six-footer or awarding him the victory at Waterloo. Yet the possibility offers itself of interpreting, though not denying, what happened in history. When they inhabit novels, historical figures need not rush pellmell into their destinies or act so resolutely as they seem to in textbooks. Fiction may cause them to hesitate and waver, may introduce the indirection and suspense that surely must have occurred and that official history has forgotten.

Again, Sir Walter serves as precedent for the writer of historical fiction. His was a practiced hand at interpreting how history happened by introducing a fictional hero, an Edward Waverley or a Quentin Durward, to thrust among real people and real events. Scott did not scruple to place his fictional characters in a position to alter history—to threaten to change events by offering advice that was ignored or interposing action that came too late. Oddly enough, when temperately applied, this is a device that makes what really happened seem all the more right and inevitable. History's near misses, the *ifs* of history, add that measure of suspense that reflects the pulse and fluctuations of observed life, all that is missing from stark chronicle. To live in the past and explore its factors of probability offers the writer of fictional narrative many prospects of creativity.

The mixture of fiction and fact introduced by the interplay of historical and fictional characters involves some intriguing problems of fair play to the reader. Since many readers are willing to encounter history only as it is mediated through the devices of fiction, to what degree may history be fictionalized? One need not agree with Napoleon that history is nothing but fiction "agreed upon," or with Henry Ford's blunt dictum that history is "bunk," to conclude that extant documentation does not circumscribe the historical event entirely. Things unrecorded may well have happened, and to invent them is not to subvert history. John Hancock may well have sneezed at the moment of appending his famous signature; Napoleon may have flexed his fingers before posing, hand thrust in jacket, for Jacques Louis David. Unrecorded minor action—historical figures were not always standing at attention—may well provide the chink in history's armor through which fiction may legitimately enter.

Putting in John Hancock's sneeze seems harmless enough; even inventing the kind of ad lib remark such a mishap would provoke from Ben Franklin should escape criticism. But what about using in dialogue—having historical figures actually deliver—sentiments that are documented historically. Would not Jefferson think and say what he would later write in the Declaration? Obviously so. Biographers would have no scruples over saying as much; the novelist should not hesitate to do so either. History, after all, is a flattering game played between the historian and the reader; neither, after all, was there; in some cases, neither was alive. The reader of history and the reader of fiction alike know how events of the past turned out—both could advise Caesar not to visit the Forum—and this is a flattering superiority both kinds of readers share over the most celebrated people who ever lived, the superiority of hindsight. The novelist has, within reasonable limits, just as much license as the historian to exploit this advantage.

The novelist, then, may reasonably claim the right to fill in the spaces the documented record leaves open to conjecture. If history tells us that two kings met in the capital city of a third and is silent as to how and under what circumstances they journeyed there, the novelist, unlike the historian and the biographer, may not only tell how it happened, but through the means of scene, show it happening. In a juvenile novel, based on the life of a real person, I was faced with a similar problem. A handwritten manuscript, written by the subject himself, recounts that when he was a boy in France, during the period of the Revolution, he buried in an empty wine bottle a copy of the last will and testament of King Louis XVI, and that after the Revolution was over and he was a young man, he dug the bottle up, only to find that as it was improperly corked part of the document had rotted away.

This was primary source material and was, as far as I was concerned, inviolable. But extrapolation from its facts was another matter. My subject was a boy in Rennes, capital of Brittany, and he lived with his widowed mother in apartments in the Palace of Justice there. He does not record the exact spot where he buried the document. I happened to notice—I had Baedeker's *Guide to Northern Europe* open at the map of Rennes as I wrote—that a hundred or so yards away from his dwelling there was a historic place called the Mound. It was here that Caesar pitched camp when his legions fought the Renati, as he tells us in his *Gallic Wars*. And it was precisely here that I had my romantically minded boy bury the wine bottle. Nothing in his deposition contradicted me, and if the place I chose was not the true one, the fictionalized action contained a poetic truth. He should in fact have broken the ground in a spot so obviously symbolic.

Having decided that much, I had no difficulty in determining what parts of the royal testament would have rotted away, and what would remain that I could quote from. I must admit that I became a little carried away at this point; I found myself deciding exactly how this young boy came upon so dangerous a document, the mere possession of which would undoubtedly have been considered treason by the Republic. (As a boy he had seen, and as a man recorded, executions by guillotine performed just below his mother's window.) As his mother was a printer's widow, and a strong-minded woman with royalist sympathies, I invented facts and wrote scenes to suggest the possibility that she herself printed the king's testament for distribution in monarchist Brittany. For all this I had nothing to go on but my imagination, but I remained with the possible, even the probable. Not a word I wrote contravened the documents I had studied.

It may be inferred from the above that, like many others, I find research, especially research for fiction, fascinating to the point of being addictive. It offers admittance to both worlds—the world of fact, with all its implausibilities and surprises, and the more disciplined world of fiction. But there comes a time—and it often comes with a wrench—when the writer must decide to cease the pursuit of facts and to call a halt to note taking. It is time to begin writing. The hunt for facts can go on for too long—a book can be talked out of existence; it can be note-carded out of ever being. As Hallie Burnett cautions in *Fiction Writer's Handbook* (Harper & Row, 1975), the writer "may start too late, when one's research and interest in the material have taken so long that the original impulse has been exhausted."

The art of writing, whether fiction or nonfiction, necessarily culminates in the science of rewriting. For some writers, revision is a stage-by-stage process; thus they come to the end of the writing and of the major revision (minor changes may be demanded as late as the final page proofs) together. For others, it is back to the drawing board again and again. Mary O'Hara wrote *My Friend Flicka* nine times before she was satisfied with it. An unhappy few find it necessary, as Fitzgerald did with *Tender Is the Night*, to transpose entire sections from one place to another. Some write in "chunks," leaving gaps that have to be returned to and reworked over and over. From original vision to final revision, the writing and rewriting of a book may occupy many long months, sometimes even years. To take three years or more to finish a lengthy novel or a thoroughly researched biography or other work of nonfiction is by no means inordinate. Finally, however, even revision must come to a stop. You arrive at the point where you must say to yourself: *Let go.*

The separation may be painful, for now Othello's occupation's gone; a life-style of long duration has come to an abrupt end. F. Scott Fitzgerald testifies to the strength of the symbiotic relationship between book and writer, recalling that while he was working on one of his novels he lived in it so intensely that he could not afterward remember what his exterior life had been during those long months of labor. Even Jane Austen, who wrote and rewrote interminably and even lived on for years with her characters and their post-final-chapter adventures vividly present to her, came decisively to a novel's end. "Let other pens," she begins the final chapter of *Mansfield Park,* "dwell on guilt and misery. I quit such odious subjects as soon as I can, impatient to restore everybody, not greatly in fault themselves, to tolerate comfort, and to have done with all the rest."

A book is not truly a book but only a manuscript until it appears in print. The process of marketing a book manuscript differs little from that of sending out any other kind of manuscript, except that reporting time is often considerably longer. The editorial prejudice against multiple submissions is equally strong in the book world. Hence it may consume a year for three or four publishers to consider your book manuscript. Sometimes—although this probably applies more to fiction than to nonfiction—a manuscript is read in a dozen houses over some years before being accepted. Many book publishers, in defensive response to the number of unsolicited manuscripts they receive each year, will not look at a complete manuscript from an unknown. For example, Doubleday, the publisher of the greatest number of titles each year, now refuses to read more than a synopsis and two sample chapters. Doubleday makes one exception to this relatively new rule: the company wants to see the full Crime Club manuscript.

Four readily available sources of information on book publishers suggest themselves: the listings in *The Writer's Handbook, Writer's Market,* and *Literary Market Place (LMP)*; also the catalogs of individual publishers. The first three sources are particularly valuable for a quick check of nonfiction categories—a large number of publishers list cookbooks, whereas a scanty handful specify poetry. Your librarian or bookseller may permit you to examine the catalogs. Even a random perusal will give you an idea of the most likely targets for juvenile or for spy and mystery novels. (Plot is definitely back in favor in book-length form, however inhospitable the magazines remain toward it.) Some publishers, you will find, tend to bring out fiction in translation; make a note to avoid these. If your novel is mainstream, study the catalog, with particular attention to the percentages. When you have decided, check *LMP* for the address and the name of an editor to send your query letter to; make this brief—you are merely asking whether or not you may submit your manuscript. "Tell us who you are," say the editors of Harvard University Press, "what is important about the book, and why you should be published by us; and include a table of contents or outline."

A manuscript deriving from long and devoted research may be no less a product of enthusiasm and inspiration than a novel, and a writer might well bring it to completion, especially if this is a first book, without having given much thought to how to go about getting it published. Getting it written seems, as one is caught up in the surprise and creative job of living in, with, and for the projected book, enough to think about. An equal but less emotional commitment might start out more calmly, with a written proposal of what the writer intends to accomplish. Acceptance of such a proposal by a publisher when the book is at an early stage can ease the writer's way, providing direction and focus. For a sample author's proposal and a copy of a book contract, consult Richard Balkin's *A Writer's Guide to Book Publishing* (Hawthorn Books, 1979). Balkin's book is a thorough, step-by-step guide to all aspects of the author-publisher relationship, from the preparation and submission of a manuscript through the processing stage to marketing and promotion.

Some books require more exacting attention to technical detail in the process of becoming than others do. A novel is innocent of apparatus, but not so works of nonfiction, which need the support of technical aids of varying degrees of complexity. An excellent guide to what is involved for the technical writer (particularly one whose book requires the support of illustrations) can be found in *Into Print: A Practical Guide to Writing and Publishing,* (Los Altos, California, William Kaufmann, 1977) by Mary Hill and Wendell Cochran. Particularly valuable for the writer of the technical or scholarly book, *Into Print* discusses in precision and depth such matters as the preparation and use of photographs, drawings, maps, and charts. More widely applicable to the problems of the beginning writer is *How to Get Happily Published* (Harper & Row, 1978) by Judith Applebaum and Nancy Evans. The authors base their sprightly and eminently practical suggestions on the provocative premise that "hardly anybody treats getting published as if it were a rational, manageable activity—like practicing law or laying bricks—in which knowledge coupled with skill and application would suffice to ensure success."

Let us assume that the manuscript is out of your hands at last, and in those of the publisher. This, you congratulate yourself, is the end of the road. But it is not. The end is only the beginning; you have much work to do before publication day. Usually there is a nine-month gestation period between your delivery of the final, fully corrected manuscript and the physical appearance, bound and jacketed, of what you may at last accurately refer to as your book. And in that interim you are not a passive, if secretly anxious, observer. The book undergoes stages of becoming that call upon you for midwifery. After house editing, your manuscript is sent to the compositor; you then see it in the form of galleys—some four pages worth of your text printed onto each long, wide-margined strip of paper. You must check and correct these galleys against your returned manuscript. Normally, you must track down the impish work of thousands of gremlins—words transposed, type jumbled, and lines set upside down; you must also correct your own errors, traceable to the manuscript.

Drop everything else you are doing to attend to the galleys; keep whatever deadline you are given for their return—usually two or three weeks. Failure to return them on time could mean a considerable delay in publication date. Very few publishers have their own printing presses; composition and printing are usually farmed out to printers who set type for many publishers. A delay in schedule often means that you go to the end of the line.

The next time you see your book, it will be in the form of page proofs. Now, and only now, the index can be made. You may pay for this to be done—it will cost two hundred dollars or more—or you may do it yourself. Unless you need a very complex index, one bristling with cross-references, you should be able to go through the page proofs and produce your own index. Several books (*Into Print* has succinct information on index making) are available to assist you on this point. Making your own index will help you to see the balance and proportions of your treatment of your subject—too late to be altered now if they are awry, but invaluable for subsequent editions. Fiction, of course, requires no index.

Your book, when it comes out, will have been published under the newly revised, thoroughly overhauled copyright law, which went into effect 1 January, 1978. This is the "life plus fifty" law. If your book or other work for which you lawfully hold copyright came out after 1 January, 1978, it is protected against infringement during your lifetime and for fifty years afterward. At the end of the latter period, such work enters the public domain and may be used in whole or in part without attribution or royalty payment. Before 1 January, 1978, copyright protection was granted for twenty-seven years, renewable for an equal period. The new law does not renew copyright protection for work whose copyright has been allowed to lapse before the effective date of the new law (known as the Copyright Act of 1976).

Copyright protection in this country, rooted in an English statute of 1710, has had a history that reflects the growing importance and complexity of the means of communication to our concept and practice of democracy. Article I, section 8 of our Constitution grants to Congress the power "to promote the progress of science and useful arts by securing for limited times to authors and inventors the exclusive right to their respective writings and discoveries." This constitutional concept places copyright protection in a position of striking relevance, one that provides a framework of the public weal and the intellectual life of the nation. Originally, interestingly enough, the "limited time" was a mere fourteen years, renewable only for another fourteen. Until 1978 copyright protection was administered under a 1909 law, itself a modification of earlier revisions of the original 1790 federal copyright statute.

In the nearly seventy-year gap between 1909 and the new law, copyright protection had become increasingly inadequate in the new communications age of radio, television, communications satellites, cable television, computers, photocopiers, videotape recorders, and the like. The amazing growth of technology in the past half century forced rethinking of the entire problem of protecting the creative artist and thinker. Clearly, a concept of "publication" wedded to hot type alone had to be discarded. Significantly, the new law establishes one system for the statutory protection of both published and unpublished works subject to copyright. The key concept for material that can be protected by copyright is that it must be in the form of a "writing"; that is to say, it must be "fixed" in a tangible form that can be reproduced. Further, the work must be both original (produced by the author's own intellectual effort, not copied) and creative (a concept including pantomimes and choreography for the first time).

The following categories of work come under the protection of the new copyright law:

1. published and unpublished nondramatic literary works
2. published and unpublished works of the performing arts (musical and dramatic works, pantomimes and choreographic works, motion pictures and other audio-visual works)
3. published and unpublished works of the visual arts (pictorial, graphic, and sculptural works)
4. published and unpublished sound recordings

Under the new classification system for copyright registration, works of the first category listed above come under Class TX.

(Forms for this and all other classifications may be obtained free of charge by writing to the Copyright Office, Library of Congress, Washington, D.C. 20559). It should be noted that the designation "nondramatic literary works" includes fiction, nonfiction, poetry, periodicals, textbooks, reference works, directories, information compilations, and advertising copy.

Under the new copyright law, a "book" is not merely a work of authorship appearing in the traditional form—printed and bound. It is also conceived of as "copy" in many forms. Thus an author may write a literary work that may find embodiment in various forms, all of them protected. Among these forms may be books and contributions to magazines; they may also take such futuristic shapes of "fixed" information as microfilm, tape recordings, and computer punch cards. It is worth emphasizing that under the new law all original works of authorship can be registered for copyright without distinction between published or unpublished work. (Up to the enactment of the Copyright Act of 1976, unpublished work could not receive copyright but had to seek protection under common law.) Now, under the new law, all types of nondramtaic literary works—including sound recordings and song poems without music—may be registered in unpublished form.

Now let us suppose that, armed with protection for the handiwork of your originality and creativeness, a security extending to your immediate posterity, you are now a published author. Your brainchild has been delivered—and it is a book. You have received a jacketed copy of an object exuding the sweetest smell on earth: the scent of the ink and paper of a brand-new book. A month after you first have the book in your hands, publication day arrives. You can scarcely believe that this is an event not universally perceived. Your book is out, and few have noticed. The earth, to your surprise, has continued turning. After brief euphoria you will doubtless turn your attention to the other matters—preferably, for the thing is habit-forming, to another book.

A time may come when the words on these pages of yours will seem strangers, the thoughts of another. But as you read them now, unable perhaps to suppress the thought that others may be perusing them also, you have a rare opportunity to look into yourself, are able to remember still the thoughts and emotions that crowded around you as page after page took its shape. At this moment, you may realize, as never before, how much of you went into the book, however impersonal and remote the treatment and the subject. This is the moment when you will, perhaps unknowingly, decide whether or not your book is to be a once in a lifetime accomplishment or whether you have found a way of being that it will be your concern and ambition to continue.

In a recent interview, shortly before the publication of her first book, author-illustrator Caroline Howe discussed with me her intention, after some years of working with film, of concentrating on writing and illustrating books for children. She feels a strong identification between aspects of her own childhood and her story, the account of the trials of a teddy bear who rounds up musical instruments and birds and beasts to play them. "The conflicts of the book are the conflicts I had as a child, coming from extreme self-consciousness," she says. She considers the mixture of fantasy and realism found in children's literature necessary. "Your environment as a child is your reality," she says. "You go to books to see other realities." A book, Caroline Howe feels, is different enough from the entertainment and information offered by the electronic media to more than hold its own. "Reading is different," she says. "With books you go off into a solitary space. When you are a child, characters in books become friends and comrades. With television they vanish suddenly; with books you can go back again and again to see if they're still there."

More than any other vehicle of communication, books can always be at hand, "still there." Therein, perhaps, lies their perennial fascination for reader and writer alike. The conclusion to be drawn from this symbiosis is clear enough.

You, the writer, must first look within, and then around you, for what you write can only come from within, from contemplation of self and from observation of and then meditation on that which is around you. Yet introspection is not communication; the *I* is rootless without the *thou*. A book cannot come into being without its writer, but it is a dead thing without readers. The need for writers and for their books was never greater than it is today. That need is worldwide. When the General Conference of UNESCO proclaimed International Book Year (for 1972), it announced as its objective "to focus attention on the role of books in society." For UNESCO the book, far from becoming in danger of being replaced by the new technology, is increasingly indispensable throughout the globe.

UNESCO introduced its "programme of action" for 1972 in these words:

> *Books today have become one of the major media of mass communication. Striking advances in production and distribution techniques have made it increasingly possible to bring low-cost, high-quality books to vast audiences. The result has been a virtual "book revolution."*

> *At the same time, the audience for books has expanded enormously. The vast increase in population, the spread of education and growing leisure time have widened markets; new distribution channels as well as the extension of libraries, particularly school and public library services, have added to the availability of books.*

> *The transformation in the role of books has taken place concurrently with the rise of the electronic media of radio and television. In the general ascendancy of the media, books have maintained their influence. Moreover, among the mass media, the book remains the essential tool of knowledge.*

Some years ago a scholarship student from an undeveloped nation who was attending the Georgetown University

Writers Conference anticipated, in questioning a speaker from the floor, with striking eloquence what was to become the UNESCO objective for IBY: "You say that in the West the novel is dead. That may be so. But you must not foreclose literary development elsewhere. Somewhere this very day, in an African village, on the South American pampas, or in a crowded Asian city, the novel is even now being born." These words have been ringing in my memory ever since they were uttered. In themselves they are enough—are they not?—to give sustenance and mission to writers everywhere.

## SUGGESTED FOLLOW-UP FOR THIS CHAPTER

### 1. *What to read*
Make yourself an authority in some field. Build upon a hobby or personal interest, preferably one of long standing. It could be a social issue or a regional problem that absorbs your reading time, a subject you find yourself injecting into conversations. It is time for you to become an expert, to take a professional interest in the subject. You become an expert in either (and finally both) of two ways. You may acquire authority from experience in the area you have chosen, from the practice of a craft perhaps. The source of your expertise may derive from living, literally, with the issue because of your occupation. Or you may have become knowledgeable through extensive interviewing (for example, of people who live in an area especially affected by "noise pollution.") In a word, you may acquire mastery of your subject through field research of varying kinds and intensities. Then there are the resources available if you have access to a large municipal or university library. You may become an expert through the intense pursuit of what previous experts have set down in books and magazines and other forms of record. Whatever the amount of your field research, you will feel and need to master your subject by reading everything you can get your hands on.

## 2. *What to write*

If your research has enabled you to determine that a new treatment of a subject of your knowledge and interest is overdue, then go ahead and plan your book. You may find that in sketching it out you have written a chapter that can be adapted to the requirements of a particular magazine. Study carefully several issues of the magazine—if it is a periodical in your specialty, you will already be aware of the magazine's coverage of and approach to the topic—and then submit the revised chapter as an article. If it is published, you will have something to show a book publisher when you write your query letter. In your prospectus, along with your synopsis of the book and a sample chapter or two, you will now be able to submit a published article. Publication of an article does not automatically give you squatter's rights to a subject, but it may well incline an editor to encourage you to continue.

## 3. *Where to send it*

Check the publisher listings in the first section of *Literary Market Place* to find out who publishes books in your category. Also check the entries in the current edition of the annual *Writer's Market*. From these two sources assemble a list of publishers who bring out books in your field. Suppose that you contemplate doing a book on a craft or hobby. A careful checking of *LMP* will disclose the names of publishers who particularly invite such books; the entries will provide addresses, telephone numbers, and the names of the appropriate editors. *LMP* also enumerates the total of titles the publisher brought out the previous year. *Writer's Market* supplies information on such matters as conditions of manuscript submission—the entire manuscript or sample chapters—royalty payment terms, advances on royalty, and, most helpfully, some titles the firm has brought out recently.

A final word: Good luck.

# A WRITER'S READING LIST*

Bates, Jefferson D. *Writing with Precision: How to Write So That You Cannot Possibly Be Misunderstood.* Washington, D.C.: Acropolis Books, 1978.

Braine, John. *Writing a Novel.* New York: Coward, McCann & Geoghegan, 1974.

Casewit, Curtis W. *Freelance Writing: Advice from the Pros.* Collier, Macmillan, 1974.

Cassill, R. V. *Writing Fiction.* 2d ed. Englewood Cliffs, N.J.: Prentice-Hall, 1975.

Commins, Dorothy. *What Is an Editor? Saxe Commins at Work.* Chicago: University of Chicago Press, 1978.

Halperin, John, ed. *The Theory of the Novel.* New York: Oxford University Press, 1974.

Holmes, Marjorie. *Writing the Creative Article.* Rev. ed. Boston: The Writer, 1976.

Janeway, Elizabeth, ed. *The Writer's World.* New York: McGraw-Hill Book Co., 1969.

Kuehl, John. *Write and Rewrite.* New York: Meredith Press, 1967.

Lubbock, Percy. *The Craft of Fiction.* New York: Viking Press, 1957.

MacCampbell, Donald. *The Writing Business.* New York: Crown Publisher, 1978.

McKenna, Eva Grice and Shirley Graves Cochrane. *New Eyes for Old: Nonfiction Writings of Richard McKenna.* Winston-Salem, N.C.: John F. Blair, 1972.

Meredith, Scott. *Writing to Sell.* 2d rev. ed. New York: Harper & Row Publishers, 1974.

Morris, Wright. *About Fiction: Reverent Reflections on the Nature of Fiction with Irreverent Observations on Writers, Readers and Other Abuses.* New York: Harper & Row, 1975.
Polking, Kirk, et al. *The Beginning Writer's Answer Book.* Rev. ed. Cincinnati: Writer's Digest Books, 1978.
Reynolds, Paul R. *The Middle Man: The Adventures of a Literary Agent.* New York: William Morrow & Co. 1972.
Surmelian, Leon. *Techniques of Fiction: Measure and Madness.* New York: Doubleday & Co., 1969.

*Exclusive of titles recommended within the text.

# INDEX